WORK IN AMERICA
The Decade Ahead

WORK IN AMERICA
The Decade Ahead

Edited by
Clark Kerr/Jerome M. Rosow

Van Nostrand Reinhold/Work in America Institute Series

VAN NOSTRAND REINHOLD COMPANY
NEW YORK CINCINNATI ATLANTA DALLAS SAN FRANCISCO
LONDON TORONTO MELBOURNE

Van Nostrand Reinhold Company Regional Offices:
New York   Cincinnati   Alanta   Dallas   San Francisco

Van Nostrand Reinhold Company International Offices:
London   Toronto   Melbourne

Library of Congress Catalog Card Number: 78-27685
ISBN: 0-422-20372-1

Manufactured in the United States of America

Published by Van Nostrand Reinhold Company
135 West 50th Street, New York. N.Y. 10020

Published simultaneously in Canada by Van Nostrand Reinhold Ltd.

15 14 13 12 11 10 9 8 7 6 5 4 3 2 1

Library of Congress Cataloging in Publication Data

Main entry under title:

Work in America.

   (Van Nostrand Reinhold/Work in America
Institute series)
   Includes index.
   1. Labor and laboring classes—United States—
1970-   —Addresses, essays, lectures.   2. Work
environment—United States--Addresses, Essays,
lectures.   I. Kerr, Clark, 1911-   II.   Rosow,
Jerome M.   III.   Series.
HD8072.W8165   301.5'5'0973   78-27685
ISBN 0-442-20372-1

TB 6/10/81

Van Nostrand Reinhold/Work in America Institute Series

Practical Management for Productivity, by *John R. Hinrichs*
Work in America: The Decade Ahead, edited by *Clark Kerr* and *Jerome M. Rosow*

VNR/WORK IN AMERICA INSTITUTE SERIES

The VNR/Work in America Institute Series is designed to provide practical insight into new and better ways to advance productivity and the quality of working life. The objective is to create heightened awareness of the opportunities for an enriched work life that can exist in innovative organizations, and to reveal the benefits of linking people and production in a common goal, through clearer understanding of the key factors contributing to worker output and job satisfaction.

The Series will provide guidance on a number of concerns that influence work performance, not only in today's work environment, but also in the even more complex world of work that lies ahead. Titles in the World of Work Series will focus on five fundamental issues affecting the work community: (1) *The quality of working life*, exploring opportunity, recognition, participation, and rewards for employees to optimize their involvement in and contribution to the work organization; (2) *Productivity*, focusing on the human factors in the productivity equation, to increase both individual and organizational output through more effective use of human resources; (3) *Education and the world of work*, discussing ways to improve the match between the entry-level worker and the job, by building bridges from education to the world of work; (4) *Employee-management cooperation*, recognizing that employees contribute important know-how and ingenuity to increase output, reduce waste, maintain product quality, and improve morale; and (5) *National labor force policy*, examining policies of the United States and other industrialized nations as they affect productivity and the quality of working life.

CONTENTS

Introduction   *Clark Kerr*   ix

I. THE WORK FORCE OF THE FUTURE

1. Work, Values, and the New Breed   *Daniel Yankelovich*   3
2. Work in the American Future: Reindustrialization or
    Quality of Life   *Amitai Etzioni*   27
3. Changing Attitudes toward Work   *Raymond A. Katzell*   35
4. The Work Force of the Future: An Overview   *Richard B. Freeman*   58
5. Manpower Policy: A Look Ahead   *Eli Ginzberg*   80
6. Minorities and Work: The Challenge for the Next Decade
    Bernard E. Anderson   92
7. Women and Work: Priorities for the Future   *Margaret S. Gordon*   111
8. Child Rearing, Parenthood, and the World of Work   *Moncrieff M.
    Cochran* and *Urie Bronfenbrenner*   138

II. THE EMERGING WORK ENVIRONMENT

9. Quality-of-Work-Life Issues for the 1980s   *Jerome M. Rosow*   157
10. Productivity Trends and Prospects   *Jerome A. Mark*   188
11. The Impact of Changing Technology on the Working
    Environment   *Wickham Skinner*   204
12. Emerging Trends in Collective Bargaining   *Irving Bluestone*   231
13. Public Policy and the Quality of Working Life   *A. H. Raskin*   253
14. Conflict and Compression: The Labor-Market Environment
    in the 1980s   *Arnold Weber*   268
    Index   281

Introduction: Industrialism with a Human Face

by CLARK KERR*

The labor force in the United States is currently experiencing its fourth period of great evolutionary change in its composition, its character, and the rules for its conduct.

The first three such periods have been:

The enormous influx of immigrants and the rise of heavy industry, beginning in the 1880s. An average 5 million immigrants entered the United States in each of the next four decades, and the total population grew at a rate of one fifth to one quarter every ten years. Many of these newcomers went into the iron, steel, and other basic industries. The new workers were largely male and willing to undertake heavy and dirty work. The American economy was profoundly changed.

The great internal migration and the depopulation of the countryside, beginning particularly with World War I. In 1920, 30 percent of the population still lived on farms compared to only about 5 percent today. Movement into the cities was accelerated by the Great Depression and then by World War II. The migrants at first were largely white and later largely black. The new workers were still mostly male and oriented toward blue-collar occupations. The automobile industry has been substantially based on a labor force so derived. The United States became highly urbanized, and patterns of life were greatly affected. Suburbs grew and ghettos spread.

The introduction of social controls over the use and conduct of the labor force, greatly accelerated by the New Deal, and again in the 1960s and 1970s. The federal government vastly increased its intervention into the labor market; trade unionism and collective bargaining came to cover most of basic industry and the historic crafts; and the states augmented their social legislation. A great redistribution of authority took place from the employer to the govern-

*Clark Kerr is chairman of the Board of Directors of the Work in America Institute, Inc. He is also chairman of the Carnegie Council on Policy Studies in Higher Education.

ment agency and to the labor union. Two and often three parties shared power where there had been only one before. Pluralistic control of the labor market came to be the dominant mode. Rules for the workplace were once made on a unilateral basis; now they are increasingly made on a bilateral and trilateral basis.

The United States has adapted to each of these vast evolutionary changes, albeit with substantial social and political stress. Each change has left its heavy imprint on American society as it exists and functions today. We are still adjusting to the continuing impacts of these old transformations even as we face a new period of fundamental change. Looking back, it may be said that the process of adaptation in each case was in the end successful both economically and politically. The nation clearly became more productive economically and at least maintained, and perhaps increased, its political coherence.

Now, new challenges are being presented. It is important to remember that, although these particular challenges are new, the experience of meeting challenges is not. I have suggested "periods" of change, but it should be noted that these periods to some extent overlap. Significant change has been the rule, not the exception, for the past century, and will continue to be characteristic of the forseeable future.

I venture the impression that the challenges of today are inherently no more difficult than those of the past, and possibly less so, and that we are better equipped with knowledge and with institutional structures to meet them. I also venture the expectation that, having met the challenges of today, the United States will have both the most productive and the most satisfied labor force since industrialization began in this nation.

THE FOURTH EVOLUTION: THE GREAT AMERICAN CULTURAL EVOLUTION IN THE LABOR FORCE

A great cultural transformation in attitudes and expectations within the labor force accelerated in the 1960s and 1970s, but its origins long antedate the past two decades. For example, the movement toward mass high school education was rapid in the decade after World War II. This was followed by more attendance in higher education beginning in about 1960. I see two main aspects to this evolution:

More people want jobs than ever before. Work for pay is becoming a more central aspect of more lives. There is no "great refusal" of jobs, rather a great demand for them. This new demand is substantial, but whether it is of the proportions suggested by Yankelovich—an additional 25 percent of people wanting jobs beyond the current size of the employed working force—remains to be seen.

More people want "good" jobs, and there is an increasing rejection of "bad" jobs, i.e., jobs in which the employee has few, if any, fringe benefits and is not covered by formal or informal seniority rules; routine factory or office jobs; and "dirty" work. The definition of a "good" job comes more and more to include some individual and small group choices about its terms and conduct, sometimes even over and beyond collective bargaining.

The new orientation may be divided into at least two major themes: personal self-fulfillment and political rights.* Of the two, the former is as yet ascendant in the United States. Political power in the workplace, as, for example, in codetermination, has not been pushed as hard as in most of Western Europe where the socialist tradition is far stronger. In the United States, in particular, over the past century more money to workers has been the dominant means by which accepted approaches to workplace accommodation have been developed rather than by giving more direct power to workers in management. This strategy depends, in part, on there being more money (in real terms). Power conflicts tend to sharpen, as in the United Kingdom today, when they are not so ameliorated by higher standards of living.

The work ethic has not disappeared from the face of America, but the aesthetics of work has taken on a great new significance. This constitutes the central theme of the new evolution. We have a *crisis of aesthetics, not ethics*—tastes have changed, and the indulgence of psychic satisfactions has increased. We also have, to a much lesser extent, at least as yet, a crisis of politics.

We are looking at this evolutionary period possibly from about its midpoint, although this is a hazardous guess. If 1960 can be taken as a very rough starting point for the sake of simplification, and if the scales were "tipped" on the side of Yankelovich's "new breed" by the early 1970s, and if one full generation (thirty years) will pass by before the full impact of this tipping is felt at all age levels, then it might be estimated that we are talking of a transition period of forty years (1960–2000) and that we are halfway through it. But the greatest impacts may still be ahead, as the transition reaches its full force.

The penetration of new attitudes and expectations into different segments of the American economy varies greatly. It is deeper where the labor force is younger than where it is older, where it is more educated than less educated, and thus also in white-collar than in blue-collar occupations (white-collar workers

*"Two themes can be said to characterize the ambience of work in America in 1977. . . . One theme can be called cultural or expressive: the concern for work as a source of self-respect. . . . The other can be called political: the concern for individual rights and power" (Rosabeth Moss Kanter, "Work in a New America," *Daedalus*, Winter 1978).

became one half of the labor force by 1978). The college, which above all other segments of American society reflects these characteristics, is the most affected. As a corollary, what is happening there may be an indication of future trends elsewhere.

Expectations and Attitudes of College Students as Signs to the Future

Some aspects of today's colleges that may indicate possible aspects of the world of work tomorrow are belief in entitlement to a place in college with adequate financing, wide choice among colleges and programs in colleges, easy "stop-outs" and reentry, easy transfers to other institutions with full credit for work done, a long period of exploration before settling down, a greatly increased range of electives and fewer requirements, a more egalitarian (and higher) grade structure, more opportunities for women and members of minority groups throughout all programs, the abandonment of the principle of *in loco parentis*, a general demand for more personal autonomy, more insistence on the right to participation in decision making (although generally not much used in practice), more checks and balances on the exercise of authority, more emphasis on the creative arts, more demand for guidance and counseling, an expectation of better buildings and facilities, more emphasis on small and self-chosen friendship groups, longer vacation periods, a mixing of education with work and leisure, a concentration on vocational interests, an acceptance of hard work, an insistence upon consumer rights and sovereignty, and a high level of satisfaction with the college experience. Some of these changes have their counterparts in the conduct of many families and in the practice of some churches as well.

It is out of this background of experience and expectations that college youth enter the labor force. What happens in college influences what happens in high school and thus also those who enter the labor force directly from high school. The college of today increasingly sets the stage for the workplace of tomorrow. Students have changed in the past and so have colleges, it should be noted, and they will continue to change in the future.

Attitudes of college students toward work are highly affirmative. A recent survey of college students shows that (in 1976) nearly eight out of ten (79 percent) agreed that "hard work always pays off," although the immediately preceding generation seems temporarily to have held contrary views. More college students are taking vocational majors—60 percent now versus 40 percent a decade ago. Over half of today's students are interested in participating in apprenticeship programs. Nearly half of today's students work full time or part time during the school year. Youth, at least, is work oriented, and there is no convincing evidence that this is not true also of older adults. (See Table 1 for data on college youth.) The attitudes and behavior of college youth toward work are of particular importance. If the work ethic were in decline, presumably it would show up first

Table 1.   Attitudes of College Students.

Attitude	Year and Source	Percentage
1. Hard work always pays off.	1967 (Yankelovich)	70
	1973 (Yankelovich)	40
	1976 (Trow)	79
2. Being well off financially is essential or very important to me (freshmen only)	1967 (Astin)	44
	1977 (Astin)	58
3. Having administrative responsibility is essential or very important to me (freshmen only)	1967 (Astin)	25
	1977 (Astin)	34
4. Want professional, technical, or administrative careers (high school seniors)	1974 (Gilford)	54
5. Want degrees beyond bachelor's (freshmen only)	1967 (Astin)	49
	1977 (Astin)	51
6. Interested in careers in law, medicine, or business (freshmen only)	1967 (Astin)	17
	1977 (Astin)	28
7. Proportion of women with probable career in law, medicine, business, or engineering (freshmen only)	1967 (Astin)	6
	1977 (Astin)	16
8. Married women belong at home (freshmen only)	1967 (Astin)	57
	1977 (Astin)	28
9. Women planning to marry within a year of completing college (freshmen only)	1967 (Astin)	27
	1977 (Astin)	17
10. Would drop out of college if not helping my job chances	1976 (Trow)	45
11. Worked at a job during college in 1975–1976	1976 (Trow)	54
12. The chief benefit of college is that it increases one's earning power	1969 (Trow)	49
	1976 (Trow)	46
13. Training and skills for an occupation is an essential goal for college	1969 (Trow)	71
	1976 (Trow)	62
14. Undergraduate enrollment in professional studies (majors)	1969 (CFAT)	36
	1976 (CFAT)	58
15. Proportion of undergraduate programs that may be taken as "electives"	1967 (Blackburn)	37
	1974 (Blackburn)	52
16. Proportion of students "stopping-out" during college	1976 (Trow)	27

Table 1.   (Continued)

	Attitude	Year and Source	Percentage
17.	Percentage of students with college grades of B or higher (average)	1969 (Trow) 1976 (Trow)	35 59
18.	Keeping up to date on political affairs is essential or very important (freshmen only)	1967 (Astin) 1977 (Astin)	51 40
19.	Developing a philosophy of life is essential or very important (freshmen only)	1967 (Astin) 1977 (Astin)	83 59

Sources:

Astin: R. J. Panos, A. W. Astin, and J. A. Creager, *National Norms for Entering College Freshmen—Fall 1967* (Washington, D.C.: Office of Research, American Council on Education, 1967) and A. W. Astin, M. R. King, and G. T. Richardson, *The American Freshman National Norms for Fall 1977* (Los Angeles: ACE-UCLA Cooperative Institutional Research Program, 1978).

Blackburn: R. Blackburn, E. Armstrong, C. Conrad, J. Didham, and T. McKune, *Changing Practices in Under-graduate Education,* A Report for the Carnegie Council on Policy Studies in Higher Education (Berkeley, Calif.: 1976).

CFAT: *Missions of the College Curriculum: A Contemporary Review with Suggestions,* A commentary of The Carnegie Foundation for the Advancement of Teaching (San Francisco: Jossey-Bass, 1977).

Gilford: Dorothy Gilford, "The Non-Collegiate Sector: Statistical Snapshots of Adult Continuing Education." Address before the American Association for Higher Education. March 11, 1974.

Trow: Carnegie Council Surveys, 1969 and 1976, conducted by Martin Trow.

Yankelovich: Daniel Yankelovich, "Turbulence in the Work World: Angry Workers, Happy Grads," *Psychology Today* (December 1974).

among young persons and particularly among those with the higher levels of education. Half of all young persons now attend college; that the work ethic among them seems to be so strong augurs well for its health throughout society today and in the near future. To the extent that educated youth is the avant-garde of American society, as it has been so often in the past, the work ethic appears not to be in jeopardy; but this, of course, can change.

Changes in Composition of the Labor Force

More of the adult population is in the labor force than ever before, and the proportion keeps on rising. More women want work, as do more teenagers, including those who combine school and work. Older people are being given more opportunities to work than in recent times, and inflation almost guarantees that more of them will take advantage of these opportunities. At the same time, the proportion of men in the labor force has gone down. Thus, work is being more equally distributed by sex and by age grouping. (See Table 2 for statistics on these and other developments.) Work is coming to be the primary way that most adults, regardless of sex and age, identify themselves, and it is the central organizing principle of their lives.

Table 2.   Changing Characteristics of the American Labor Force.

Characteristics	Period of Time	Change
1. Proportion of population 16 and over in labor force	1947–1976	58.9 to 62.1%
2. Percentage of women 16 and over in labor force	1947–1976	32 to 47%
3. Percentage of married women in labor force	1947–1976	20 to 45%
4. Women as a proportion of labor force	1947–1976	28 to 41%
5. Teenagers (16–19) employed	1970–1976	42.3 to 44.3%
6. Student civilian labor force participation rate (ages 18–24 for 1947, 16–24 for 1974)	1947–1974	23 to 45%
7. College student labor force participation rates:		
Male full-time students	1962–1974	31 to 43%
Female full-time students (rates for part-time students do not differ greatly from those of nonstudents)	1962–1974	21 to 40%
8. Proportion of men 16 and over in labor force	1947–1976	86.8 to 78.1%
9. Proportion of men 16 and over out of labor force	1947–1976	13.2 to 21.9%
10. Proportion of labor force from minority groups (blacks and other nonwhites)	1954–1976	11 to 12%
11. Labor force participation rates for men 55–64 years of age	1947–1976	90 to 75%
12. Illegal immigrants as proportion of labor force	1974	8%
13. Percentage of employees on a part-time basis	1950–1975	16 to 21%
14. Median years of education of members of labor force	1910–1977	8.1* to 12.6
15. Percentage of labor force who have attended college one year or more	1910–1977	6.5† to 33%
16. Percentage of labor force who have completed four or more years of college	1910–1977	3.5† to 17%

*1910 figure is median years of education of population 25 years of age and over, which is slightly lower than the educational level of members of the labor force.

†Figure for 1910 is for male population aged 25 to 64 years, which represents most of the male labor force.

Table 2.   (Continued)

17.	Percentage of employed labor force in white-collar occupations	1870–1976	18 to 50%
18.	Expressed job satisfaction	1949–1976	69* to 86%
19.	Areas of comparatively low job satisfaction: operatives, farm and nonfarm laborers (clerical workers were only slightly less dissatisfied)	1966–1973	No change. Less than 50% expressed "high satisfaction."
20.	Job turnover: average number of jobs held over male's work lifetime	1900–1966	6 to 12
21.	Absenteeism for wage and salary workers	1957–1976	Little or no change
22.	Holders of two or more jobs as proportion of all employed persons	1956–1975	5.5 to 4.7%
23.	Self-employed persons as proportion of total nonfarm labor force	1900–1975	27 to 7%
24.	"Traditional worker" as proportion of total labor force (married male wage earner, wife present but not employed)	1960–1977	30 to 14%
25.	Composition of the American labor force in terms of household arrangements	1977	
	Wage earners in multi-wage-earner households		64%
	Wage earners in single-person households		12
	Wage earners who are sole source of support for dependents		24
			——
			100%
26.	The "three-tier society"	1976	
	Households with multiple wage earners; and households with a single wage earner with no dependents		57%
	Households of two or more persons dependent on one wage earner		25
	Households with no wage earner		18
			——
			100%

*1949 figure is for whites only; comparable figure for blacks was 55%. Job satisfaction of blacks rose to 76% in 1969; the 1976 figure here does not distinguish by race.

Sources:

1. *Employment and Training Report of the President* (Washington, D.C.: U.S. Government Printing Office, 1977), Table A-1, p. 135. (Hereafter cited as *ETR*.)

2. Richard B. Freeman, "The Work Force of the Future: An Overview," Chapter 4 in this volume.

3. *Ibid.*

4. *ETR*, Table A-3, p. 139.

5. "Labor Month in Review," *Monthly Labor Review* 100, No. 9 (September 1977): 2.

6. Carl Rosenfeld, "Special Labor Force Report: The Employment of Students, October 1960," *Monthly Labor Review* 84, No. 7 (July 1961): Table 3. Anne McDougall Young, "Students, Graduates, and Drop-outs in the Labor Market, October 1974," *Monthly Labor Review* 98, No. 8 (August 1975): Table 1.

7. Kopp Michelotti, "Young Students: In School and Out," *Monthly Labor Review* 96, No. 9 (September 1973): 13. Anne McDougall Young, *op. cit.*

8. *ETR*, Table A-1, p. 135.

9. *Ibid.*

10. *ETR*, Table A-3, pp. 139, 141.

11. *ETR*, Table A-2, p. 138.

12. Michael Piore, "Impact of Immigration upon the Labor Force," *Monthly Labor Review* 98, No. 5 (May 1975): 42.

13. *ETR*, Table B-14, p. 212.

14. Clark Kerr, "Educational Changes: Potential Impacts on Industrial Relations," in Gerald G. Somers, ed., *The Next Twenty-Five Years of Industrial Relations* (Madison, Wis.: Industrial Relations Research Association, 1973), p. 188. Kopp Michelotti, "Educational Attainment of Workers, March 1977," *Monthly Labor Review* 100, No. 12 (December 1977): 53.

15. John K. Folger and Charles B. Nam, *Education of the American Population*, A 1960 Census Monograph (Washington, D.C.: U.S. Government Printing Office, 1967), p. 167. Michelotti (1977), p. 53.

16. John K. Folger and Charles B. Nam, *Education of the American Population*, p. 167. Michelotti (1977), p. 53.

17. *Employment and Training Report of the President* (Washington, D.C.: U.S. Government Printing Office, 1976), p. 150. (Hereafter cited as *ETR*.) Freeman, *op. cit.*

18. Gallup Polls, as reported in George Strauss, "Is There a Blue-Collar Revolt Against Work?" in James O'Toole, ed., *Work and the Quality of Life* (Cambridge, Mass.: MIT Press, 1974), p. 43. Raymond A. Katzell, "Changing Attitudes toward Work," Table 1, Chapter 3 in this volume.

19. *Job Satisfaction: Is There a Trend?* U.S. Department of Labor, Manpower Research Monograph No. 30 (Washington, D.C.: U.S. Government Printing Office, 1974), pp. 9–10.

20. Stanley Lebergott, "Labor Force and Employment Trends," in E. B. Sheldon and W. E. Moore, eds., *Indicators of Social Change: Concepts and Measurements* (New York: Russell Sage Foundation, 1968), p. 125.

21. Janice Neipert Hedges, "Absence from Work—Measuring the Hours Lost," *Monthly Labor Review* 100, No. 10 (October 1977): 22.

22. Howard V. Hayghe and Kopp Michelotti, "Multiple Jobholding in 1970 and 1971," *Monthly Labor Review Reader*, U.S. Bureau of Labor Statistics Bulletin 1868, Washington, D.C., 1975, p. 163.

23. *ETR*, 1976, p. 149.

24. Calculated from data in Howard V. Hayghe, "Marital and Family Characteristics of Workers, March 1977," *Monthly Labor Review* 101, No. 2 (February 1978): Tables 1 and 4.

25. *Ibid.* U.S. Bureau of the Census, Current Population Reports, *Marital Status and Living Arrangements: March 1977*, Series P-20, No. 323 (Washington, D.C.: U.S. Government Printing Office, April 1978), Table F (for those maintaining a family without spouse present). Primary individuals computed from U.S. Bureau of the Census, Current Population Reports, *Households and Families by Type: March 1977 (Advance Report)*,

Series P-20, No. 313 (Washington, D.C.: U.S. Government Printing Office, September 1977), and from U.S. Bureau of the Census, Current Population Reports, *Money Income and Poverty Status in 1975 of Families and Persons in the United States (Spring 1976 Survey of Income and Education)*, Series P-60, No. 111 (Washington, D.C.: U.S. Government Printing Office, April 1978), Table 1A.

26.   U.S. Bureau of the Census, *Money Income and Poverty Status in 1975, op. cit.*

Important changes in the composition of the labor force include the following:

• Women today constitute 41 percent of the labor force, and all forecasts predict a continuing upward trend in the 1980s.

• The post-World War II baby-boom cohort has come of age and, as a result, large numbers of young people have moved into the labor force. Because of the lower birthrate of the 1960s, the number of people in the labor force between the ages of 16 and 24 will decline in the 1980s by over one million, and their share of the labor force will be reduced by six percentage points.

• In 1975 there were 39 million workers in the 25–44 age bracket; by the end of the 1980s there will be 60 million workers in this category, a 55 percent increase. The proportion of the work force which is aged 25–44 will have increased by ten full percentage points.

• There has been a sharp decline in the percentage of older men, those aged 55–64, in the labor force, with a greater percentage of these men retiring early. Their drop from a participation rate of 90 percent in 1947 to 75 percent in 1976 is somewhat of an enigma, although several possible reasons for the decline have been advanced: Some were laid off and were unable to reenter the labor force due to age discrimination; others were encouraged to leave through early retirement or severance payments; still others quit due to the nature of their jobs; and more people are asking for and receiving disability compensation.

• The number of nonwhites in the labor force has increased only slightly in recent years, with the decline in the participation rate of nonwhites relative to white workers balanced by increases in the population of nonwhites relative to that of whites. Efforts to promote equal job opportunity, however, have resulted in shifts of minorities within the labor market, with more white-collar employment now open to members of this group.

• Although precise numbers are not available, it has been estimated that the labor force includes about 7 million illegal aliens, totaling perhaps 8 percent of the employed labor force; and the United States has the longest border in the world between a developed and a largely underdeveloped economy.

• Persons in the labor force now average a little more than a high school education. For the younger generation, about one half attend college for some period of time, and half of these become college graduates.

The Rise of the Three-Tier Society

The income of different groups of persons varies substantially with the composition of the household. The number of workers and their dependents can now be of as much or even more importance as a factor in determining income for most households (and per capita within households) than the occupation of the traditional "main" and only wage earner of the household, and it is easier and quicker to change the composition of the household than to accumulate skills in order to change occupations.

These changes have given rise to a three-tier society in terms of incomes of different groups in the population:

- The multiple wage-earner household, with or without dependents; *and* the single wage-earner household without dependents (approximately 57 percent of all households in 1976).
- The household of two or more persons dependent on one wage earner (approximately 25 percent).
- Individuals or families with no wage earner (approximately 18 percent).

The first type of household tends to be more affluent, to have more discretionary income, other things being more or less equal, than the second type, and the second type more than the third.

Changing Attitudes toward Work

Most employed persons continue to be reasonably well satisfied with their jobs and to be willing to work reasonably hard at them. However, the overall picture conceals growing discontent among those segments of the labor force that are performing dead-end, low-paying jobs; and, throughout society, more education, more knowledge about jobs, more mobility, and more financial resources all mean that individuals are more eager and free to decline "bad" jobs and to search for "good" jobs.

Jobs generally have been getting better in many ways—higher incomes, more leisure, more security, better working conditions.*

The long-term trend in work satisfaction (1949–1977) has been an upward one, particularly among blacks as better jobs have become available to them. There are, however, some pockets of comparative dissatisfaction, particularly involving laborers and persons with routine assembly-line and office jobs. As other jobs become better, such jobs become comparatively worse.

The great bulge in workers of middle age will intensify competition for promotions and for better jobs generally. This should encourage orientation toward effective working performances. Some persons, however, will have disappointed expectations and this undoubtedly will affect their morale negatively.

*See Peter Henle, "Worker Dissatisfaction: A Look at the Economic Effects," *Monthly Labor Review*, February 1974; and Robert J. Flanagan, George Strauss, and Lloyd Ulman, "Worker Discontent and Work Place Behavior," *Industrial Relations*, May 1974.

Paralleling this positive orientation toward work is a more tolerant attitude toward different life-styles away from work, and more engagement in such life-styles. There are, of course, no entirely separate compartments for "work" and for "life," and life-styles have their impacts on work-styles, requiring many personal, interpersonal, and organizational adjustments. These impacts may increase in the future. There are inherent contradictions between emerging life-styles and old-fashioned attitudes toward work. The work ethic in the longer run may yet turn out to contain within itself the "seeds of its own destruction": hard work leads to affluence; affluence leads to new life-styles; new life-styles diminish the work ethic. But what seemed like affluence yesterday tends to become for many people the minimum acceptable standard of living today, and affluence remains somewhere ahead. Aspirations seem always to run ahead of attainments.

Although attitudes toward work remain generally affirmative, many people are more selective about their choice of specific jobs:

- Social and geographic mobility have increased, particularly for those members of minority groups with advanced levels of education.
- The cost of refusing a specific job has been reduced through unemployment compensation, food stamps, and other forms of social support. Also, as standards of living have been raised and as there are more multiple-earner families, individuals can survive longer waiting periods on their own resources. Young persons, in addition, have a more readily available choice between continuing their education and taking whatever job is available.
- More people want more options in connection with the jobs they do choose. Women often want part-time work. Men sharing household work often want flexitime. Couples or friends increasingly want to share jobs. Students want hours of work that accommodate their school schedules. Older people want reduced hours of work.
- A more educated labor force wants more interesting jobs, and more control over jobs,* and a greater variety of jobs, and more alternation of education, work, and leisure. "Interesting" jobs are now more in demand and "secure" jobs less.

Productivity

During the last ten years the rate of increase in the productivity rate within the private business sector has fallen dramatically to 1.8 percent per year from the 3.2 percent per year of the twenty-year period following World War II. The slowdown is partly due to cyclical factors, to shifts in the types of industries in the

---

*"Job control" is, as a result, not just a feature of American trade unionism, as Selig Perlman so persuasively argued long ago, but also increasingly of working life in its entirety (*A Theory of the Labor Movement* [New York: Macmillan, 1928]).

private sector and their level of output, and to the large numbers of relatively unskilled youth and women entering the labor force in the past decade who have been employed mainly in less productive, service-type occupations. There are ample explanations for this decline in rate of increase other than any diminution in work effort. The United States will not decline economically, if decline it does, because of any now evident new unwillingness of the labor force to work reasonably hard.

Absenteeism has not increased over the past two decades, even with the introduction of so many nontraditional workers.

IMPLICATIONS FOR THE WORLD OF WORK

The world of work is already reflecting the impacts of this fourth great evolutionary change in the labor force and its conduct. Management and unions are both making adjustments, and more are in order. But there is also a lot of perplexity. The cold wind of change is blowing in the faces of managers— private executives, trade-union officials, and government administrators—and there is still some uncertainty about the directions from which it is coming and particularly about how to take shelter from it.

The following are some of the apparent implications for labor-market policy of the cultural and attitudinal changes now taking place.

Providing Full and Equal Employment Opportunities

Many more jobs will need to be created. There will be more "voluntary unemployment" and thus it will be harder to obtain "full employment." New definitions of full employment will be needed, for example, one for persons wanting full-time work on a permanent basis, another for persons wanting part-time work on a permanent basis, another for those wanting full-time work on a variable basis, and still another for those wanting part-time work on a variable basis. There will be "ratios" of unemployment, not one rate.

Employers, especially in the private sector, will need to restructure work to create more jobs for the growing number of people who are in or who wish to join the work force, and these jobs will have to be more challenging and offer greater psychic rewards.

Women, many of them married, will continue in greater numbers to strive for more and better positions in middle- and upper-level management and in the professions. They will continue to need the help of antidiscrimination and affirmative-action programs to meet their goals, but many of them will also benefit from reforms in other areas: availability of better day care for children, more part-time jobs, and more recourse to flexitime and other alternative work patterns that will assist them in meeting obligations at home and at work.

Blacks have moved in increasing numbers into the clerical and sales levels of white-collar occupations and in more modest numbers into the managerial levels of white-collar employment and into the crafts and professions. But affirmative-action efforts must continue in order to ensure access to education, and to more satisfying and well-paying occupations for minority-group members.

Competition for jobs among young, inexperienced workers is intense. Young blacks in central cities, in particular, are suffering from a staggering unemployment rate, estimated at up to 60 percent. As the numbers of youth decline in the 1980s and entry-level jobs become more available, employment prospects for young people should improve.

Older workers may seek more part-time work to augment retirement incomes or seek second careers. Both of these options should be easier due to antidiscrimination legislation in the newly enacted law which, with several exceptions, extends the mandatory retirement age to 70. The reentry of this group into the labor force may even be welcomed in the 1980s as the number of available younger workers declines.

Adjusting Work to Changing Expectations

Jobs can be improved, job satisfaction in many occupations can rise, and society can accept a "new breed" that is willing to work hard on "good" jobs, provided they have freedom to influence the nature of their jobs and to pursue their own life-styles.* Many now "bad" jobs will need to be improved in their working conditions or in terms of their comparative compensation, or they will need to be filled by a constant flow of new immigrants, whether legal or illegal, since no one else will take them. Bad jobs fall mainly in three categories: "structureless" jobs in which the incumbent is unprotected by formal or informal seniority rules and is not subject to much in the way of fringe benefits; routine work in a factory or office; and "dirty" work, such as agricultural labor or garbage collecting. † Historically such jobs have often been poorly paid and most still are, although some

---

*Although the "new breed" in general seems oriented toward holding jobs and working on them, more men are now in the category of "out of the labor force"—some of them, presumably, rejecting work altogether. Thus there may be three cultures instead of two: old breed, new breed, and the opt-out breed. It is the new breed, particularly, that lives split-level lives: more or less "square" on the job but "counterculture" off the job. The size and composition of the "out of the labor force" category deserves continuing attention.

† Eli Ginzberg ("The Job Problem," *Scientific American*, November 1977) has defined half of the jobs in the private sector of American society as "bad" in the sense that they are found in industries in which average earnings are below the national average, mainly in services, retail trade and finance, real estate, and insurance. Our definition of a bad job is different. It is one that is bad because it is

have by now risen substantially in their comparative compensation. The wage and salary structure of the nation should be, and sporadically is being, stood on its head with once bad jobs being paid more than "good" jobs. To some extent, but to a limited extent, bad jobs can be made into good jobs.* The alternative to more money or to job improvement is to keep on allowing ever new waves of immigrants to fill these jobs, with substantial cumulative consequences.

We now have the anomaly of substantial unemployment and substantial numbers of job vacancies, not so much because of lack of skill but because of lack of acceptance by large numbers of Americans of the "total package" of costs and benefits that many jobs now offer. The revolt against bad jobs by an increasingly highly educated and sophisticated labor force is one of the fundamental forces of this stage of industrialization. Some very hard choices loom ahead.

Even though jobs may be "good," there will be employees who are overqualified by education for the jobs they hold. This group may easily run to 5 to 10 percent of the labor force. †

Nontraditional workers bring with them nontraditional arrangements, just as nontraditional students do in the colleges. The "traditional" worker, a married male who is the sole source of income for his family, is now in the small minority (about 15 percent).

There is more job turnover—it has already doubled since 1900. More second careers must be facilitated; more exceptions must be made to rules; more options must be created affecting terms and length of work, fringe benefits, and codes of conduct. These developments have impacts on the personnel office and also on collective bargaining contracts. One way to avoid irreconcilable differences of interests among workers is to give them several options among which to choose within the terms of the contract.

structureless and/or routine and/or dirty, and these characteristics are not offset by above-average pay. Reviewing occupation by occupation, it appears that perhaps somewhere around 25 percent of the jobs in the private sector are bad according to this definition. The proportion in government employment is considerably lower, both according to the Ginzberg definition and this definition.

* Some jobs are of necessity "routine" or "dirty," but they must not necessarily be low paid; and with high enough pay, they would no longer be viewed as bad. And it should be noted that structureless jobs do fit some members of the labor force who want a chance to enter the employed labor force and gain experience, or who want only intermittent or part-time work permanently without any ongoing attachments, or who are between employment at more regular jobs. Structureless jobs are only really bad when they are too low paid or otherwise too exploitative, or offer no chance to move out for those who want to move on.

†If we add together the groups in which many of the members are likely to be disadvantaged or disenchanted, we get a very sizable number of persons involved: 18 percent of households without a wage earner; over 5 percent of active members of the labor force without a job; 25 percent of wage earners who have "bad" jobs; 5 to 10 percent of the wage earners who are clearly overqualified for their jobs; and about 24 percent of wage earners who have dependents and are the sole source of income in the household. There is substantial overlap among these categories; and many persons in some categories (particularly the last) could not be considered disadvantaged or so likely to be disenchanted by their position in society; but the net numbers, after such adjustments, must be substantial.

Maintaining Productivity Increases

The Bureau of Labor Statistics forecasts indicate that productivity rates will increase in the decade of the 1980s, but probably will not return to the high rate of increase of the two decades following World War II.

Productivity could be further improved, however, by programs that encourage the development of human and capital resources, and by improvements in technology. Also, the formation of labor–management committees to attack such problems as how to eliminate excessive waste of energy, materials, supplies, or equipment will undoubtedly result in higher productivity. Similarly, careful choice of equipment and process technology to enhance the work environment as well as to provide better direct means of production will also improve productivity.

The expected changes in the composition of the labor force in the coming years should also have a positive effect:

- The prime age group, which is gaining experience, will increase in number.
- The smaller growth in the total labor force with continuation of capital growth should result in continued improvements in capital–labor ratios.

Retarding the growth of productivity, however, will be an increase in the amount of investment related to environmental standards, occupational safety and health standards, and energy conservation. Also, few further gains are likely to emerge from shifts from the farm to nonfarm sectors of the economy.

THE GREAT UNCERTAINTY: THE FUTURE CONTEXT

The 1980s are now just ahead. Plans are already being made for this decade by private corporations, by unions, and by government. What will the factual situation be? What old policies should be changed and what new ones should be adopted? Little is predestined. One significant aspect of industrial society, as compared with earlier societies closer to raw nature, is that so much is left open to human choice. What may be the main axes of development that will help shape the future? Where are we going in terms of a central theme or themes?

It is clear that some visions of the future that stirred debate as little as a third of a century ago no longer agitate our minds and passions. Socialism has been decisively rejected as a path for social advancement in the United States, as has the idea of the corporation-as-community of Elton Mayo,* and the contrary view of

---

*Elton Mayo, *The Human Problems of an Industrial Civilization* (New York: Macmillan, 1933).

the union-as-community of Frank Tannenbaum.* Not the state alone, nor the corporation alone, nor the trade union alone will lead the way into the society of tomorrow.

Several interesting scenarios are set forth in the chapters of this book:

The *"quality of life"* prospect of Etzioni. Resources become less available. The work ethic undergoes an erosion in "a slow but not a slack America." Society becomes more decentralized; the introduction of larger and larger scale technology is rejected. Quality of life becomes more important than quantity of goods.

The *new problems to solve* challenge of Bluestone. Much remains to be done—secure full employment, reform the authoritarian workplace, attain the four-day workweek, create better jobs, among other goals. The presumption is that the resources will be available and that legitimate wants have not yet been satisfied; there is a new world still to win.

The *hard bargaining ahead* expectation of Raskin. Many difficult issues exist, including stagflation, foreign competition, technological displacement of workers, reduced hours of work, affirmative action. These issues are set within the context of a growing hostility among corporations, trade unions, and government. "Conflict and confrontation" and a new era of bad feeling may lie ahead; but there is no prospect of a Marxian-type class war.

The *"new breed"* script of Yankelovich. The past decade was a "watershed in American social history" and half of all adult Americans now belong to the "new breed." Members of the new breed want jobs in a quantity not previously imagined, but the challenge is to get them to work at the jobs once they have them. "Success" and "self-fulfillment" have parted company. The "psychology of entitlement" will triumph. There could be a "disaster in the making," but it can be avoided if the new breed of managers can devise "diverse incentive packages" that are sufficiently attractive to draw forth effort. The new breed will "change the very nature of modern industrial society," in the course of a "value revolution."

The *"democracy at work"* vision of Rosow. Political democracy in the state will find its counterpart in economic democracy within the plant. This is already the clear tendency in almost all the nations of Western Europe, led initially by Germany.

There are other scenarios around, including:

The *heaven on earth* version of Kahn. † Standards of living all around the world will surpass those currently enjoyed in the United States by several times over.

*Frank Tannenbaum, *A Philosophy of Labor* (New York: Knopf, 1951).

† Herman Kahn et al., *The Next 200 Years* (New York: Morrow, 1976).

The *new hell* vision of Heilbroner.* Resources will run out and all social systems deteriorate. There will be a new war of "every man against every man"—the Hobbesian nightmare.

The *last fling* vision of Leontief.† The world economy has about another twenty years before major current sources of energy are exhausted or near exhaustion.

The *slow strangulation* thesis of Schumpeter.‡ Innovation grinds to a halt under growing burdens of controls.

And still other scenarios are being enacted now: *slow growth* in the United Kingdom; *growing social anarchy* in Italy—"red guerrilla islands" proliferate; and the *"hard hat society"* in Sweden where the labor-market "partners" in production largely determine what happens to the economy and guide even government itself—"consensus" in advance by the "social partners" takes the place of pluralistic initiatives by many elements of society.

There are many scenarios. Which one or which combination will prove to be the one that is actually played? That depends, in part, on what is desired but also on what major decision makers, and even the people at large, come to expect. The future, to some extent, determines the present as expectations about it affect current actions. What assumptions are made about the future, in turn, affect the future as they first affect the present.

Free Individuals—Controlled Organizations

I should like to venture one more view of what basically is happening to American society that particularly relates to the future of work in America. It is that we are rejecting what Sidney and Beatrice Webb once called the "device of the common rule," which replaced the "anarchy of individual bargaining."§ Not only unions but also large employers and the government came to prefer fixed rates and standards "uniform in their application": one rate of pay, one length for the workweek, one set of job descriptions, one rate of output, and so on down a long list. The common rule was the chosen instrument of the private and public bureaucracies that resulted from the large-scale endeavors of industrial society.

The nontraditional worker, the educated worker, the mobile worker, the "new breed" worker lead to pressures for many variations around the common rule; to "electives" at the place of work as in the school; to special arrangements in the

---

*Robert L. Heilbroner, *An Inquiry into the Human Prospect* (New York: Norton, 1974).
†Wassily Leontief et al., *The Future of the World Economy* (New York: Oxford University Press, 1977).
‡Joseph A. Schumpeter, *Capitalism, Socialism, and Democracy* (New York: Harper, 3rd ed., 1950).
§*Industrial Democracy* (printed by the authors, London, 1897) pp. 715, 734.

office just as there are individual "learning contracts" in college; to options in working time, in retirement plans, in job tasks; to choices about when to work, when to learn, when to take leisure time, when to retire, rather than follow a set schedule; to the multiple-option society instead of the society of the common rule. I agree with Yankelovich about the new demand for "self-fulfillment" as part of this; but I part company with him when he suggests that hard work per se is now being widely rejected.* Thus I see more that is creative in this development and less that might lead to possible "disaster," although Yankelovich also notes the possibility of "constructive" results. A race, however, certainly is taking place between more education and new life-styles on the one side, and more progressive personnel policies and practices on the other.

We are heading, I believe, toward a society that might be identified as one of *free individuals* and *controlled organizations*. Clearly organizations are being subjected to more and more controls, as Schumpeter feared, but individuals are being liberated in many ways. We are building what might be called "industrialism with a human face."

---

*". . . millions . . . are no longer motivated to work hard." (See page 3.)

WORK IN AMERICA
The Decade Ahead

I.
THE WORK FORCE OF THE FUTURE

1.

Work, Values, and the New Breed

DANIEL YANKELOVICH

President, Yankelovich, Skelly and White, Inc.

A New Breed of Americans, born out of the social movements of the sixties and grown to majority proportions in the seventies, holds a set of values and beliefs so markedly different from the traditional outlook that they promise to transform the character of work in America.

Here are just a few consequences of New Breed values:

- The desire to hold a paid job has become so compelling that some 24 to 27 million people not now employed in full-time paid jobs—women, young people, and old people in particular—are waiting to take jobs if they become available. The traditional method of creating jobs is through growth in the economy at the average rate of 2 to 2.5 million new jobs a year; at this rate, supply has no chance of catching up with demand. The official unemployment figure of about 7 million therefore grossly understates the potential demand for jobs. As we move closer to our national commitment to guarantee jobs for everyone who wants to work, we are confronted with the awesome task of creating millions of more new jobs than those that will be generated by normal or even superheated growth in the economy.[1]

- Competition for jobs has already grown so fierce that young blacks, the prime target group for many policy planners, are the most deprived; they now suffer from an unemployment rate estimated at 46 to 60 percent. If our approach to the job market does not change, their plight will grow worse. And yet, millions of jobs that are considered undesirable or "dead end" cannot be filled.

- Today, millions who do hold paid jobs find the present incentive systems so unappealing that they are no longer motivated to work hard.

3

As a consequence, not only do they withdraw emotional involvement from the job, they also insist upon steady increases in pay and fringe benefits to compensate for the job's lack of appeal. The less they give to the job, the more they seem to demand, a process that cannot continue for long without breaking down. A deep flaw in the incentive system, signified by the failure of the old incentives to catch up with the new motivations, leads inexorably to deterioration in the workplace, threatening the position of the United States as the world's foremost industrial nation.

No one wants these distressing consequences, least of all the New Breed of Americans. But they have to be reckoned with. And reckoning with them is, after all, the principal task of those who manage the economic system. My aim in this chapter is to demonstrate the need to break through the rigid economic mind-set that now dominates policy thinking about work and jobs in order to gain a broader perspective, one that adds psychological and social insights to traditional economic categories. If we can broaden our policies to take into account systematically recent changes in the American value system, perhaps in the 1980s we can turn a potential disaster into a positive opportunity to build a more vital economy *and* a more humane society.

In this chapter, I first comment briefly on the general relationship of value systems to economic principles and then describe how traditional values affected the workplace in the past. The subsequent section shows how these values are being transformed, and the final section discusses the consequences of New Breed values for the unemployment problem and the incentive system.

VALUE SYSTEMS AND ECONOMIC PRINCIPLES

More than a half century ago Thorstein Veblen argued that the laws of economics are not fixed and independent but depend totally on the value system of the society. When social values change, economic principles must also change. If, for example, the majority of Americans suddenly ceased to value economic growth, as appeared possible just a few years ago, our thinking about jobs, productivity, and the direction of the economy would be thrown into disarray and, because of the political consequences, would have to be rethought along fundamentally new lines. Veblen's argument that the economy cannot exist as an island isolated from the society at large is clearly basic to economic policy. Yet policymakers have ignored it with impunity for years.

If Veblen and those who followed him—Schumpeter, Heller, Okun, Heilbroner, Galbraith, and others—are correct, how can so fundamental a point be ignored? There are several possible explanations. One is that Veblen's dictum is an empty truism, correct in the abstract but without measurable consequences in the practical, everyday world of jobs and work. Another possibility is that the American value system had not changed in ways essential to the economy until quite recently. Therefore policymakers could have been lulled into a sense of false security.

I favor this latter explanation. For most of this century, right up to the 1970s, the social values of the majority of Americans, insofar as they bear on work and jobs, had remained essentially stable. Economists could therefore give lip service to Veblen's insight but brush it aside in practice because it had so few practical consequences. The everyday rules of thumb with which policymakers operated as they examined the labor market, unemployment, work incentives, productivity, and other work-related issues could be applied as if the value system did not count.

Assuming that the value context was fixed and immutable, we could also assume that our economic models could function in splendid isolation: "Variables" that do not change are, by definition, not variables—until they suddenly and unexpectedly stir to life.

Then, in the 1970s, the values of Americans changed dramatically. The "constants" suddenly turned into variables, and everyone was caught unprepared. We will be busy throughout the 1980s, and perhaps the 1990s as well, with the problem of integrating this new factor into our thinking about jobs and work and, more difficult still, into our formal tools of measurement.

The first signs of significant change appeared in the 1960s with the emergence of the students' movement and the women's movement. In the 1960s these were merely premonitory; they affected a bare handful of the population. Appearances to the contrary, the majority of Americans in the 1960s held fast to traditional values. It was not until the 1970s that the New Breed majority significantly shifted their value orientation. Unless we understand these New Breed values correctly, we cannot answer any of the following tantalizing questions:

- Why do so many jobs go begging when so many people are looking for work?

- How large is the pool of people who would take jobs if they were available? What kinds of jobs?
- Why does the unemployment rate of young people in general, and young blacks in particular, continue to rise even when the economy outdoes itself in creating new jobs?
- Why are so many women flooding into the labor force?
- In the future will old people want to retire, or will they want to go on working?
- What should we do about the so-called undesirable jobs that are now being done by illegal aliens, or not being done at all?
- How important is money as an incentive to people to work hard and be productive?
- Does job satisfaction lead to improved productivity?

TRADITIONAL VALUES AND THE WORKPLACE

In the last half century the field of psychology has added greatly to our understanding of what contributes to people's feelings of well-being. A variety of studies have demonstrated that psychological well-being is a complex structure. Among its chief building blocks are a sense of self-esteem and conviction of one's worth as an individual; a clear-cut sense of identity; the ability to believe that one's actions make sense to others as well as to oneself; a set of concrete goals and values; feelings of potency and efficacy; enough stimulation to avoid boredom; a feeling that one's world is reasonably stable; and an overall sense of meaning and coherence in one's life. People for whom these needs are met often experience a joy in living and a conviction that they are successful as human beings. Their lives may be marked by suffering and frustration—such is the human condition—but, psychologically speaking, they are the fortunate ones.

Because psychologists focus so sharply on the *individual*, their writings imply that it is up to each person to achieve his or her psychological well-being through inner resources. Unfortunately, psychologists fail to appreciate how dependent all of us are on the ability of the society and culture to create the conditions—social, economic, political, and cultural—in which personal ego strengths can be nurtured.

For most of this century, and in particular in the quarter century following World War II (roughly up to 1970), the value system of most Americans centered around a number of powerful, culturally derived symbols that drew their strength from their ability to "deliver" at least some of the essentials of psychological well-being. In particular, they proved capable of giving people a sense of self-esteem, a clear identity, concrete well-defined goals and values, a sense of effectiveness, and a conviction that their private goals and behavior also contributed to the well-being of others.

Most of these symbols are strikingly middle class in character. They became dominant values in the 1950s and 1960s as more people were able to move into the middle class through education, a booming economy, and a steady rise in the median income of all but the poorest 20 percent of the population. Though these symbols are familiar to everyone, it is useful to outline the key ones to underscore how fundamental is the current change in values. Let me simply list a few of the leading success symbols of the recent past:

- The nuclear family symbolized a successful haven of refuge from a rough world, the major source of joy in life, and the basic socio-economic unit.
- Within the family, a rigid division of labor carried powerful symbolic overtones. The principal male role was to be a "good provider." The responsibility of the woman was to be a good wife, mother, cook, housekeeper, and residual legatee of all responsibilities except those of making a living and being "handy" around the house.
- Certain key possessions also played a vital symbolic role, notably the ownership of a single-family home, a large automobile, various labor-saving appliances, a television set, and such status symbols as diamond rings, wall-to-wall carpeting, and silver flatware. In the 1950s, the General Motors line symbolized to perfection the social mobility values of the period. As one moved up the ladder of success, each rise in rank could be symbolically celebrated by moving up the General Motors line—from Chevrolet to Pontiac, to Buick, to Oldsmobile, to Cadillac.
- Among the most important social symbols of success were those representing respectability. Respectability was achieved through such visible symbols, reinforced through advertising, as a well-kept lawn, a spic-and-span home in which floors were "clean enough to eat from," well-scrubbed children, sheets "whiter than white," appearing clean and neat at all times, "saving for a rainy day," "bettering oneself" in the world, and providing a good education for one's children. In private, one was required to avoid the appearance of violating the norms

of conventional sexual morality, i.e., by keeping homosexuality in the closet, as well as by hiding pregnancy or abortion for unmarried daughters, and by not condoning sexual relations between unmarried adults in the family home.

• Subordinating oneself to a complex network of obligations to others was also replete with symbolic meaning: One was expected to sacrifice oneself for the sake of children and family; to be loyal to the expectations of employers; to carry out one's responsibilities to the community, friends, and neighbors; and in general, to observe those social and moral norms that supported these values.

For years to come, social critics will be debating whether the post-World War II period, from 1945 to 1970, was a "golden age" of stability and fulfillment in American life, or an era of repressive conformity, or both, in some paradoxical sense. We are still too close to this period, even though it is rapidly receding, to offer any valid judgment. But for our present purposes, I would like to underscore how marvelously ingenious, flexible, and democratic this value system was. So abundant were the symbols of success and psychological well-being, and so accessible were most of them to the average American during a period of rapid economic growth that almost everybody could be a "success" in some terms. In the postwar period, the median disposable income of Americans doubled from $5,600 in 1950 to $12,000 in 1973 (in 1970 dollars), so that a majority of Americans could experience self-fulfillment by means of a steady annual increase in their standard of living. It is true that people complained about the competitiveness and strain of "keeping up with the Joneses." In many ways the postwar period *was* a highly competitive era. But it was also an era in which the symbols of success were available to the majority rather than to the select few. Almost everybody could belong to a family, observe the rigidly prescribed sex roles in marriage, have children, sacrifice for them, buy a car, own a TV set, be respectable, keep their lust confined to their hearts, and observe the rules—and, in doing all these things, participate communally in a culturally defined consensus of what constitutes success.

Moreover, success symbols were clear-cut and concrete. People found it easy to know when they were being successful and to let others know as well—no small virtue in a symbol. Through hard work and a little luck, Americans achieved a high degree of self-esteem for themselves and also gained the approval of others.

From a sociological point of view, the indisputable virtue of the 1945-

to-1970 era was that individual aspirations for success and the socioeconomic trajectory of the society toward ever greater growth fitted together harmoniously. The individual wanted what the society was prepared to reward. When people worked hard, earned money, and spent it unstintingly on consumer goods, it brought them self-esteem and the approval of others as well as material comfort. Crucially important, people were able to feel that they were advancing the goals of the larger society as well as fulfilling themselves. (This is a point to keep in mind as we begin to discuss changes in the value system since 1970.) To maintain psychological well-being, people *must* feel that what they are doing makes sense not only to themselves but to others as well. When they do not have this feeling, they may not know precisely what is missing in their lives, but they feel off-balance, confused, uncertain.

Some of the consequences of the old value system for the world of work can be summed up as follows:

- If women could afford to stay home and not work at a paid job, they did so.
- As long as a job provided a man with a decent living and some degree of economic security, he would put up with all its drawbacks, because it meant that he could fulfill his economic obligations to his family and confirm his own self-esteem as breadwinner and good provider.
- The incentive system, providing mainly money and status rewards, was successful in motivating most people.
- People were tied to their jobs not only by bonds of commitment to their family but also by loyalty to their organizations.
- Most people defined their identity through their work role, subordinating and suppressing most conflicting personal desires.
- For all practical purposes a job was defined as a paid activity that provided steady full-time work to the male breadwinner with compensation adequate to provide at least the necessities, and, with luck, some luxuries for an intact nuclear family.

Under the onslaught of a new value system, these consequences of the old value system have already changed or are in the process of changing.

CHANGES IN THE VALUE SYSTEM

Since the beginning of the 1970s, the American people have been struggling with a confusing shift in the relationship between "success" and "self-fulfillment," as each of these terms takes on new forms of cultural definition. As we have seen, in the postwar period, the meaning of success was clear and unambiguous. Moreover, for most Americans, success and self-fulfillment were synonymous. People found their self-fulfillment through the pursuit of success: the psychological satisfactions sought through self-fulfillment—self-esteem, a firm sense of identity, feelings of autonomy, freedom, achievement, effectiveness, and general well-being—were pursued and achieved for millions of Americans by means of the symbols of success I have described.

In the 1970s, the aspirations for self-fulfillment of millions of Americans split away from the traditional symbols of success. This happened for many complex reasons having to do with the sexual revolution, the effects of the women's movement on the family, the dying off of the generation scarred by the Great Depression of the 1930s, a growing disillusionment with the ability of our institutions to deliver the goods, the failure of the economy to live up to people's expectations of a steady annual increase in income, a questioning of whether the values of a consumption economy are worth the nose-to-the-grindstone way of life that pays for all the goodies, an almost subliminal awareness that energy shortages and environmental hazards call for a new orientation, and a further evolution of individualism into the quest for less conforming personal life-styles. For whatever reason, once self-fulfillment was severed from success, it began to acquire its own cultural meanings, some of which still partly overlap with success, but many of which do not.

Simply put, a New Breed of Americans have come to feel that success is not enough to satisfy their yearnings for self-fulfillment. They are reaching out for something more and for something different.

I estimate that, at the present time, the New Breed, those who feel that their aspirations for self-fulfillment can no longer be wholly satisfied through conventional success, constitute a majority of the American people (approximately 52 percent).[2] Not surprisingly, the younger, better educated, and more affluent parts of the population are disproportionately represented in the New Breed, whereas the older, poorer, less well-educated segments of the population cling more tenaciously to the old value system and to traditional success symbols.

The relationship of the New Breed to older symbols of success is complex. Several different patterns can be discerned. One pattern, the clearest, involves an outright rejection of success, but only a small minority of the New Breed conform to this pattern. Those who opt out of the system to find new life-styles in rural Maine or Vermont or in the Colorado mountains are heirs to the counterculture of the 1960s. They abhor and reject most traditional symbols of success. In contrast with the majority of the New Breed, as well as with those who cling to tradition, their quest for self-fulfillment leads to an emphasis on "less": less money, simpler life-styles, fewer possessions, smaller institutions. Most New Breed people, however, do not reject success outright. On the contrary, they value it, but they also find it wanting. Somehow, the conventional symbols no longer satisfy their deepest psychological needs nor nourish their self-esteem nor fulfill their cravings for the "full rich life." Their choice leads not toward *less*, but toward *more*. In effect, they demand full enjoyment as well as full employment.

What is the nature of this "something more"? Significantly, the New Breed themselves cannot answer concretely and specifically when this question is put to them. In surveys conducted in the 1950s and 1960s, the majority of Americans could readily tell you what their goals were. People spoke of their family life, their plans for a new home or new car, the education of their children, and their desires for modest but steady increases in their standard of living. Today, the New Breed speak a different language. They speak vaguely of "fulfilling their potential," of the need to "keep on growing" psychologically, spiritually. They speak of having "a duty to themselves."

In contrast to older symbols of success, the new self-fulfillment symbols seem amorphous and elusive. They do not have the clear, tangible reality of obtaining a ten-dollar-a-week raise in pay, buying a new Oldsmobile, having a son or daughter accepted at Michigan State, moving to Scarsdale, or throwing a successful Tupperware party. As a result, many people do not know today whether or not they are being self-fulfilled, nor are they able to communicate that state of grace to others through readily recognized symbols.

Such vagueness creates disorientation and confusion. People constantly ask themselves: "Am I happy?" "Am I being self-fulfilled?" "Am I doing what I really want to do?" In the pursuit of the elusive goal of self-fulfillment, Americans today restlessly uproot themselves. They shuttle from one end of the continent to the other. They break up perfectly good marriages and form new ones. They leave one job for another. They change careers. They redecorate. They diet. They jog. They read Gail Sheehy's book *Passages* to find out how they are doing in comparison with others in their age group. Self-assertively, they wonder out loud whether they are being assertive enough. Complaining of other people's narcissism, they elbow other egos out of the way to make room for their own. Obsessed with self-fulfillment, they pull the plant from its soil over and over again to make sure its roots are healthy.

Although the New Breed's inchoate desire for something beyond the old symbols of success is hard to pin down, several general features can be discerned. New Breed people assume that self-fulfillment, unlike success, is to be found *within* the self. In the old success philosophy, what counted lay *outside* the self—a new car, an achieving child, a job promotion; in the new philosophy, the searcher turns inward.

Typically, also, the New Breed feel they are obliged to give more attention to their own needs and desires than to what other people expect of them. As parents, they convey this message to their children: "I have my own life to live. I am prepared to take care of you and do all I can for you, but I will not live my life vicariously through you. For this you should be grateful, because you too have your own life to live, and you should not have it burdened with obligations to others, including obligations to us, your parents." And if they are young people, they say to their parents: "I appreciate what you have done for me, but please leave me alone to make my own mistakes and live my own life. I may not know what I want to do with it, but whatever it is, it's what *I* want to do and not what others expect of me. It's ridiculous to conform to a lot of rules that no longer make sense in our kind of society."

In the New Breed we see the beginnings of an ethic built around the concept of duty to oneself, in glaring contrast to the traditional ethic of obligation to others. In reaching for "something more than success," the New Breed also press for greater freedom for the individual, freedom to express impulses and desires that people have been accustomed to suppress. Sexual desires are the most obvious, hence the greater openness of homosexuality, pornography, nakedness, and casual sexual encounters. But other forms of freedom "to do what I want to do" are almost as prominent: freedom to enjoy life now rather than in some distant future; freedom to elevate one's own desires to the rank of entitlements; freedom to give one's own ego more room in which to maneuver; freedom to pull up stakes and move on without having to pick up the pieces.

The New Breed values are expressed in the world of work in some ways that are obvious and others that are quite subtle. Let me call attention to three of the more striking manifestations of New Breed work-related values: the increasing importance of leisure, the symbolic significance of the paid job, and the insistence that jobs become less depersonalized.

Leisure

Along with family life, work and leisure always compete for people's time and allegiance. One or the other is usually the center of gravity; rarely does the individual strike an equal balance among all three. For the New Breed, family and work have grown less important and leisure more important. When work and leisure are compared as sources of satisfaction, only one out of five people (21 percent) state that work means more to them than leisure. The majority (60 percent) say that while they enjoy their work, it is not their major source of satisfaction. (The other 19 percent are so exhausted by the demands work makes of them that they cannot conceive of it as even a minor source of satisfaction.[3])

This is not a purely American phenomenon. A recent study in Sweden produced this striking set of findings.[4] When Swedish men, 18 to 55 years of age, were asked way back in 1955 "What gives your life the most meaning—your family, your work, or your leisure?" only 13 percent answered leisure, 33 percent named work, and 45 percent said their families gave their lives the most meaning. In 1977, when the same question was asked of a new cross section of Swedish men, the proportion of men naming work as the main source of meaning in life had been cut in half, from 33 percent to 17 percent. The position of family life had also eroded slightly, from 45 percent to 41 percent. But dedication to leisure had more than doubled, from 13 percent to 27 percent!

The Symbolic Importance of a Paid Job

If for men leisure grows more important as the domain within which self-fulfillment is to be pursued, for New Breed women the symbolic significance of a paid job has greatly intensified. Let us acknowledge at once that most women work for money: Many women have no other source of economic support but their own work, and increasing numbers support their dependent children through paid work. Even when the burden of making a living falls mainly on the man, the money earned by the woman in most families has proven indispensable to maintaining a standard of living the family considers satisfactory. Yet, even though work is often an economic necessity for women, one of the essential points of the women's movement is the symbolic meaning of a paid job.

In recent years unpaid housework has suffered a severe loss in social status. For women today being "just a housewife" is a poor means of maintaining self-esteem. For New Breed women, exclusive confinement to the unpaid work of homemaker and mother somehow implies being cut off from the full possibilities of self-fulfillment. A paid job has become a badge of membership in the larger society and an almost indispensable symbol of self-worth. It is also a practical means of achieving autonomy and independence. The woman with a paid job, however menial or poorly paid it may be, feels that she no longer has to be totally dependent on the will and whim of a man. No longer is she obliged, because she is trapped in a status of total dependency, to stay with an unsatisfactory marriage. Divorce rates have shot up because divorce is now a practical option for millions of women. They now have, or can acquire, the "price of admission" to independence in our society—a paid job. This does not mean that only women are choosing divorce and are solely responsible for high divorce rates; many women do not choose divorce because they are able to find work, but find work because they are forced to support themselves after men leave to "fulfill themselves."

To observers, and indeed to many women who work, exchanging the security of a homemaker for a poorly paid job seems like a bad bargain. Often it *is* a bad bargain. Probably, therefore, women in the 1980s will grow more discriminating about the jobs they take. But even when this occurs, as seems inevitable, the pendulum will not swing all the way back. Unfortunately, many women seem to have accepted unquestioningly the male-dominated values of the old era; instead of bringing men to a greater appreciation of the values of home, family, and child care, women have endorsed the male values associated with paid work.

The Subjectivity Factor

More complex and intangible is the New Breed's refusal to subordinate their personalities to the work role. To understand this refusal is to grasp the essence of the New Breed's quest for self-fulfillment.

One of the most striking characteristics of the old value system is the tendency for people to identify themselves with their work role. European visitors to the United States are often startled when Americans identify themselves mainly with their work. "I am a car dealer"; "I'm assistant manager of the local bank"; "I'm a housewife"; "I manage the personnel department at J. C. Penney's." Thus do Americans quickly and readily label themselves. There is no greater source of discomfort to the New Breed's sense of self-fulfillment than this traditional equation of identity with the work role. In the eyes of the New Breed, when an individual is subordinated to a role, he or she somehow is turned into an object, and individual humanity is reduced in some indefinable but all-important sense. In the new value system the individual says, in effect, "I am more than my role. I am myself." The New Breed person demands that his or her individuality be recognized. "Yes," says the New Breeder, "I am a secretary, but first and foremost I am a human being." When we ask people in our surveys which aspects of their work are becoming more important to them people stress above all else "being recognized as an individual person." They also stress "the opportunity to be with pleasant people with whom I like to work." Significantly, for the majority of people these demands come ahead of the desire that the work itself be interesting and nonroutine.

Perhaps no flaw of the old value system is felt more deeply by New Breed Americans than the conviction that, for all of its indisputable merits, the old value system depersonalized the individual. It is fascinating to watch this theme, a theme that has played a central role in both the existential critique of modern society and the Marxist critique of capitalist society, reemerge in a new form as a semiarticulate popular value held by a majority, rather than as an abstract philosophical generalization advanced by intellectuals. Many intellectuals have long held that modern industrial society, either in its capitalistic form or in its bureaucratized socialistic form, is inherently incapable of treating people in their work role as subjects rather than objects. Often this view is put forth as part of an elite ideology and critique of modernization. Yet here we have a mass movement, unrelated to any fixed ideological position, and largely uncritical of the system as a whole, demanding in the name of individual self-fulfillment that an old flaw in the system be repaired, unrelated to any political or ideological program of action.

When people insist that they not be subordinated to their role, this demand conflicts directly with traditional concepts of managerial efficiency. In the 1980s, we shall see this confrontation played out in thousands of forms and in millions of day-to-day decisions whose cumulative effects are destined to change the very nature of modern industrial society.

CONSEQUENCES OF THE VALUE REVOLUTION

Reality imposes many constraints on New Breed values—in the forms of limits to the economy's capacity to create new jobs; international competitive pressures; traditional practices that pit labor against management, business against government, consumer against producer. So sharply do New Breed values conflict with the realities of the workplace that confrontation seems inevitable. Two fronts will bear the brunt: the employment system and the incentive system.

The Employment System

With each passing year, the consensus in the country grows stronger that a paid job at fair rates of compensation should be guaranteed to everyone who wants to work. This commitment to full employment has developed slowly over the past three decades, but its tempo is now accelerating. (As of December 1977, 61 percent of the public endorsed it.[5]) Unfortunately, this commitment is based on certain assumptions that the new values are rapidly rendering obsolete. If we assume that an unemployment rate of about 7 percent accurately reflects the present level of demand for jobs, and if we further assume a "full employment" objective of 4 to 5 percent unemployment, then the objective does not seem beyond our grasp.

Under the impact of the new values, however, the official unemployment rate of 7 percent does not nearly begin to measure the size of the potential work force. Based on a reanalysis of Bureau of Labor Statistics projections, Eli Ginzberg has estimated that 24 million people would take full-time jobs if they were available, more than three times the number counted in the official 7 percent unemployment figure.[6] Using a somewhat different set of calculations, I arrived at a similar estimate of 24 to 27 million people waiting for jobs.[7] The arithmetic is simple and overwhelming. To meet a national commitment to full employment, if our estimates are approximately correct, the economy would have to create more than 20 million new jobs.

These estimates say nothing about the kinds of jobs people prefer or the conditions under which they would accept work. But they do help to explain why a policy of reducing unemployment through normal economic growth cannot possibly be successful. This lesson was painfully brought home to the Ford administration. Indeed, one of Mr. Ford's chief economic advisors[8] attributes the Republican loss of the 1976 presidential election to its failure to grasp early enough the true nature and magnitude of the unemployment problem.

Sweden, which also is undergoing a new-values phase of development, is already experiencing more of its practical consequences. To reduce unemployment in rural areas, the Swedish government has recently built factories in locations in which unemployment is high. Astonishingly, the government found that unemployment in the target areas was higher after the new factories were built than before. People who were not officially included in the labor force appeared out of nowhere to take new jobs as fast as they were created.

Clearly we confront a vastly different unemployment problem than in the recent past. There is no way to create 20 million new jobs through a business-as-usual approach, conservative *or* liberal.

What is likely to happen in the years ahead?

The most obvious possibility is that we will back off from our national commitment to guarantee jobs for all those who want to work. Though this is the clearest choice, I think it is also the least likely. Curiously, both the old and the new values converge to reinforce the symbolic power of a paid job in our society. For those who remain faithful to the old values, particularly adult men with families, a paid job is the classic road to self-respect—the chance to discharge one's obligations to others, to achieve identity, respectability, economic security, material comfort, and social mobility. Under the new values, a paid job symbolizes independence, freedom, challenge, belonging, a chance for self-fulfillment, and hope for the future, not just for the family man but also for women, single men, and young people of both sexes.

The new values strengthen our national commitment in other ways as well. The preoccupation with self inexorably carries with it this message from those with jobs to those without them: "If I have to carry *my* share of the burden, I'll be damned if I will let you get away without carrying *yours.*" As the national debate on tax reform, redistribution of income, and reverse discrimination intensifies, as it must, certain outcomes seem inevitable. To the psychology of entitlement that dominates New Breed thinking, a job is not a privilege, but a right. Here once again liberals and conservatives, Old Breed and New, converge. Americans may disagree on who should get what, but there is universal agreement that everyone has the right to take a grab at the brass ring of success and self-fulfillment through hard work. This points to a strengthening of the traditional concept of equality of opportunity as the fairest way to decide who should get what, in contrast to the pressure for an equality-of-results approach currently favored by many policymakers. In the future, however, equality of opportunity will be interpreted more generously to give more people an equal chance at the starting line. And inevitably, the starting line will be defined in terms of paid jobs, supplemented by various educational programs.

Americans are an intensely practical people. To most Americans it makes no sense to have a fifth of the potential work force remain idle and partly dependent on government transfer payments that have to be financed by taxes on those who do work. The idea that tens of millions of our fellow citizens want jobs may give the economists a giant headache, but from the man in the street's point of view, this fact will be greeted with a loud hurrah as a harbinger of future economic health and productivity.

For these and other reasons I suspect that our commitment to guarantee jobs to all who want to work will be strengthened in the 1980s, not weakened, even if far-reaching new approaches are required to achieve a full-employment economy.

A second possibility is that we may back off from New Breed values. Perhaps we will go back to the traditional division of labor: the man as chief breadwinner and good provider and the woman as economically dependent mother and homemaker. I suggested earlier that women will surely become more discriminating in the kinds of jobs they take, and some may rediscover the homemaker's role to be a more satisfying alternative than menial paid work. But these are minor adjustments, ripples in the tide. The prospect of any large-scale return to the dominant family/work patterns of the fifties and sixties is, I believe, negligible.

Consider just one fact. At the turn of the century, a woman's life expectancy was forty-seven years, eighteen of which were spent in childbearing. Women married young and spread their childbearing years over a much larger proportion of their total life span than they now do. Today, the average woman's life expectancy is seventy-seven years, and women spend only about ten years of this long life in childbearing. It is true that child *rearing* takes a lot longer, but many women with young children apparently have concluded that the children do not need their full-time attention and can be cared for by surrogates. There is simply no way that, with an ever-increasing level of education, women are going to return to a setting that occupies their full energies for only a small fraction of their lives. The essence of the new values resides in people's conviction that all options for self-fulfillment must remain open. One of the most attractive and realistic options, from many points of view, is the paid job. It is not likely that this conclusion will weaken in the 1980s; on the contrary, it will probably grow stronger.

The country's most likely response to the unemployment problem, and it is the worst of all possibilities, is no response. We will probably drift into the future, refusing to make any but small patchwork adjustments.

Few institutions seem ready to confront the problem in its full magnitude. Government is not adept at finding creative solutions to politically divisive problems. The ideological positions of our two major political parties lock them into obsolete and inadequate approaches. Businessmen fear all interventions that experiment with the workings of the private economy. (How otherwise can one explain the endorsement of massive transfer payments to those unable to find work by such well-credentialed conservatives as Milton Friedman?) Trade unions fear all changes that might jeopardize the job security of their present members. Economists have few creative ideas for dealing with structural unemployment, or for creating new jobs through methods other than managing aggregate demand or traditional public-works programs. In combination, all these forces work toward drift, inaction, unresponsiveness.

Drift will benefit few. Through costly transfer payments, we will continue to support many of those who cannot find jobs, particularly if they are out of work through no fault of their own. As in the past, these payments will not be large enough to permit those who do not work to live in comfort, but at the same time will be too large to be politically acceptable to the overburdened taxpayer. Besides, able-bodied men and women who find themselves "kept" like dependent and unwanted pets will grow ever more disaffected. The competition for jobs will become fiercer and perhaps even vicious, with young people, blacks, women, and old people pitted against each other for second-rate jobs. Our massive social needs in connection with the cities, transportation, housing, and conservation, will go on being neglected. And to these old sources of neglect we will add new ones: the neglect of young children whose parents are working; the neglect of old people who retire unwillingly because we do not have the social imagination to invent vital roles for them; the neglect of increasing millions of middle-aged singles who are the losers in the game of musical chairs we are currently playing with family life.

The great challenge of the 1980s will be to prevent this drift from occurring. To meet it we need more political will and intellectual understanding than we now have. I suspect we will have to invite into the tight circle of policymakers a broader representation of talents. We will need the best thinking of humanists, scientists, architects, engineers, philosophers, sociologists, artists, anthropologists, psychologists, community leaders, and above all, the general public. The public holds the key. If we can create public understanding of the alternatives and trade-offs and launch a real diaglogue on the value choices involved, we may have a chance of avoiding the drift and of inventing new ways to give people what they want most: a job to do, and a fair wage for doing it.

Incentives

More intangible, but no less serious, is the clash between New Breed values and the incentive system. Perhaps no question will dominate the workplace in the 1980s more than how to revamp incentives to make them a better match for the work motivation of the New Breed.

One might assume that because so many people want paid jobs, they are therefore motivated to work hard. This is true for some people, but the desire for a paid job and the motivation to work hard are independent factors.

Just *having* a paid job meets important human needs: for income, independence, self-respect, and belonging to the larger society. In principle, a person might be richly satisfied merely by holding a job without working at it seriously.

And in practice, this is what a great many do. People will often start a job willing to work hard and be productive. But if the job fails to meet their expectations, if it does not give them the incentives they are looking for, then they lose interest. They may use the job to satisfy their own needs but give little in return. The preoccupation with self that is the hallmark of New Breed values places the burden of providing incentives for hard work more squarely on the employer than under the old value system.

Unaccustomed to this burden, employers are angry and frustrated. Under the old value system employers relied on the carrot-and-stick approach, the carrot being money and success, the stick being the threat of economic insecurity. This combination still works, but not as well as in the past. With the advent of New Breed values the motivational context has changed drastically.

The workplace in America is among the most conservative of our institutions. It has been highly resistant to change, particularly to the successive waves of individualism that have swept over so many other areas of American life. To be sure, at the stratospheric levels of giant corporations, trade unions, government bureaucracies, hospitals, and other institutions, individualism flowers for top-level executives. In these great baronies of our society, the self-fulfillment needs of those at the top of the hierarchy are given full play, but all other employees are expected to conform to rigid rules of group behavior. On ceremonial occasions, obeisance is paid to them: "Our people are our greatest resource and we must pay attention to their needs." But in everyday life, attention is paid to everything but people—capital requirements, technology, material resources, managerial techniques, political pressures, cost controls, and markets.

As long as the traditional carrot-and-stick approach worked well, those at the top could afford to pay less attention to the human side of the organization. Perhaps the chief lesson we should draw from the changes shaped by the new values is that concern with the human side of the enterprise can no longer be relegated to low-level personnel departments. In the 1980s knowledge of how the changed American value system affects incentives and the motivation to work hard may well become a key requirement for entering the ranks of top management in both the private and public sectors. If this occurs, we shall see a New Breed of managers to correspond to the New Breed of employees.

In the light of the emerging value system, where precisely does the dominant incentive system go wrong and what should be done to change it?

The incentive system as it exists today is marred by three crucial faults. The first and most obvious is that the system is uniform where it should be diverse. The New Breed values are, in essence, an extension of individualism to the workplace, where today's individualism can be defined as the quest for life-styles that suit each individual's unique needs, potentials, and values. Some people care mainly about money. Some would rather be compensated by more leisure. Others seek status opportunities. Still others derive their satisfaction from the inherent challenge of the work itself. There are even some who still place the well-being of the organization or the society ahead of purely personal goals, and future rewards ahead of present ones.

These varied motivations are not uniformly distributed. The mix in every organization we have studied is different: It depends on the type of work, the demographic composition of the employees, and the local subculture. Many organizations know that people do have differing needs and desires, and informally they make some effort to accommodate these, particularly at the executive level (for example, permitting some executives to pursue outside interests on company time). But the formal incentive structure is kept uniform and intact. It is easier to administer. The work of managing diverse incentive packages poses an administrative and bureaucratic nightmare. Understandably, therefore, most managers choose to ignore the problem. Under the old value system they could do so with impunity; under the new value system they cannot. In the 1980s they will be obliged to face this new reality.

The second flaw is that in its uniformity, the incentive system relies too heavily on economic incentives. Earlier I stated that money and economic security are as important as ever, but that the overall value context had changed. Let me explain. In recent years many people have lost confidence that employers can meet their demands for money and security. Up to the mid-1970s Americans had grown accustomed to steady annual increases in their standard of living. But these increases have not been forthcoming in the past few years. Also, many workers had negotiated arrangements that they thought enhanced their economic security, such as the United Auto Workers' supplemental unemployment benefits. But the severe recession of 1974–1975 proved to them that their hard-won economic security benefits could be wiped out without warning. Supplemental unemployment benefits turned out to be a thinner cushion than anyone had anticipated. If we add to the trauma of this recession the eroding effects of inflation, an increasing tax burden, a high unemployment rate, and the failure of the economy to deliver an ever-improving standard of living, we can better understand what has caused a sharp drop among workers in the credibility and good faith of employers.

In addition, under the old values, many men were willing to put up with frustration on the job for the sake of carrying out their responsibilities as exclusive breadwinners for the family. In many surveys conducted in the 1950s and 1960s, most men (75 to 80 percent) would say in response to direct questions that they were indeed satisfied with their jobs. However, when one probed for the reasons, most would, in effect, reply, "Well, it's really a lousy job, but at least it's a living. As long as it lets me take care of my family, I'm satisfied." But today, sweeping social change has undercut this once powerful motivation. Remarkably, only about 15 percent of all households today consist of a male breadwinner who has exclusive responsibility for supporting a nonworking wife and minor children living at home. Male self-esteem is no longer bound up as extensively as in the past with the need to sacrifice personal desires for the sake of the family. In other words, most men are no longer rewarded by their families with the respect and pampering that often came with the old prerogative of being the exclusive breadwinner. In the fifties and sixties, seven out of ten men and women defined a "real man" as a breadwinner and a good provider, not one with sexual prowess or physical strength or force of character. In today's society, the cultural meaning of masculinity is no longer mainly economic.

Another contextual change relates to the devaluing of traditional success symbols. Put simply, the things that money can buy—automobiles, appliances, homes—remain important for their *use* value, but they no longer are as significant as status symbols. Such symbols no longer automatically confer heightened self-esteem on the individual. And, since self-esteem is crucial to self-fulfillment, "money" success no longer motivates people as powerfully as in the past. Paradoxically, in the new motivation context people often demand more money from employers as a form of revenge if other satisfactions are not forthcoming. If the only advantage of a job is that it brings in money, if it frustrates the individual in all other ways, if it fails to meet needs for self-esteem or demands for meaningful work, then employees will demand more money even if they know it is not deserved. Thus, employers form the mistaken impression that money has grown more important to people, even though it has, in fact, become less so.

A third flaw is that quality-of-life motivations are not well understood by employers and, even when they are, large organizations do not know how to balance these motivations with their requirements for efficiency and productivity. As mentioned earlier, employees want recognition of their worth as individuals as well as of what they do on the job. Ideally, people would prefer to work in small groups in which they can form close human ties. Many want more responsibility and authority early in their careers, even though they may not be ready for it. Most people want a chance to learn new things, to find interest in their work, to be with pleasant and agreeable people, and to find new ways to express themselves on the job. They also want to make shorter commitments and more one-sided commitments; that is, they want the employer to be more obligated to them than they are to him.

To employers, these attitudes add up to a formula in which employees want more and give less. By and large, this perception is correct. Furthermore, there is no assurance that even if the New Breed's needs could be met, greater productivity would result. In some cases it would and in others it would not. We know that frustration of needs leads to *decreases* in productivity; there is less evidence that satisfaction leads to increases.

Many New Breed desires seem farfetched. What people feel entitled to and what a recalcitrant world will give them may bear little relationship to each other.

Employers yearn nostalgically for the good old days when people worked hard because they went hungry if they did not. Such nostalgia is, in its own way, as unrealistic as the more exaggerated claims to entitlement of the New Breed.

What, then, is the prospect for the future? Surprisingly, it might be more attractive than the picture I have painted. Without attempting to put an artificially rosy glow on gloomy realities, we must not overlook other factors that change the meaning of the whole. Social change is dialectic; it does not proceed in a straight line. People swing from one extreme to another before settling at some midpoint. In revolting against the depersonalization of jobs, people may seem unrealistic and unmindful of the constraints on the employer. But the lack of realism is superficial. Deep down, the American people know how hard it is to make a living and to succeed in today's world. They are ready to negotiate a "work contract" that will preserve the gains of the past and keep this country as productive as ever. But they want to negotiate a *new* contract that defines their job within a context in which their new self-fulfillment needs will be acknowledged, within realistic constraints. If employers will give a little, they will give a little. Employers should not assume in advance that they cannot, in fact, give people what they truly want. Perhaps we have been misled by the job-enrichment movement, which has overstated and to some extent misinterpreted the work requirements of the majority. It is true that for a large minority (about 35 percent of the work force), particularly the better educated, the substance of the work itself must be inherently interesting and challenging.[9] The majority, however, are not demanding "meaningful work" in this sense. What most people mean by "interesting work" and "challenge on the job" is not what an artist or a research scientist means. It is astonishing how little it takes for most people to feel wanted, needed, challenged, useful in their work. To overstate somewhat, it is possible that there are very few *inherently* undesirable jobs. But in millions of jobs today people are treated shabbily and paid poorly besides. And this combination makes their jobs undesirable.

SUMMARY

In retrospect, the 1970s will be seen as a watershed in American social history. The great changes taking place in the value system have consequences for *all* aspects of American life, but none more so than for the workplace. Our traditional economic categories lead us to false conclusions. Within their framework we seem to be confronted with a disaster in the making: a mass of would-be workers far in excess of the normal capacity of the economy to create new jobs to accommodate them, and an incentive system that no longer motivates people. But disaster looms only if the situation is seen within a narrow economic perspective. If we broaden our vista to take new psychosocial realities into account, the "disaster" looks more like an opportunity. Ever larger numbers of people are willing to share the burdens of coping with our advanced industrial society and its problems. A better educated work force refuses to accept the old alienations assumed by past thinkers to be inherent in modern society. The employees' challenge is essentially constructive; and if it is properly understood and acknowledged, we may emerge with a better society as well as a healthier economy. We may have to prod our institutions to mobilize their political will, but no one ever said that the purpose of people is to suit the convenience of institutions. It is supposed to be the other way around.

Up to now our policymakers have not understood and have not responded well to the great forces that are reshaping the American value system. Adapting successfully is partly a matter of political will, partly a question of proper understanding. It is the failure of understanding I find most disturbing. We can, I believe, muster the political will to reduce apparent conflicts of interest between employer and employee, because both stand to benefit if we do so. But we will drift into even sharper political conflict in the future unless we have a better grasp on the revolution in values.

NOTES

1. See note 7 for a full explanation of how the author arrived at the estimate of 24 to 27 million jobs needed.
2. The Yankelovich Monitor, 1977.
3. *Ibid.*
4. Hans Zetterberg, Karin Busch, and Mats De Uham, "Work as a Life-Style in Competition with Other Life-Styles: Some Observations from the Swedish Scene." Unpublished manuscript, 1977.
5. Yankelovich, Skelly and White, Inc., "Soundings," *Time* (November 1977).
6. Eli Ginzberg, "The Job Problem," *Scientific American* (November 1977).
7. The estimate of 24 to 27 million jobs needed is based on the following statistics, taken from publications of the Bureau of Labor Statistics and the *Employment and Training Report of the President (1977)*:

A. Those who answer that they "want a job" in the BLS monthly surveys:

	Millions
Official unemployment	7.0
Those who have a part-time job but want a full-time job	3.5
Those who want a job but, for various reasons (health, school, home responsibilities), are not looking for one	4.1
Those who want a job but are no longer looking for one because they are discouraged	0.9
Total	15.5

B. Those who say that they "do not want a job" in the BLS monthly surveys but who might want to enter the labor force if the right kinds of incentives and jobs were available:

	Millions
From 1/10 to 1/7 of those (predominantly women) who have home responsibilities	3.0–4.2
From 1/7 to 1/5 of those men and women (predominantly over 60 years of age) who are retired	1.2–1.7
From 1/5 to 1/3 of students	1.4–2.2
Total	5.6–8.1

C. Three groups not reflected in the BLS surveys but included in the *Employment and Training Report of the President* (1977):

	Millions
Employable recipients of welfare and food stamps	2.0
Enrollees (largely inner-city inhabitants) in federal training programs	1.0
From 1/4 to 1/3 of men 25–54 years of age who do not fall into any of the preceding categories	0.5–0.7
Total	3.5–3.7
Grand Total	24.6–27.3

Note: For further discussion of rationale and estimates see

Frank F. Furstenberg and Charles A. Thrall, "Counting the Jobless: The Impact of Job Rationing on the Measurement of Unemployment," *The Annals of the Academy of Political and Social Science* (March 1975).

Bertram Gross and Stanley Moss, "How Many Jobs for Whom," *Public Service Employment and Analysis of Its History, Problems, and Prospects,* Alan Gartner et al., eds. (New York: Praeger, 1973).

8. Private conversation with William Seidman.

9. The Yankelovich Monitor, 1977.

2.

Work in the American Future: Reindustrialization or Quality of Life

AMITAI ETZIONI

Professor of Sociology
Columbia University
Director, Center for Policy Research, Inc.

Predicting the future, especially in educational, social, and cultural matters, is at best a very tricky endeavor. Since our past record is rich not only in mistaken expectations and misleading forecasts but also in a tendency to focus on the wrong factors, it seems only prudent to limit ourselves to heuristics, that is, to seek to clarify what alternative futures *might* be, building on the alternatives already discernable in our present condition.

Aside from reducing our margin of error to zero (no prediction is made), this technique also helps us in shaping the future. Once alternatives are identified, we can attempt to help the one (or ones) we favor and seek to hinder the other (or others). After all, one reason the actual future is so elusive is that our predictions of what it will be like affect the actions which make it so.

To explore productively the present and future status of the labor force in America and the role of the more educated versus the less educated within, it seems useful to ask first about the societal context. Indeed, one of the greatest insights of modern sociology is that societies function like systems, like semiorganic beings, that is, that the course of developments in one part of the society cannot be charted without an understanding of the main links between that part and the other main segments of society. The image often employed is that of a bunch of matches tied together with a rubber band. If you move one out of place, whether it will snap back or move the others out of place or rearrange the pattern depends only in part on the initial dislocation. The rest is up to the rubber band and the other matches. Thus, the effect of a continuing increase in the proportion of the college-educated in the labor force, if, indeed, it does continue, depends only in part on the effect of college education. The rest will be determined by such diverse societal factors as technological changes, retirement policies, women's movements, and many others.

Although the relevant factors are numerous, one stands out because it provides the context for most of the others, namely, the society's project. A society's project may be viewed as those endeavors around which the principal efforts of its members are organized. For Tanzania, the central project may be the furtherance of economic and social development; for Nazi Germany, war and conquest. For most Western societies since the Industrial Revolution, the central project has involved the mass production of consumer goods and services.

The term "project" is adopted from the French existentionalists, who used it to refer to individuals rather than to social groupings. Accordingly, persons are characterized by what they are endeavoring to become, not by what they are at present: not a student, but a physician in the making; not a neurotic, but an individual in search of ways to manage anxiety; and so on. While the project is aimed at realizing a future state, its influence and force are very much in evidence (and measurable) in the present, because the future vision entailed by the project serves as a principal source of meaning and organization for current efforts. Thus, the student–physician, in anticipation of the day he or she will earn a high income, treat the poor, or eradicate an illness, is borrowing money, staying up nights, and sacrificing current income and pleasures. What explains a person's conduct, then, is not so much the current circumstances as the future goal he or she is trying to realize.

We suggest that it is fruitful to view societies as if they were organized around one or more projects. This contrasts with the view that societies are communities, groups of groups, or populations arranged in stratified structures. To present society as a project is to see it as capable of collective action, of directing its efforts toward shared purposes. True, no society is ever completely mobilized. Even in the extremities of war, as when Britain was severely threatened in 1939–1940, a significant part of its activities as a society did not involve the defense effort. But project-related activities are those that provide the society with its unique characteristics and direction, as well as forming the context within which other activities are conducted.

For America since the 1890s, particularly during peacetime, the central project has been to mass-produce ever more goods and services. Of course, some members have accrued a significantly larger share than others; nevertheless, the standard of living for all Americans has risen over the years. In recent years, however, this project has come under serious challenge. It is true that, at least since the 1890s, there have always been a few intellectuals who were not enamored of the worship of material success, the cult of "more," the definition of the good life as the production and consumption of more and more consumer goods. But in recent years, these sentiments have gained a much greater following. A combination of the counterculture residue and the energy crisis has led a majority of Americans to question the value of the industrial consumption project. Two Harris polls taken in the 1970s are particularly illuminating. Asked about choices America has to make, only 17 percent of a national sample favored setting the goal at "reaching higher standards of living," whereas 79 percent chose "teaching people how to live more with the basic essentials." Further, 15 percent favored "improving and speeding up our ability to communicate with each other through better technology," whereas 77 percent preferred "spending more time getting to know each other better as human beings on a person-to-person basis." Twenty-two percent endorsed the search for bigger and better things, whereas 66 percent favored more "humanized" living, and so on. Similarly, an August 1977 Harris survey showed that many of the values that only ten years ago were regarded as the province of the younger generation have now been adopted by the mainstream of Americans. Thus, 65 percent believe that modern technology "furthers the program of society more than the progress of the individual"; 61 percent, that such technology creates as many problems as it solves. Sixty percent are antibigness. Seventy-three percent would rather live in open country than in a city.

Although it is true that public-opinion polls can be misleading (for example, people may express their nobler sentiments in answer to a pollster, while actually continuing in their old pursuits), the very fact that no new consensus is emerging as to what is considered "good" is significant. And there are other indications that Americans feel this way. Thus, whereas there is still a substantial increase in the number of women who are joining the labor force, there is a tidal wave of voluntary retirement—before the age of sixty-five. In addition, millions are choosing "second careers" which are often less lucrative (and therefore allow for fewer purchases of goods and services) than their original jobs, but are seen to be more intrinsically satisfying. Still others devote less zeal to their work and more toward improving their understanding of self and others, toward cultivating their "inner space," and pursuing leisure activities that require relatively few purchases. The list of the most popular American hobbies for 1977 was headed by gardening (36.5 million families participated); stamp collecting (16 million); bridge, chess, and genealogy (10 million each).

What is the significance of these changes for orientation to work? The initial values, which served to legitimate the work effort that industrialized America in the 1880s and 1890s, and which shaped self-discipline, deferment of gratification, saving (to form capital), and hard work (to build and fuel the industrial machine), initially drew their ultimate justification from religious values. Economic success was seen as reflecting religious status. With the greatest emphasis on productivity and not on consumption, self-indulgence was deemed socially detrimental and morally undesirable. Then secularization set in. For a while the glorification of building the tools of production was carried by inertia, but this was like improving a highway leading to a ghost town. Max Weber referred to this stage as the "irrationality of rationality" and David Riesman called it "mad rationality." Gradually, God was replaced by consumer goods. The same endeavors that originally promoted hard work and frugality as a contribution to industrial development were increasingly being justified as generating a high standard of living on both the individual and societal levels. Indeed, the evolving industrial America did produce ever more of the promised golden eggs.

However, the increasing emphasis on the hedonistic *result* triggered a growing interest in a hedonistic *process*. With the preponderant value system leaning toward the pursuit of self-satisfaction, the challenging of deferred gratification—labor now for the promise of future rewards—was an unsurprising consequence. The concept of toilsome work as necessity gave way to a concern for enjoyable labor, if not the avoidance of work altogether. This phase resulted from the seeming ability of the post-World War II capitalist machine to provide abundance without excessive effort.

The diligent labor and monetary frugality of past generations were paying off, and the new generation, less concerned with self-discipline, the future, or transcendental values, was more eager to enjoy the available goods and services immediately.

This celebration of materialism, which resulted from the unleashing of one element of the pattern of values and meanings produced by mature capitalism, that of hedonism and its end results, in effect conflicted with the core of early capitalist values and meanings: hard work, self-discipline, and saving. These were also challenged by hippie hedonism, which with its isolated communes, love of nature, and Zen Buddhism, had quite different roots from materialistic hedonism. Hippie hedonism stressed sensualism or nirvana, that is, activities which required little labor or investment, such as sex, rapping, contemplation, cheap wine, and voluntary poverty. It thus rejected both industrious endeavors and their outcomes.

In the clash of values that resulted, the hippie counterculture, as a distinct, active cult posing an alternative future, quickly burned out. However, like many other societal cults, it left behind a much more moderate version that is easier to integrate with previous values and that commands a much wider following among Americans. Millions came to question the traditional imperatives: economic progress, science and technology, success, and materialistic abundance.

These challenges to the major components of the legitimation of the industrious society were reinforced by environmentalists, who questioned the compatibility of a hyperactive industrial society with harmonious coexistence with nature. Condemning the demolition of our natural elements by strip mining, industrial pollutants, and car fumes, the environmentalist philosophy advocates conservation of resources and moderation of economic activity. The same orientation has found support in a variety of contemporary psychosocial movements, which stress relaxation, inner peace, and harmonious relationships with others, rather than the conquest of nature and outer space.

A vision of an alternative society, a "quality-of-life" society, has risen, where the main focus is on social values, all the way from concern with the environment, health, culture, and public affairs, to the development of self and meaningful relationships with others. Here, work is not so much avoided as it is placed in a secondary position and judged in its relation to these priority values.

True, the continuing trend of greater participation by women in the labor force is a counterforce, and there is much less slack in the demand for goods than there is disapproval of the quest for more. Still, in the final analysis, there is little room for doubt that capitalism, of both the early and mature types, now holds less sway than previously.

Where do we go from here? Three alternatives for future societal development seem plausible. One is a continual erosion of the legitimacy of work, saving, materialism, science—in short, the *erosion of modernity*. Such continual decline does not spell imminent collapse, however. The notion that the United States will suffer an "end" similar to that of the Roman Empire is rather unlikely. Societies very rarely come apart, and even Rome ultimately fell to invading barbarians and only indirectly to its domestic hedonists. But it is quite possible for North Americans to become slower-paced, more content with pleasure and relaxation, less driven, less mobilized, less productive, less efficient, more corrupt, and more politicized.

Or, the United States may enter an age of *restoration* in which old virtues, values, and taboos will be injected with new potency. Futurologist Herman Kahn referred to this alternative as a "counterreformation"; columnist Kevin P. Phillips, as a "traditionalist resurgence"; and writer Walter Lippman, as a "deep reaction against the Rousseauistic philosophy." A challenged society sometimes employs its old repertoire to reestablish an era and its traditional set of normative elements to recommit itself. Thus the Catholic church, faced with internal decomposition at the Protestant challenge during the Counter Reformation, did not so much try to preempt the Protestant effort by providing its own members with some of the same innovations, but returned to its own earlier, purer traditions.

In contemporary America this option is what conservatives and neoconservatives are, in effect, championing. The emphasis on constitutionalism, which was one element in the furor over Watergate, is an example of this revival. Others would favor a return to old taboos against premarital sex, extramarital sex, divorce, homosexuality, and other activities now gaining increasing acceptance.

Reindustrialization, although less explicit in normative terms, is probably the most effective means of achieving restoration. Industrialization typically proceeds along three main stages: first, an era in which an infrastructure or prerequisites for industrialization are emphasized, including the extensive development of transportation (for example, railroads); finding energy sources (coal mines, oil wells); and providing national communications (for example, wire services), which then lead to mass production of consumer goods and services.

The suggestion by former Vice-President Nelson Rockefeller that the United States should invest $100 billion in the development of new energy sources as a down payment to be followed within ten years by $535 billion to $700 billion, in effect calls for a return to the infrastructure era, to the United States of the 1880s and 1890s. Hence, those most concerned with energy development would have little consideration for other values, from environmental protection to social justice, all of which "cost" resources. The return would be not merely, or even finally, a matter of economic resources, but would necessitate a recommitment to the work-and-save ethos and a parallel rededication to technological efficiency, productivity, and economic progress.

In direct contrast is the third alternative, which proposes a positive vision, a *quality of life* society. It raises the image of a new America, in which the current set of secure normative elements (behavioral and institutional embodiments) become the primary set, with the industrious set taking a secondary place. Here priority is given to energy conservation, not development. A slower but not slack America, a more "continental" society, would focus on culture and recreation with less concern for materialism. Society would trade some driving and some being driven for greater appreciation and commitment to living in harmony with the environment and with one another. There would be more emphasis on inner peace and the development of relations with others rather than on a conquest of the environment and exploitation of nature.

This quality-of-life society would foster a greater willingness to invest in social rather than in economic progress. This does not mean a return to poverty or, as it is sometimes characterized, the Stone Age. Nevertheless, a slow economic growth, drawing on America's very high GNP per capita, would allow a most comfortable standard of living by almost any other country's standard, or even by earlier American ones.

This differs from the hedonistic, anomic America by its new, positive affirmations, its new commitments. To illustrate: work may be made more self-actualizing and labor time may be cut, but work undertaken would be pursued with renewed dedication. There would be more studying for its own sake and less for the purpose of "making it."

It is unclear at this point where the United States is headed—toward a more slow-paced and less industrious society, reindustrialization, or a quality-of-life society—or even what the core project will be. One matter, however, is quite clear: Whatever direction, these or others, the societal context does take, it will significantly affect the place of work in society and its importance versus other activities; the rewards given for self-discipline, dedication, and effort; and the kinds of persons who will be attracted to, or alienated from, labor.

3.
Changing Attitudes toward Work

RAYMOND A. KATZELL
Professor of Psychology
New York University

Anyone who has paid the slightest attention to weather forecasts or football predictions will be properly skeptical about an attempt to discern the state of mind of the nation's work force ten years from now. In fact, one would be inclined to laugh it off, were it not such a serious matter. That assessment derives from the proposition that the success or failure of many future policy decisions will depend on the degree to which they coincide with the mood of the working men and women of the time—policies pertaining to compensation, job design, organization structure, work schedules, and retirement, to name but a few. So we must do the best we can, duly mindful of the hazards and uncertainties.

The major uncertainty stems from the absence of a satisfactory data base. All predictions that aspire to a semblance of science naturally entail the projection of trends from the past. This subject, however, suffers from a dearth not only of firm facts, but of comparable facts collected at various times past.

The major temptation that we must try to avoid is that of oversimplification. There is certainly more than one attitude that is important. Furthermore, those attitudes are not now identical in all segments of the working population, nor can we assume that they will follow parallel paths in the future. And even if we could project their probable future courses, we must be mindful of perturbations, that is, changes in economic, political, or social conditions that could divert them from their projected paths.

Those caveats suggest a sequence for our inquiry. Let us start by clarifying the principal worker attitudes of concern. Second, let us chart what is known of their past trends and present status, and then, in light of that plus what we can anticipate concerning relevant future circumstances, make our best guesses about what the future holds.

THREE KINDS OF ATTITUDES

It is easy to speak glibly about "worker attitude," as if it were some uniform or aggregate property such as worker age or take-home pay. Actually, of course, a worker has many attitudes pertaining to his or her work, and any two of them may not be closely correlated. For example, a person may like a job pretty well, but not care much about being productive in it. Both of these are attitudes that the worker has regarding the job, but they are quite different and may be largely independent of each other.

What various work attitudes do have in common is that they are stable cognitions or awarenesses that people have of their work, and these all have an evaluative or dispositional aspect, that is, like–dislike, pro–con, and similar connotations.

We can identify three major classes of such attitudes, somewhat but not completely separable from one another. They pertain to (1) how important a person's work is to him or her, called "job involvement"; (2) what a person wants, needs, or expects from a job, which may be termed "work values"; and (3) how strongly a person likes or dislikes a job, called "job satisfaction."

We will consider each of these types of work attitudes in turn, paying particular attention to evidence of present trends and current status. Obviously, it is only when we have readings of where we have been and where we are now that we can plot a future trajectory. Later, we will discuss what the future may hold for these attitudes.

THE IMPORTANCE OF WORK

Perhaps the most fundamental attitude toward work is whether a person wants to work at all. Traditionally, in industrialized societies, a person's work role has been perceived as central to his or her entire *persona*—who the person is has been defined pretty much by what he or she does for a living.

Some authorities have suggested that this will or perhaps should change in a postindustrial culture. The economist George Soule wrote not so long ago that one of the key problems confronting our civilization will be how to reconcile the social and psychological requirements of working with its lessening economic necessity.

The dedication to work was illustrated by a survey done about twenty-five years ago of a sample of white male workers. When asked whether they would continue working if they were to inherit enough money to live comfortably without it, four out of five answered in the affirmative. That ratio was a bit higher for middle-class workers (86 percent) than for working-class people (76 percent). Most of the middle-class workers wished to stay in the same kind of job (61 percent), whereas only about a third of the working-class people expressed that desire. Apparently, the desire to work is not contingent on infatuation with one's job, but on some more general reason; for most of the middle-class people, it turned out to be interest in accomplishment, whereas for most working-class people it was mainly to keep occupied.

Essentially the same question was later repeated in several national surveys as recently as 1977. The proportion who would continue to work has declined to about seven out of ten. Because of sampling differences, we cannot be certain that the twenty-five-year decline in fact reflects a reduced national involvement with work, although the suggestion is rather apparent. Nevertheless, the percentage of those opting to work remains high.

A 1973 study by the Survey Research Center also contained several questions designed to measure job involvement or investment of energy in one's work. About three out of four workers responding to a summary question described themselves as strongly or moderately involved, which is not inconsistent with the picture yielded by the approach just discussed.

Research on people who differ in their levels of job involvement has shown that it varies both with the characteristics of the worker and with the work situation. The person to whom work is more important is, as already noted, more likely to occupy a middle-class than a lower-class type of job; more specifically, the job is likely to be one that people regard as stimulating and "enriched." The job is also likely to be one that affords the worker opportunities for participation in decisions. As to personal qualities, the more involved workers tend to be older, to have a sense of personal responsibility for what happens to them, and to subscribe generally to the hard-work ethic; they also have had a history of success and tend to be more satisfied with their jobs.

The traditional American commitment to work apparently even survived the "greening" of college students, which occurred in the late 1960s. A Yankelovich survey showed that in 1969 41 percent of college students did not think that the emphasis on work should be reduced, but by 1973 that percentage had gradually risen to 50 percent and was apparently continuing to head upward. Furthermore, a whopping 84 percent believed that it was very important to do one's job well.

If one turns from survey data to see what attitudes may be reflected in actions, the following points are noteworthy:

- The average age at which workers have opted to retire from the General Motors Company has been decreasing gradually, so that it now stands at less than 60 for both salaried and hourly employees; nationally, about half the people who retire are under 65.
- Pressure is mounting to change or even eliminate mandatory retirement age.
- Women are becoming more insistent about their right to work, even if they have or once had family responsibilities.
- The rate of increase in labor productivity has generally been declining over the past ten to fifteen years.
- The 1970s have witnessed a resurgence of enrollments in such career-directed university curricula as business, engineering, and medicine.
- The armed services are having difficulty in recruiting personnel, in spite of high levels of unemployment among eligible youth.

The foregoing picture seems full of contradictions. On the one hand, there are indications that many, probably most, people are at least moderately involved with work, want to stay with it, and believe that it is worth doing well. On the other hand, there are signs of disenchantment and some indication that many people are dropping out, slacking off, or not availing themselves of work opportunities.

That confused picture becomes clearer when we recall that differences in job involvement may be explained by certain personal characteristics and by certain properties of the work situation. In short, it looks as though there are segments of our work force who are relatively turned off by work and others to whom it is important—and there are probably some people whose disaffection is growing, whereas there are others for whom work is becoming increasingly important.

WORK VALUES

In the past fifty years, there have been more than fifty studies bearing on the question of the attitudes that people have regarding what they are looking for in their jobs and careers. One would think that this would give us an adequate basis for discerning trends, but that is not the case. The results of the various studies are not closely consistent; the various factors differ in importance from time to time, but changes are not progressive. It would seem, therefore, that the variations are due to differences in the samples surveyed and in the methods of inquiry and not to meaningful developments unfolding over time.

With respect to the contemporary picture, the most comprehensive overview is found in the Survey of Working Conditions, taken in 1969–1970 by the University of Michigan for the U.S. Department of Labor. This was a survey of a systematic national sample of approximately 1,500 American workers. On the average, that sample rated various comfort factors (such as working hours and work load) as relatively less important than job challenge, financial rewards, relations with co-workers, and resources to get the work done. The single factor receiving the highest rating was "The work is interesting," the lowest was "I am not asked to do excessive amounts of work." The authors concluded that, in addition to conventional economic factors, American workers are more concerned with obtaining jobs that are interesting and challenging than with avoiding such jobs. A 1976 survey by the National Opinion Research Center confirms that general picture; a factor that emerged as particularly salient is the belief that the job is important and gives the worker a feeling of accomplishment.

The Survey Research Center sample comprised nearly equal numbers of blue-collar and white-collar workers. The former corresponded in their responses more closely to the stereotype of economic man, since financial considerations headed their ratings. Among white-collar workers, intrinsic factors, such as interesting work and opportunity to develop abilities, headed the list, whereas economic factors, although still not unimportant, lagged on a relative basis. However, the differences between these occupational groups were not very great and, to a considerable degree, were associated with differences in educational levels. Consistent with that interpretation is the 1973 survey of college students reported by Yankelovich, in which the two highest ranking factors in career choice were challenge of the job and ability to make meaningful contributions, whereas financial, and especially comfort, factors lagged on the list. Differences in educational levels, of course, imply differences in various other sociocultural factors, such as occupational levels, family background, and affluence, and such influences doubtlessly help explain what is happening as well.

Another factor that has been found to be associated with differences in work values is the worker's sex. Women have generally ascribed relatively greater importance to social and emotional considerations (such as having pleasant co-workers) than have men. That difference is also probably associated with sociocultural factors, such as the traditional women's role as more the harmonizer of social relationships and less the leader or primary breadwinner. As women's work roles change, so may their work attitudes.

Age, too, may play a role here; there is some evidence that younger workers place greater weight than do older ones on intrinsic job factors, such as degree of challenge, diversity, and freedom. There is some evidence also that such factors are more salient to people from middle-class cultural backgrounds and, more generally, to those motivated by "higher order" needs for achievement, self-expression, and self-control.

Hard data are scarce regarding time trends in work values. The Yankelovich research on college students reported earlier did detect some evidence of an increasing emphasis on work and careerism in the early 1970s, apparently reversing what was generally believed to have been the trend during the 1960s. In some other surveys that are not strictly comparable, there are also evidences of recent increases in the importance of intrinsic work factors compared to two or three decades ago. That trend is especially noticeable in younger people.

In the absence of adequate hard data, it may be instructive to consider the opinions that numerous social observers have voiced on the subject. By and large, their consensus has been that American workers, especially young adults, have become increasingly prone to reject the traditional values of workmanship, career advancement, and financial success in favor of self-determination, self-realization, and creating the good society.

For example, the noted personnel consultant, Robert McMurry, is reported to have said that the nation's value system has been drastically eroded, with permissive attitudes replacing the Protestant work ethic (*New York Times,* October 2, 1970). Journalist Harry Bernstein wrote that work is being treated more casually than in the past (*Washington Post,* January 1, 1973). Addressing a meeting of the American Management

Association, psychologist David Whitsett observed that American workers are increasingly concerned with emotional and social values in contrast to the economic aspects of their jobs (*Journal of Commerce,* February 18, 1976). An article in *Business Week* (May 10, 1976) suggested that social values are now based not on the traditional work ethic but on the desire for improved leisure and quality of working life. Futurologist Herman Kahn has discerned a general evolution of our culture away from "Yankee business ethics" toward one featuring public welfare, comfort, leisure, and avoidance of risk (*Miami Herald,* December 14, 1976).

These are just a small sample of similar statements that have been appearing in various media during the past decade. From such views has emerged a picture of what has been called "the new breed" of American worker—one who is even further tilting the scales away from the traditional definition of a good job as one providing steady work, good pay, comfortable and safe conditions, and, possibly, opportunities for getting ahead. This new breed is seen as taking those elements for granted and as now desiring jobs that offer, in addition, freedom, interesting and challenging work, and a substantial voice in what goes on.

That picture, since it is based largely on personal observations and impressions, can be and has been disputed as the projection of middle-class intellectuals. The counterargument is that the vast majority of American workers in nonmanagerial, nonprofessional occupations still subscribe pretty much to the traditional conception of what comprises a good job: One that offers good pay and pleasant conditions without too many headaches, especially if there is plenty of time off and a retirement plan under which one can enjoy one's leisure.

Nonetheless, there is something compelling about the hypothesis of the "new breed." For one thing, it is so widely held by so many people who are in a position to know, that it is difficult to dismiss as a mass delusion. For another, as we have already noted, it is not without some support from empirical research. Furthermore, it is consistent with the value patterns which research has particularly detected as predominating among younger, better educated workers in white-collar occupations. Since the postwar trends in the labor force have been toward larger proportions of such workers, it is reasonable to infer that more of today's workers resemble that new breed than was true in the past. Finally, such shifts in work values would be congruent with changes that appear to be going on in general social values, where there seems to be lessening stress on efficiency, growth, and material achievement and increasing emphasis on social responsibility, personal fulfillment, ecological balance, and consumerism.

In short, the proponents of the new breed hypothesis and of the traditional view of American workers are probably both partly right and partly wrong. It depends on which worker one is talking about. However, the current trend seems to be for a growing proportion of the population to place greater stress on intrinsic factors, such as job meaningfulness and challenge, whereas extrinsic factors, such as comfort and security, are becoming relatively less salient. We will return later to the question of what this implies for the future.

JOB SATISFACTION

How well a person likes his or her job depends on the discrepancy between the individual's work values (what is wanted, needed, and/or expected from the job) and what the job delivers—or at least what he or she thinks it delivers. Changes in job satisfaction can therefore result from changes in either or both of those terms—changes in workers' values and/or in the jobs themselves.

The subject of job satisfaction has been studied extensively in the past forty years, so that by now literally thousands of books and articles have been written about it. Some of the more salient and dependable conclusions that can be extracted from that literature may be summarized approximately as follows:

- About 80 percent of the work force describe themselves as rather satisfied with their jobs as a whole, with a little more than 10 percent expressing active overall dissatisfaction.
- Job satisfaction can be disaggregated into satisfactions with various facets of the job, the major ones being financial features, promotional opportunities, supervision, co-workers, and the work itself.
- The figures on levels of satisfaction vary somewhat with how the questions are phrased; for example, only about half the respondents when asked say that they would continue in the same kind of work if they had a choice, in contrast to the aforementioned 80 percent who say they are satisfied, suggesting that there may be more dissatisfaction than meets the casual eye, or the interviewer.
- Job satisfaction is lower on average among disadvantaged minor-

ities than among whites; however, this appears to be due to the fact that they generally have less desirable jobs, for blacks and whites in the *same* jobs have quite similar attitudes toward the conventional subjects of pay, supervision, working conditions, and so on.

• Job satisfaction of women and men is also generally about equal; however, the ingredients making for satisfaction or dissatisfaction may not be identical for the two sexes.

• Job satisfaction is generally lower among those under 30 years of age.

• Among the characteristics of jobs that have been found to be associated with higher levels of satisfaction may be noted:

- higher occupational level, with greater satisfaction in managerial and professional jobs than in factory, clerical, or agricultural ones;
- higher pay, especially when it is perceived as related to performance;
- "enriched" jobs, providing relatively higher amounts of challenge, diversity, autonomy, meaningfulness, and social contribution;
- considerate, democratic supervision;
- participation in decisions affecting one's work or working conditions;
- interaction with others, especially those who are influential or significant;
- relatively small organizations and/or work groups;
- adequate resources (equipment, materials, procedures, etc.).

• Job satisfaction is correlated with numerous off-the-job factors, tending to be higher, for example, among those who are more satisfied with life in general, those who work in nonurban communities, and those women who do not have small children.

• It is also generally higher among the better educated; however, there are strong signals pointing to the importance of proper utilization of education and ability: (1) *within* a given occupational level, those who are more educated are generally less satisfied, and (2) among the least satisfied are those who have had some college education but did not graduate.

• The connection between job satisfaction and job performance is complex and convoluted: Each to some extent causes the other, but each also is affected by other factors and is, therefore, somewhat independent of the other; it can be said, however, that when both are elevated, workers are truly motivated, but when both are low there exists a classic syndrome of apathy or demoralization.

So much for the current picture. But what do we know of trends in job satisfaction, especially during the recent years? Here, too, in spite of the voluminous literature on the subject, our data are disappointingly flimsy. In order to plot a meaningful trend, it is manifestly essential to have comparable facts collected from equivalent and representative samples at various times. The unfortunate fact is that nearly all of the thousands of studies consist of one-shot glimpses of special samples obtained by means of measures improvised for the immediate purpose at hand. Indeed a recent review sponsored by the U.S. Department of Labor discovered only fifteen national surveys conducted between 1958 and 1973 that can furnish relevant facts,[1] and even these are not entirely satisfactory because of variations in wording and sampling. However, it is instructive to review the resulting picture, as listed in Table 1. To these findings, we have added those of similar surveys conducted in 1974, 1975, 1976, and 1977.

The data came from national surveys conducted by four different organizations, all of which contained a question corresponding to "On the whole, how satisfied are you with the work you do?" As can be seen, the percentage of respondents who could be classified as "satisfied" runs at or slightly above the 80 percent figure reported earlier. There was a slight increment between 1958 and 1964, after which the level remained at a reasonably stable high plateau throughout the following years. The authors of the Labor Department review therefore seemed justified in concluding in 1974 that "There has been no substantial change in overall levels of job satisfaction."

That conclusion was at variance with what many other knowledgeable people believe to be the case. For example, George Gallup, Jr., whose organization is one of those contributing data to table 1, has been quoted as saying that its 1973 results indicated "a greater degree of discontent now than has been found for a number of years—particularly among youths," and that this poses a threat to future industrial output in the United States.

The disparity between the two views may well be due to whether one looks at overall averages, or whether one looks at certain parts of the whole. Table 1 takes the former perspective and finds stability. But, when

Table 1.   Percentage of "Satisfied" Workers, 1958–1977.

Year	Source	Percent "Satisfied"
1958	Survey Research Center*	81
1963	Gallup Poll*	89
1962	National Opinion Research Center	83
1964	Survey Research Center, University of California	91
1964	National Opinion Research Center*	92
1965	Gallup Poll*	87
1966	Gallup Poll*	92
1966	Gallup Poll*	89
1969	Survey Research Center	85
1969	Gallup Poll*	92
1971	Survey Research Center	91
1971	Gallup Poll*	88
1971	Gallup Poll*	86
1973	Gallup Poll*	88
1973	Survey Research Center	90
1974	National Opinion Research Center	85
1975	National Opinion Research Center	87
1976	National Opinion Research Center	86
1977	Survey Research Center	88

*Males only; all others comprise both sexes.

the attitudes of certain segments of the labor force are examined, evidence of change may be found. For example, an analysis by Opinion Research Corporation (ORC) of surveys conducted in client companies indicates a growing gap between managerial and nonmanagerial employees, with the attitudes of the latter showing deterioration, while those of the former remain stable or even improve. Comparing the 1977 results reported by the Survey Research Center with those of 1973 indicates no further decline among workers under 21, but significant deterioration among older workers. That survey also reveals greater decline among blue-collar than white-collar employees.

Furthermore, it is possible that dissatisfaction with certain aspects of work is growing, whereas dissatisfaction with other aspects is diminishing. The increasing emphasis on the challenge and meaningfulness of work, and the accompanying deemphasis of extrinsic factors, may reflect growing satisfaction with the latter and dissatisfaction with the former. Those two trends in satisfaction might well be canceling each other out, so that, misleadingly, the average is unchanged. In support of this possibility, the Survey Research Center's analysis of satisfaction with various facets of the job finds that certain attitudes deteriorated between 1973 and 1977, such as those pertaining to job challenge and to promotions, whereas attitudes toward co-workers remained the same. The ORC surveys also find such irregularities.

Illustrative of the difficulty over interpreting such findings is one in the Survey Research Center data indicating that satisfaction with compensation declined between 1973 and 1977, although the respondents reported that actual earnings (corrected for inflation) remained about the same. The probable explanation is that, in the interim, workers' values regarding compensation changed. This was possibly due to a general escalation of expectations of what a job should deliver. Another, not necessarily conflicting, possibility is based on evidence that as growth and fufillment values remain unsatisfied, material ones increase in salience.

In sum, although levels of general job satisfaction remain high, and impressions of its decline may at times be exaggerated, the impression of stability may be misleading in two ways. First, job satisfaction may in fact be deteriorating among certain important segments of the population, but those declines may be masked by the stable level in the majority of workers. Second, its deterioration with regard to certain aspects of work may be offset by satisfaction with other factors. Even if one accepts at face value the reading that "only" about 10 percent of our work force is persistently discontented, this translates to some 10 million people who are functioning in life at levels that are less than desired, and desirable. Those concerned with improving the nation's quality of working life must, therefore, strive to identify those job facets that are the chief sources of growing discontent, and those groups of workers who react most strongly to them.

FUTURE TRENDS

Preceding sections of this chapter have attempted to portray recent trends and current status with respect to three major types of attitudes toward work: job involvement, work values, and job satisfaction. By and large, the average American worker has been found to be at least moderately involved with work, to desire a job that offers both material amenities and personal gratification, and to describe his or her job as satisfactory even if not deeply satisfying. Certain classes of workers, or people in certain kinds of jobs, deviate from these averages: for example, younger workers are more likely to emphasize the importance of having work that is challenging and fulfilling, to be less involved with their jobs, and to be less satisfied with them; factory operatives, generally, are not as much involved with their jobs, are more concerned with material prerequisites that provide social or ego gratifications, and are somewhat less satisfied. When we examine trends over the past decade or two, we cannot detect drastic changes in the overall figures. On the other hand, the views of certain segments of the working population may be changing more rapidly than most—especially those who are under 30, over 55, underutilized, female, or black. Moreover, whereas attitudes toward certain aspects of work are stable, or improving, other attitudes appear to be deteriorating.

In short, it is possible to interpret the evidence as indicating that worker attitudes in the United States are really rather stable, that workers still view work in pretty much the same way that they have in recent decades, and that they are still reasonably well satisfied with their working lives. But to do so would be to overlook the dynamic factors suggested when we compare the data with respect to different attitudes and from different segments of the work force. Then we discover evidence of differences in current work attitudes and in recent trends among different groups of workers.

The Dynamics of Attitude Change

Both common sense and theory lead us not to be surprised by that picture of variety and change. Attitudes, after all, are acquired through experience, and as experience changes, so will attitudes. Attitude change is, however, typically rather slow, partly because the outer world does not often change dramatically, and partly because the attitudes we have are anchored firmly in many previous experiences.

The experiences that give rise to attitudes stem from two sources: (1) the experiences of others, transmitted to members of a society via its "culture," and (2) the personal experiences of each individual, largely growing out of the roles and statuses he or she occupies in society. Hence we may predict changes in work attitudes from projections of changes in these two sources of experience. The former may be illustrated by a decreasing emphasis on "success" as a goal of life that is passed on to members of society, the latter by the realization of an individual that more enjoyment is being derived from social life than from a job. Either could be a source of reduced job involvement.

On the personal level, in addition to the mechanism of associative learning just mentioned, there may be a developmental sequence through which people tend to pass. People who look both for material and psychological rewards tend to give the former consideration priority in their working lives until those requirements begin to be reasonably well met. Thereafter, intrinsic considerations, such as status and challenge of the job, may take on greater significance for them.

To some extent, we can therefore estimate possible changes in work attitudes of a population by projecting changes in cultural values, beliefs, and behavior patterns. Changes resulting from the experiences of individual members of a population can be predicted from the projected changes in the work environment and/or in the demography of the work force. That is, experiences tend to be associated with social and economic statuses and roles, so that changes in the nature of statuses and roles may be expected to alter the experiences and hence the work attitudes of individuals. An example is the changing work role of women, which is likely to bring about associated changes in their work attitudes, and in those of men also.

Cultural Changes

Social analysts are by no means in agreement concerning the directions in which our Western culture will evolve. However, the relatively short-term outlook with which we are concerned here is generally expected to witness an extension of certain trends that have been developing over the past decade—provided, of course, that no major perturbation occurs, such as a war, severe depression, or political upheaval.

Daniel Yankelovich and other social analysts have noted the following contemporary cultural trends that are likely to affect work attitudes:

- Reduced concern with economic insecurity.
- Revised definitions of success, with less emphasis on material achievement and more on personal fulfillment.
- More flexible and equal division of work roles between the sexes.
- Growing psychology of entitlement to the good life.
- Greater questioning of efficiency as a criterion of goodness.
- Shifting emphasis from bigness and growth to smallness and conservation.
- Rising concern with ecological balance and the environment.
- Growing beliefs that work organizations are obliged, not only or

even mainly to make profits, but also to contribute to the quality of life and of society.

- Rising concern with the welfare of consumers.
- Greater awareness of issues pertaining to health, both physical and mental.
- Greater social acceptance of ethnic minorities.
- Growing conviction that there is more to life than working.

To the extent that the foregoing developments in fact take place, they will, of course, not affect all people equally. But, on the whole and in combination, they are likely to stimulate shifts in work attitudes such as the following:

- Economic well-being may increasingly be taken for granted (except for those newly emerging from poverty), with benefits becoming increasingly important relative to take-home pay in the compensation package.
- Workers may become more attuned to the long-range career implications of their jobs, in contrast to here-and-now considerations.
- Hitherto disadvantaged groups—women, blacks, and others—will press especially hard for better jobs, higher pay, more training, more of the action.
- Autonomy, responsibility, achievement, and related psychic rewards may continue to gain in importance relative to material or comfort considerations (which is not to say that the latter will fade).
- The social and ecological significance of jobs and organizations may become a matter of greater import in attracting workers and maintaining their job satisfaction.
- More workers may want more of a voice in what goes on in their companies.
- Concern with satisfying use of leisure time may grow.
- The importance of hierarchical status may decline, both as a source of power and as a source of satisfaction.
- Workers may demand more attention to conditions furthering mental and physical health and well-being—"quality of working life"—even at the expense of productivity and profits.
- People may become less motivated to work long and hard just out of habit or conscience; increasingly, they may expect explanations and payoffs in both material and psychological terms.

Trends in the Work Force

As was noted earlier, a second major avenue of attitude change is comprised of changes in personal experiences associated with alterations in the status and roles of the work force. Hence, a useful way of anticipating what future changes may occur in worker attitudes therefore consists of analyzing the changes that are expected in the composition of the work force. If the work force changes in ways that have already been found to be associated with differences in attitudes, we may infer that future attitudes would tend to shift accordingly, all other things being equal.

There seems to be consensus among most labor economists regarding the following changes that can be expected over the next decade in demographic attributes of the work force:

- A larger percentage of workers will have been born and raised in a middle-class, urban, American cultural milieu than has been the case previously.
- The average age will increase; the proportions of workers in their teens and early twenties will decrease sharply, whereas those in the 25- to 44-year-old bracket will increase; changes in mandatory retirement may further increase the proportion in their sixties.
- The black portion of the labor force is expected to increase by about one third, compared with a gain of only one fifth for whites.
- Women are likely to increase their rate of participation in employment from the present level of approximately 40 percent, especially in professional and managerial occupations.
- The average educational level will continue to increase, as a result of fewer workers with less than a high school education and more workers with at least some postsecondary education.
- The average level of income and associated socioeconomic factors will rise.

Implications for Attitudes

Several interesting developments are suggested for the 1980s, when we superimpose on the expected changes in the characteristics of the work force the work attitudes that have been found to be associated with those characteristics. These may be quickly grasped by reference to Table 2, which shows for each of the aforementioned work force changes the associated shifts that are implied in involvement with work, in work values, or in job satisfaction.

Table 2.   Attitudinal Implications of Work Force Changes.

Work Force Changes	Implications for		
	Job Involvement	Work Values	Job Satisfaction
Sex			
More women	Work more important to many women, less to some men	More emphasis on career opportunities, self-fulfillment	Satisfaction with promotion prospects
		More concern with arrangements permitting home-making and careers	Dissatisfaction with "lock-step" jobs
Age			
Fewer under 30	Work more important to some, less to others	More emphasis on security, earnings, benefits	Less tendency to be dissatisfied, provided that material rewards
More over 65		Less emphasis on self-fulfillment more concern about leisure time and retirement	are good and a person has developed leisure interests
Education			
Higher average level		More emphasis on self-fulfillment	Greater overall satisfaction
More post-high school		More emphasis on work that uses abilities	More dissatisfaction with under-utilization and lack of challenge
Socioeconomic status			
More middle-class, urbanized	Work more important	More emphasis on challenging and socially signifi-cant ("meaning-ful") activities	More dissatisfaction with socially irrelevant work
	Second careers become more important		
		More interest in leisure, less emphasis on sub-sistence	Greater diversity of satisfaction–dissatisfaction
		Greater diversity	

Table 2.   (Continued)

| Work Force Changes | Implications for | | |
	Job Involvement	Work Values	Job Satisfaction
Ethnic mix			
More blacks	Work more important for those trying to "make it"	More emphasis on material aspects, security, and promotions	More dissatisfaction with low-paying, dead-end jobs

As can be seen, the aggregate of these developments points to divergent changes in the importance of work. The presence of more women, especially those seeking careers, more older people, and a generally higher level of affluence portend greater involvement in work for a sizable portion of the work force. Women who have reared their children, along with both men and women whose initial careers have provided them with financial security but not with a sense of accomplishment, will be increasingly likely to be interested in second careers. On the other hand, the importance of work may diminish for a growing number of men whose wives have become primary wage earners. The same may well be true for an increasing number of people in their fifties and early sixties who have the resources and the opportunity to consider early retirement. We may expect that there will be many among the growing black segment of the work force who will increasingly value work as a way of escaping ghetto life. Thus, levels of involvement are likely to shift in a variety of directions among different groups of workers.

Diversification seems to be the prospect for work values as well. A work force that features fewer younger people and more minorities emerging from impoverished backgrounds is likely to have significant numbers of people to whom such material considerations as security, compensation, benefits, and future prospects will be dominant considerations. A more highly educated work force implies growing interest in jobs that provide opportunities for use of abilities, self-expression, and fulfillment, along with the traditional economic and material rewards. The growing number of career women should intensify that emphasis, as well as the search for jobs that provide promotional and growth opportunities. On the other hand, the general rise in socioeconomic, educational, and cultural levels implies that fewer people will be willing to settle for jobs that serve mainly subsistence needs, and more will be seeking work that is socially meaningful and affords opportunities for use of abilities and self-fulfillment. The rise in sociocultural level also portends diversification of outlooks and interests, so that we can expect the work force to have a wider range of values not only in employment but in leisure; as a consequence, people will be less alike in what they want out of life and work.

The picture of the 1980s that we have projected thus far is an admixture of trends that vary in direction: diversity is the essence.

Trends in job satisfaction will depend on how effectively the world of work succeeds in coping with the multiplicity of needs and demands of an increasingly heterogeneous work population. The final column of Table 2 suggests the varied forces leading to satisfaction or dissatisfaction among different segments of the work force. For example, it will not be enough for many women to have a job that offers only good intrinsic and extrinsic rewards; flexibility, which permits women to dovetail a job with homemaking responsibilities, will also be important. As the number of middle-class workers expands, there will be increasingly widespread dissatisfaction with low-skill jobs that provide only steady work and good pay; however, many blacks newly emerging from poverty and marginal in education will readily accept exactly such employment. The increased representation of employees in the 25 to 44 age bracket is likely to increase competition for higher status, better paying jobs; the impact on job satisfaction will depend on whether the evolving technologies and job market will expand those opportunities at a sufficiently rapid rate.

The picture is even more complicated by individual differences within these demographic and social classes. Workers with some postsecondary education are generally among the most dissatisfied, since their lack of a college degree often bars them from the more challenging occupations. However, not all of these workers desire jobs that impose more responsibility and a greater degree of self-management; some will be looking for minimum hassle, with high wages. Similarly, not all older workers will seek jobs that provide good retirement benefits after twenty-five years of service; there will be many who resist the idea of retiring even at age sixty-five, especially among those who have not developed strong leisure interests.

Moreover, these individual differences are likely to become even more prominent in the 1980s than they are today. There are several factors in contemporary culture encouraging such a trend. One is that our expanding media of information and education are exposing more people within a given segment of the work force to a wider variety of socializing influences. Another is that our society has become less insistent on uniformity, more tolerant of idiosyncracy. Finally, there is the growing belief in the *right* of each person to be an individual and get what he or she wants—what has been termed the rising "psychology of entitlement." The convergence of these forces was neatly described in a recent report of Yankelovich, Skelly and White, Inc.: "Thus, the emergence of greater plurality of work styles becomes translated into a *demand for the individualization* of the work environment."[2]

To summarize our projections of work attitudes of the future, the changes anticipated herein may be telescoped into the following broad trends:

- The traditional economic significance of work will be supplemented by a rising concern with its psychological quality and social meaningfulness.
- More workers at all levels will want a stronger voice in decisions affecting their jobs and to be less subject to hierarchical control.
- A shrinking proportion of the work force will be content to have routine, unchallenging jobs.
- More people will think in terms of long-range careers and even multiple careers, not just in terms of immediate jobs.
- The importance of nonwork (family, community, retirement, leisure) will increasingly rival that of work.
- The work force will exhibit a wider diversity of attitudes toward work, portending numerous departures from the foregoing.

How far those trends will, indeed, unfold in the 1980s is far from clear. There are strong stabilizing influences: force of habit, comfort with the familiar, discomfort with the unfamiliar, and the tremendous capacity of most people to adapt. But, always subject to the absence of a major upheaval, sooner or later the foregoing trends are likely to emerge, if not in the 1980s, then perhaps by 2000.

RISING WITH THE TIDE

The trends in worker attitudes just noted do not necessarily spell disaster. In fact, with ingenuity, they can be converted into forces making for an even healthier, more viable social and economic system than we have today. However, the phrase "with ingenuity" implies changes in social institutions to keep pace with the changes in attitudes. In this concluding section, some suggestions are offered as to the nature of those changes.

Listed in the following are some features of work that, singly or in combination, are likely to make jobs more harmonious with the attitudes of the work force of the future:

- Structuring jobs so that workers make more visible contributions to others and perceive the consequence of what they do.
- Redesigning jobs in order to increase the proportion that utilize higher levels of ability and education.
- Creating more job-sharing opportunities, that is, dividing a traditionally full-time job so that it can be covered by two or more part-time workers.
- Increasing the flexibility of rewards (pay, benefits) available to workers, so that each person may have wider options to meet particular needs and preferences.
- Increasing the flexibility of work schedules by flexitime (hours in the day), days off, vacations, and other methods.
- Establishing more part-time jobs, especially for homemakers, retirees, and those needing supplemental income, such as actors, writers, and others.
- Offering sabbatical leaves for those who wish to study, try out something else, or just replenish themselves.
- Using job rotation, both on an informal basis within work teams, or on a scheduled basis across departments or even employers (such as intergovernmental assignments, loans of personnel from industry to education, and so on).
- Providing more and better mechanisms for sharing power up and down the line, such as task forces, labor–management committees, works councils, collective bargaining, Management-by-Objectives programs, autonomous work teams, fewer levels of hierarchy, "linking-pin" arrangements, and so on.
- Creating more and better opportunities for use of leisure, coupled with avocational counseling and education.
- Providing more flexible arrangements for retirement, including early retirement, exceptions to mandatory retirement, and partial or phased retirement. These arrangements should be accompanied by resources for retirement counseling.

- Using affirmative action to recruit and prepare women and disadvantaged minorities for jobs and careers.
- Improving corporate citizenship via additional attention and weight given to effects on consumers, local communities, and society.
- Experimenting with nontraditional rewards, such as time off for good performance, or giving eligible workers opportunities to try out new jobs.
- Creating new careers in areas of heightened public concern, such as conservation, consumer protection, or mental health; such developments could be doubly advantageous if they were made accessible to underemployed groups, such as youth, minorities, or women.
- Increasing the flexibility of career structures, so that people may have choices at key points in their careers—for example, choosing to advance in either managerial or technical channels, or opting to change careers altogether.
- Improving the match between people and jobs, taking into account potential attitudes as well as proficiency of the worker; the techniques for doing this may, in fact, be farther advanced than are the mechanics of and commitment to implementation.

None of the preceding items is altogether novel. Many have been devised in recent years precisely in attempts to cope with the deterioration in worker attitudes, with at least preliminary evidence of utility. For example, experiments in job enrichment and in participative management have often shown good results when introduced in the right way in the right situations. What is being suggested here is that the need for such alterations in our work systems will be greater in the 1980s than they were in the 1960s and 1970s, given the evolution predicted earlier in worker attitudes. And the solutions, to be effective, will need to be more than superficial or piecemeal; a sufficient number of elements will have to be changed so that in aggregate they will constitute new systems of work.

Ingenious managers and behavioral scientists will no doubt be able to devise additional programs to cope with those attitudes. For example, in addition to the foregoing we possibly should be thinking in terms of subdividing some mammoth organizations or increasing the opportunities for self-employment; both of those kinds of work settings are likely to appeal to many of the workers of the future.

In sum, the 1980s are likely to witness further evolutions in worker attitudes along lines initiated in the 1960s and maintained through the

1970s. Experiments in the reform of work systems, initiated partly in response to those changes, indicate directions for future development. Creative thinking is likely to improve further on such programs. Depending on our collective success in designing and instituting reformed systems, the future may either be populated largely with workers who are involved and satisfied with their working lives or who are demoralized and frustrated.

NOTES

1. R. P. Quinn, G. L. Staines, and M. R. McCullough, *Job Satisfaction: Is There a Trend?* Manpower Research Monograph No. 30, U.S. Department of Labor (Washington, D.C.: U.S. Government Printing Office, 1974).
2. Yankelovich, Skelly and White, Inc., Corporate Priorities, "The New Worker," Briefings for Management, November 16, 1977.

4.
The Work Force of the Future: An Overview

RICHARD B. FREEMAN
Professor of Economics
Harvard University
National Bureau of Economic Research

The American labor force will undergo considerable change in the decade ahead. Some changes are likely as a result of the continuation of past labor-force trends. Other changes, however, will diverge from past developments and create new labor-market conditions and problems. The purpose of this chapter is to identify the most important potential future changes and to evaluate their impact on the economy. The chapter begins with a brief review of the major post-World War II labor-force developments and the extent to which they were foreseen by analysts, and then examines the socioeconomic forces that appear to have caused the most important changes. On the basis of likely future changes in the causal factors, an effort is made to predict the nature of the labor force in the 1980s. The analysis identifies the *coming shortage of youth* and the enormous *increase in the number of prime-age workers* as the two most important potential labor-force changes in the decade ahead, though other likely changes are also discussed.

THE CHANGING LABOR FORCE

Before trying to forecast changes in the work force, it is necessary to have some knowledge of the composition of the current labor force and of the ways it has changed in recent years.

In 1976 there were over 96 million persons aged 16 and over in the

U.S. work force, of whom 94.7 million were in the civilian work force. Forty-one percent of the work force were women, nearly half were less than 35 years of age, and almost one fourth were between 16 and 24.[1] Approximately one in three had attended college for at least one year and one in six was a college graduate; over 70 percent were high school graduates.[2] In terms of employment, 50 percent of the work force worked in white-collar jobs, with one in four employed as a professional and manager, whereas only 15 percent were the factory "operatives" of a traditional industrial society.[3] One fifth of the work force were members of trade unions or related associations.[4] One seventh were part-time

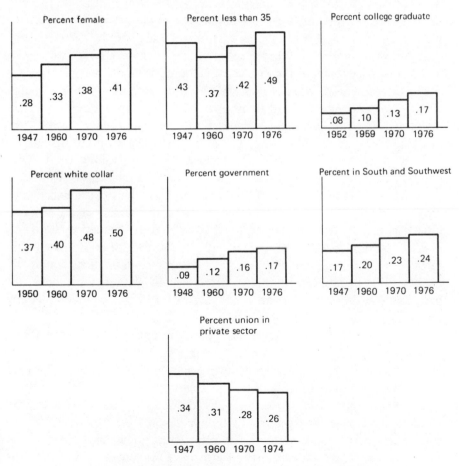

Figure 1.   Major changes in U.S. work force, 1947–1976.

workers[5]; one sixth worked for governments.[6] About 35 percent resided in the South or Southwest.[7]

Thirty years earlier the composition of the labor force was quite different, with relatively fewer women, young persons, highly educated workers, government workers, and white-collar employees, and relatively more full-time workers and union members. In the span of only three decades the work force had changed to a remarkable extent.

Figure 1 provides a graphic snapshot of the major patterns of change in the post-World War II era, beginning with demographic developments and proceeding to changes in the composition of employment.

The most important change in the period was the extraordinary increase in the female proportion of the work force, which jumped from 28 percent in 1947 to 41 percent by 1976. At the outset of the period 31 percent of women aged 16 and over participated in the work force; in 1976, 47 percent did. Over three fifths of the growth in the total work force from 1947 to 1976 was the result of the increased amount of female participation.[8]

The movement of women into the work force involved major social changes in the composition of families and in the nature of jobs. Much of the growth in participation took place among married women, whose rate of participation in the labor force more than doubled, from 20 percent in 1947 to 45 percent in 1976, with marked increases among those with children 6 to 17 years old (26 to 54 percent) and among those with children under 6 (11 to 37 percent).[9] Presumably, partly as cause and partly as effect, the fertility rate fell while at the same time an increasing proportion of homes, especially among blacks, came to be headed by women, many of whom worked. In regard to jobs, the growth of the female work force was associated with a marked increase in part-time jobs, which are largely filled by women. In 1950, 16 percent of persons with work experience over the year were part-time workers; in 1975, 12 percent, and in 1976, 21 percent.[10]

There was a striking (and little noticed) difference in the growth of the female work force in the thirty years under study. In the 1950s and early 1960s the bulk of the increase occurred among older women, many of whom were returning to work as their children reached school age. Nearly 80 percent of the growth in the female work force between 1947 and 1965 resulted from increased numbers of women aged 35 and over, whose labor force participation rate rose sharply. By contrast, in the late 1960s and early 1970s, the major source of growth of the female work force was among younger women, with 77 percent of the increase coming from persons less than 35 years old. From 1965 to 1976, the participation rate of women aged 20 to 24 rose from 50 percent to 65 percent while that of women aged 25 to 34 rose from 39 percent to 57 percent.[11] The divergent sources of growth in the female labor-force participation rate in the two periods raise important questions about the causal factors at work and make a simple unicausal explanation difficult.

The age structure of the work force also underwent sizable change, though for much more readily comprehensible reasons. In the 1950s, the proportion of the work force below 35 years of age fell, the result of the decline in birthrates during the Depression. In the mid-1960s, the number of younger workers began increasing, raising the proportion of those under 35 years of age from 35 percent to 50 percent in the span of only one decade, the result of the post-World War II baby boom. Because of the increased proportion of the young going on to higher education in the period, much of the growth in the labor force of younger workers occurred among the college-trained. In 1966 there were 0.49 male college graduates aged 25 to 34 per graduate 35 years of age and over; by 1976 the ratio had jumped to 0.78. One important consequence of the shifting age distribution of the work force, especially among highly educated men whose age–earnings profile traditionally is relatively steeply sloped, was a marked twist in the relative earnings against the young. In 1968 men aged 45 to 54 earned 1.18 times as much as those aged 25 to 34; by 1975, the age premium had risen to 1.26. For college graduates, the rise was even more striking, from 1.38 to 1.63.[12]

The principal change in the qualitative dimension of the labor force was the increase in educational attainment. During the 1960s, the college and university system enjoyed an unprecedented expansion, a veritable golden age for academe, with enrollments, expenditures, academic salaries, and job prospects rising rapidly. From 1966 to 1974, the number of bachelor's degrees granted doubled, while the numbers of master's degrees and doctorates increased almost as rapidly.[13] Estimates by Schultz, Denison, and others attributed a sizable fraction of overall economic growth per capita to the increased educational attainment of the labor force.

The great boom in higher education and the increase in the numbers of those enrolled came to an end in the 1970s, as the enormous increase in supply outstripped the growth of demand for college graduates. Between 1968 and 1973 the rate of return for investing in a bachelor's degree fell by perhaps as much as four percentage points (from 11 to 7 percent);

graduates in teaching and liberal arts had severe difficulties in obtaining work commensurate with their education, while those with doctorates faced a "new depression" in the market for academicians. As a result, enrollment rates leveled off (among women) or fell (among men), often by remarkable amounts. In 1969 44 percent of men 18 to 19 years old went on to higher education; in 1974 just 34 percent did. In 1969 the ratio of graduate school enrollments to college graduates 22 to 29 years of age was 0.50; by 1975, the ratio had fallen to 0.40.[14] Whether the reduced rate of college enrollment will be maintained in the next decade represents one of the major questions about the future labor force, to be addressed later.

The stabilization or drop in enrollment rates among the young did not, however, reduce or even greatly affect the rate of increase in the overall educational attainment of the work force. Even with the rates of the 1970s, the average education of the labor force rose noticeably. This was because of the large difference in years of schooling between retiring and entering workers, which remained sizable even with changed influxes to higher education. The proportion of college workers among the young but not in the work force as a whole stabilized.

Turning to the characteristics of employment, the figure highlights three significant changes in the period. First is the shift in employment from blue-collar to white-collar jobs, particularly professional and technical and clerical positions, and a concomitant drop in the less skilled share of jobs. The growth of white-collar workers was especially marked among nonwhite workers, where the proportion of white-collar workers nearly doubled from 1965 to 1976, and professionalization cut the historic gap between black and white representation in the professional and technical group by over 50 percent.[15]

Second, there was a near doubling in the governmental share of the labor force, though here the rate of growth declined markedly in the 1970s. By 1976 one in six workers was employed by some governmental body, largely at the state and local level. One third of the growth of employment over the entire 1948–1976 period is attributable to expansion of the public sector. At the other end of the spectrum was a continued shift of the work force out of agriculture, leaving just 3.8 percent of employed workers in that sector in 1976, and a drop in the self-employed nonagricultural labor force.[16]

The third important and widely heralded shift in the period was in the geographic distribution of employment, with a marked shift in jobs away from the eastern and midwestern industrial belt. The fastest growing regions of the country were the South, Southwest, and to a lesser extent, the West Coast. Many industries moved into the South and Southwest in the period, locating new plants in such states as Texas, Louisiana, Florida, and Arizona. Industrialization of those areas and loss of employment in New England and the Midwest became the subject of considerable controversy, due in part to the federal government's spending decisions allegedly favoring the Sun Belt over the Snow Belt.

In addition to the gross changes in the composition of employment shown in Figure 1, there were other marked shifts in employment. The coal industry, a declining "sick" sector in the 1950s and 1960s, became an expanding growth sector in the 1970s. The education industry underwent the opposite pattern of change, as did aerospace. There was rapid growth of employment in computing machinery and losses in such areas as textiles, shoe manufacturing, and steel. Upwards of one third of the work force changed their detailed occupation category from 1965 to 1970.[17] What is important toward understanding the nature of the labor force and predicting future patterns is the remarkable magnitude of these shifts, which points to a *highly mobile and flexible labor force*.

In terms of the institutional structure of the work force, the most important development in the period was the *dwindling of private-sector unionism* and *growth of unionism among governmental employees*. In 1953, 34 percent of the nonagricultural labor force was organized; in 1974, 26 percent was organized. This striking eight-point drop actually exceeded in terms of percentage points the drop in the fraction unionized in the 1920s. Decomposed by sector, the decline is seen to occur entirely in private employment. Several traditionally organized sectors of the economy, such as coal and construction, underwent marked drops in the fraction unionized, while even in manufacturing the union share of production labor fell.[18] Although some of the drop can be attributed to the shift of the labor force to the less organized regions of the country, or to the increased number of historically less organized women, much is also due to more subtle socioeconomic forces, including increased managerial opposition and the advent of more sophisticated tools for combating unions, the quantitative effect of which remains to be evaluated. The only sizable area of union growth was in the public sector, where the teachers moved from almost entirely nonunion to primarily union status in the 1960s, with their professional association, the National Education Association, becoming an effective union organization; and where the Police and Firefighters Association also began negotiating collective contracts in large numbers; and where large numbers of other workers came to be organized by the State, County and Municipal Workers Union. Whether these patterns will continue into the future, effectively changing the face of unionism in the United States, is another major question regarding the work force of the 1980s.

Finally, the ethnic composition of the U.S. work force also underwent some change in the period. The nonwhite share of the labor force remained roughly constant over the entire period, as declines in the participation rate of nonwhite relative to white workers were counterbalanced by increases in the population of nonwhites relative to that of whites. The major change was in the supply of "illegal aliens," largely from Mexico and Latin America. Although, for obvious reasons, precise estimates of the number of illegal aliens are unavailable, experts have claimed that perhaps 6 million workers fit into this category in 1976.[19] These workers would amount to 4 percent of the measured labor force and, assuming that most entered in the late 1960s and 1970s, 30 percent of the growth of the work force from 1965 to 1976. Because of the apparent importance of illegal aliens in the past growth of the work force and their potentially greater role in the next decade, much more knowledge is needed about this component of the work force.

Past Changes versus Past Forecasts

The nature of the problem of predicting the labor force of the future can be most fruitfully gauged by examining the extent to which some of the major changes just described were or were not adequately foreseen in the past. If the rise of the female work force, changed age structure, increased educational attainment, and related changes were at least roughly predicted by past analysis, we could reasonably expect to be able to predict some important future changes. If most of the major developments were unexpected, the task of prognostication for the decade ahead would have to be judged more difficult and the ensuing efforts viewed with some trepidation.

Table 1 contrasts predicted and actual changes in the number or fraction of workers with varying characteristics in several time periods and also gives predicted and actual changes in the future work force. The figures do not tell a very sanguine story about our ability to foresee major changes in the labor force. The most important development in the period covered, that is, the massive movement of women into the work force,

Table 1.   Predicted and Actual Changes in the Labor Force, 1960–1975.

Group, Initial Period when Forecast was Made and End of Period	Change in Absolute Numbers (in Thousands) or in Percentage of Work Force		Percentage Changes	
	Predicted	Actual	Predicted	Actual
1. Female workers				
1960–1970	6,962	8,578	31.1	36.3
1965–1975	6,712	11,133	25.2	41.8
2. Work force less than 35				
1960–1975	14,818	19,059	51.4	65.8
3. Doctorate degrees				
1969–1976	14.2	7.2	54.2	28.0
4. Percentage of work force 1960–1975				
Professional and managerial	0.051	0.045	24.2	21.4
Craftsmen	0.000	0.001	0.0	0.8

Sources: Projections:
1960–70 *Manpower Report of the President 1964*, Table D-8, p. 179;
1965–75 *Manpower Report of the President 1966*, Table E-2, p. 215;
1960–75 *Manpower Report of the President 1966*, Table E-2, p. 215;
1969–76 *National Science Foundation, 1969 and 1980 Science and Engineers Doctoral Supply and Utilization* (May 1971), Table B-1, p. 26;
1960–75 *Manpower Report of the President 1966.*

Actual figures:
Employment and Training Report of the President 1977, Table A-2, p. 137 with 14-15 year-olds added to totals for comparability, Table A-15, p. 162;
National Academy of Sciences, National Research Council, *Doctorate Recipients from U.S. Universities, 1976*, p. 5, Table A.

was grossly underestimated in nearly every forecast, even those made in 1965 when an upward trend was apparent. The inability to project the growth of the female work force is perhaps best illustrated by the failure of the Bureau of Labor Statistics (BLS) to foresee the rise in the participation of younger women in the 1960s and 1970s, thereby missing that major behavioral development.

A second major labor-force change in the period, that is, the growth in the number of younger workers, was also not foreseen by analysts despite its dependence on demographic factors. One reason for the surprising failure to forecast the number of workers less than 35 years of age with greater accuracy is the difficulty of forecasting the proportion in school and the participation rates of students. Another is the inability to predict the aforementioned growth of the young female work force. If illegal aliens, many of whom are below 34 years of age, are included, the magnitude of the error grows sizably. Because of demographic factors, which do not translate directly into labor supply, and because of the influx of illegal (and legal) young immigrants, the age composition of the work force turns out to be more difficult to project accurately than might have been thought.

As can be seen in Table 1, line 3, one of the most egregious forecast errors occurred at the top of the educational ladder. National Science Foundation forecasts of the growth of Ph.D.'s, made as late as 1969, far overstated the actual growth of the early 1970s, essentially by missing the downturn in the doctorate market and its impact on the supply of new doctorates. Such errors in forecasting educational development are by no means rare. In 1949 Seymour Harris published a book which predicted that if more young persons went to college in the 1950s the market would be glutted, while even as prescient a seer as Allan Cartter expected the rapid growth of enrollments and degrees of the sixties to continue into the seventies.

Forecasts of the gross structure of employment have been much more accurate (Table 1, line 4), although this in part represents the wide range of groups included under the one-digit categories. As the level of disaggregation is increased, the standard "fixed requirements" method of forecasting employment runs into increasing problems. The general direction of change is usually correct, but forecasting errors are large (Freeman 1977).

As for institutional changes, no major analyst expected the union movement to run into the problems of organizing workers that characterized the 1960s and 1970s. In 1947, just as union growth was beginning to level off, political scientist Charles Lindblom in fact predicted that widespread organization of the work force was going to transform the society, creating a syndicalist economy. In 1957 Dunlop did foresee some problems in future organization, but he failed to identify the dwindling of private-sector unionism as the main tendency of the ensuing two decades. The problem is not that these or other analysts missed "obvious clues" to future changes due to incomplete or erroneous analyses, but that it is intrinsically difficult to foresee structural changes in labor-market institutions.

The lesson to be learned from this review of forecasts is that it is no easy task to make good predictions of the work force of the future. Both in terms of absolute size and composition, the labor force changes dramatically in relatively short time spans—often in ways that, at least in the past, were not foreseen by standard forecasts. The attempt to discern the size and composition of the work force of the 1980s later in this chapter must be viewed in light of the sizable unpredicted changes of the past. Although, given increased knowledge of labor-force behavior, we may be able to do better than past analysts, the record suggests caution and modesty.

DETERMINANTS OF THE LABOR SUPPLY

Before attempting to predict changes in the labor force in the next decade, it will be valuable to consider the economic determinants of labor supply and the extent to which economic analysis can account for the changes described earlier.

To begin with, the overall supply of labor can be decomposed into three basic components using the accounting identity:

$$L_E = \sum_i POP_i \; LFPR_i \; EL_i$$

where

L_E = labor measured in "effective units"

POP = population in group i

LFPR = labor-force participation rate in group i

EL_i = average qualifications of workers, as reflected in the human capital of group i

i = index for demographic groups

The economic analysis concentrates on the factors that determine the labor-force participation (LFPR) and investment in qualifications or human capital (EL_i) dimensions of workers.

Consider first the determinants of the participation decision, which can be modeled fruitfully in terms of responses to two wages, the market wage facing an individual and the "shadow" wage that reflects the value of nonmarket activity. As depicted in Figure 2, when the wage exceeds the value of nonmarket time, the individual will decide to participate in the work force; whereas when the wage falls short of the value of nonmarket time, even when the individual remains at home, he or she will choose to stay out of the labor force. The market wage includes nonpecuniary as well as pecuniary components and is conceptually measurable with market data. The shadow wage, which is not directly observable, will be a function of nonmarket production and consumption possibilities. It will depend on the level of the income of other members of the household, on nonwork income, and on the technology of household production; it will be closely intertwined with the composition of the home, particularly the presence of children.

Changes in labor-force activity are explicable in this model by changes in the wage or shadow wage and their underlying determinants. For persons out of the work force, an increase in the wage will have a substitution effect, raising the value of working and possibly inducing entrance into the work force. For persons in the work force, an increase has both a substitution and an income effect, as their overall income is raised by the higher wage. The number of hours worked may increase or decrease depending on the net of these two effects. Increases in the income of other family members, such as husbands in the case of married women, will affect participation through the shadow wage, which rises as long as household goods have a positive income elasticity, inducing less labor-force activity through the standard income effect. Improvements in household technology, which take the form either of new machines or techniques or of lower prices for given techniques, can increase or decrease work activity depending on the extent to which they substitute for household time, among other things.

The traditional encouraged worker–discouraged worker dichotomization of labor-force behavior can be captured readily by the model. Changes in the wage, with all else the same, would give rise to discouraged (or encouraged) worker behavior as the substitution effect induces persons to leave or enter the work force. Changes in other income that affect the shadow wage underlie the additional worker behavior, which depends on the income effect. When wages and other income change, the discouraged worker pattern would dominate, provided the substitution effect exceeds the income effect, that is, that the shadow wage is less responsive to the changes than the wage, while the additional worker pattern would predominate under converse circumstances.

The missing component to this model is changes in attitudes, which may very well be important in actual changes in participation over time. In general, the economic model takes attitudes as given to trace the effects of income, price, wage, and related market factors on behavior. In the absence of clearly specified measures of attitudes and any theory of changes, attitudinal issues should be brought into the story gingerly, for

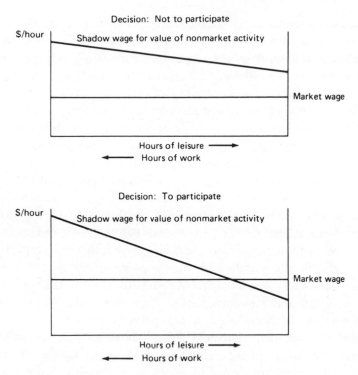

Figure 2. The labor participation decision.

there is great danger in using attitudes as a *deus ex machina*. As will be seen shortly, however, it may not be possible to exclude them in considering past changes in female labor-force behavior.

The Economic Explanation

To what extent can major labor-force changes be explained in terms of responses to economic incentives?

The basic effort to explain participation rate patterns in terms of income and substitution effects, intiated by Mincer in the 1960s, involves a two-stage procedure. First the effects of factors on participation are estimated, using cross-sectional (more recently, longitudinal) data. Then the estimated model is applied to the time-series changes by multiplying the estimated effect of variables (such as the wages of women and of men) by the actual change in these explanatory factors to obtain a predicted change. The prediction is then compared to the actual change to assess the importance of the factors under study.[20] Although Mincer's first set of estimates suggested that most of the long-term growth in female participation could be attributed to responses to the wages of women and their husbands, ensuing work by Cain attributed a much lower impact to these economic forces: The estimated parameters for female and male incomes were found to differ substantially in different cross sections, suggesting possible attitudinal or other changes, and to explain only a small proportion of the long-term changes. Because the wages of men and women have risen at roughly the same rate over time, the simple model requires *much* larger substitution than income effects, which are not found in the cross sections nor in recent work treating individual observations on large data tapes.[21] The addition of other factors likely to affect wages and shadow wages, such as education and number of children, does not greatly improve the results. Estimated parameters from time-series studies, most of which have focused on cyclic rather than on long-term changes, also do not greatly improve the power of the model.[22] Perhaps most discouragingly, the most recent results for the 1970 census of population show that the economic factors "which together once explained three-quarters of the variation in wives' participation rates across SMSAs [Standard Metropolitan Statistical Areas], now account for only about one-third of it. Many of the variables are no longer significant, and the strength and explanatory power of all except the unemployment variable have declined."[23] We are far from accounting for the rise in the participation of women in terms of simple economic forces.

One possible missing element from standard models, which may enhance the power of the wage–shadow-wage approach, is the nature of household technology. The household sector is surprisingly capital intensive. In 1975 the average household had, for example, $6,990 in consumer durables. From 1952 to 1975 the accumulation of durables increased by 5.4 percent per annum.[24] Refrigerators, washing machines, and related equipment became increasingly prevalent in the home. Although cause-and-effect cannot be readily disentangled, the growth of fast-food services and other restaurants came to offer a more readily available (and chosen) alternative for one of the main household products. In the absence of hard estimates of the quantitative effect of these factors, of substitution between time and goods in household production, and of the key elasticities of substitution, however, we can do no more than speculate about the effect of technology in "freeing" women's time.

Another possible missing element, which must be brought into the story with care, is attitudinal changes, potentially associated with the women's liberation movement of the late sixties and seventies. That there were significant changes in attitudes over the period is apparent from diverse opinion surveys. As late as 1967, 44 percent of first-year college women and 67 percent of first-year college men thought "a woman's place is best at home." In 1974, only 19 percent of entering college women and 40 percent of men agreed with that view.[25] Clearly, it had become (for whatever reason) more socially acceptable for women to devote themselves to careers as opposed to marriage and family. The extent to which these changes in attitudes were caused by or caused some of the labor-force patterns is difficult to determine. Given the problem of explaining patterns over a period of time in terms of income and substitution effects, their possible role deserves some attention.

Older Men

The basic economic model appears to be somewhat more successful in accounting for the decline in the labor participation of older men, where the principal force at work has been Social Security laws. As an increasing proportion of the male work force has come to be covered by Social Security, which places a 100 percent tax on earnings above a modest amount, the participation of men 65 and over has dropped. The possibility of receiving some benefits at age 62 has induced further declines into the next age group. In this case, studies of individuals have found sizable response parameters for the effect of economic variables (including Social Security benefits) on retirement behavior, with older men estimated to be more sensitive to wages or nonwage income than men in general (Cain and Watts 1973). Although detailed analysis of the effect of Social Security on retirement is just beginning, the evidence seems to support the attribution of a considerable effect to the Social Security mode of retirement pay (Boskin and Hurd 1977).

Qualifications of the Labor Force

The human-capital analysis of investment in skills provides a reasonably successful explanation of the changes in the qualifications of the work force shown in Figure 1 although, as in other problems, it is also necessary to consider the demand factors at work as well. In the human-capital model, decisions to obtain a certain level of schooling or skill are made by comparing two income streams: the stream that results from the investment and the stream that would obtain in its absence. If, at a given interest rate r, the present value of the former exceeds the latter plus the direct cost of the investment, the individual is expected to choose the investment. Because about two thirds of the private cost of education turns out to consist of foregone income, as opposed to direct costs, the analysis directs attention to differences in the wages of more and less qualified persons as the major factor in investments in schooling.

Time-series analyses of enrollment patterns suggest that much of the postwar expansion and the seventies' contraction in the higher education system can be attributed to changes in wages and rates of return. As figure 3 documents, a relatively simple model of the economic incentives for investing in college tracks the increase and decrease in the enrollment ratio of 18- to 19-year-old men in post-World War II years with surprising success. More complex models, focused on specific groups, have yielded comparable results. The slowdown in doctorate production appears explicable in terms of the economic factors at work in that market although, in this case, nonprice signals, notably the difficulty of obtaining work, appear to be the prime causal factor of changes. The selection of particular fields of study has also been found to respond to market factors with, for example, relatively many students choosing education majors in the 1960s and many fewer choosing this major in the 1970s when the teachers' job market deteriorated. [26] In sum, though by no means without problems, the economic analysis does appear to provide a good handle on the changing educational attainment of the work force.

Turning to occupational and industrial deployment of workers, the most important economic factor appears to be shifts in demand, which operate along relatively elastic supply curves to direct labor to different sectors. The principal technique for analyzing these changes is fixed requirements analysis, which focuses on the industrial mix of the economy as the prime identifiable force altering demand for labor. The BLS and other agencies provide fixed requirement forecasts for broad and detailed occupations and industries quite frequently. The forecasts appear to be reasonably on target for one-digit occupations or industries and provide some clue to changes among more detailed groups as well, though with large forecast errors. Although the technique has clear-cut problems and shortcomings, since it is incapable of capturing such dramatic shifts as the growth of demand for mathematicians in the fifties and sixties and changed demand for coalworkers in the sixties and seventies, it offers some guide to the future industrial–occupational composition of the labor force.

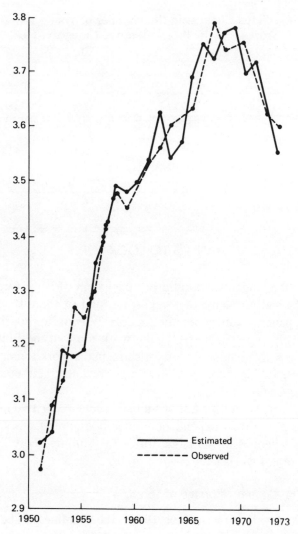

Figure 3.   Logarithm of proportion of 18- to 19-year old men enrolled in college and proportion estimated from economic incentives, 1951–1973. Based on regression estimated in R. Freeman, "Overinvestment in College Training?" *Journal of Human Resources* (Summer 1975): Table 5.

Table 2.   Predicted Changes in the Number of Young Workers and Workers in the Promotion Age Category, 1975–1990.

	Total Civilian Labor Force 16 and Over	Persons 16–24	Persons 25–44
Number, 1975	92,613	22,265	39,091
Number, 1990	114,517	20,918	60,533
Percentage change, 1975–1990	23.7	−6.0	54.9
Share, 1975	100.0	24.0	42.0
Share, 1990	100.0	18.0	52.0
Change in share, 1975–1990	—	−6.0	10.0

Source: *ETR*, Table E-2, p. 253.

CHANGES TO LOOK FOR

Having given the reader some notion of the extent of labor-force change, of the failures and problems of forecasting, and of the difficulty of explaining past patterns with economic models, it seems appropriate to consider, tentatively and speculatively, the work force of the future. In this section I identify five potentially major shifts in the work force, set out the reasons for regarding them as likely, and consider their potential economic consequences.

Table 2 presents Bureau of Labor Statistics data on the two most important and, because of their dependence on demographic factors, most reliable "likely" changes in the labor force: the coming shortage of youth and the plethora of workers at promotion age.

Shift No. 1. The Coming Shortage of Youth

Because of the low birthrates of the 1960s, the absolute number of young workers is expected to fall sharply in the 1980s. In terms of absolute numbers, Table 2 shows a decline of over 1 million persons between the ages of 16 and 24, which will reduce the share of the labor force below the age of 24 by 6.0 percentage points. The absolute and relative drop in the number of young workers are likely to have sizable economic consequences, reversing many of the patterns of the 1960s and 1970s. With relatively few young workers, the age–earnings profile can be expected to twist in favor of the young, reducing the premium to older workers. Assuming, as seems reasonable, that younger and older workers can substitute more easily for each other at the lower rather than at the upper educational levels, the rewards for attending college should rise for persons of college age in the decade, with consequences to be developed further under shift 3. The problems of teenage and youth unemployment, which have been especially severe for blacks, ought to diminish, though to what extent is not clear. At the least, the employment prospects for less qualified young persons will improve greatly, as companies find it difficult to fill entry-level positions. In addition, as Cartter first pointed out, the shortage of youth will mean severe problems for the educational system and a reduction in employment of teachers and college faculty, at least relative to the overall work force.

The only possible factor which could ameliorate the coming shortage of youth would be a marked inflow of young immigrants, illegal or legal.

Shift No. 2. The Plethora of Workers at Promotion Age

Perhaps even more remarkable will be the demographic bunching of the prime-age work force in the 25–44 age bracket, in which persons are typically in the process of competing for various promotions and supervisory positions. Whereas in 1975 there were 39 million workers in the 25–44 age bracket, in 1990 there will be 60.5 million—an extraordinary 55 percent increase. The proportion of the work force aged 25 to 44 will increase by ten full percentage points. This remarkable age bunching of the work force will have far-reaching consequences for the job market. On the one hand, it implies a more rapid overall rate of economic growth and, because the number of persons of working age will be so large, an easing of the burden of redistributive taxes from workers to nonworkers. On the other, it suggests fierce competition for promotions, coupled with substantial career disappointment for many and the possibility that persons in the 25–44 cohort of 1990, some of whom have already entered the job market and already suffered from being born in a large group, will receive especially low relative income for their entire lives. The "excessive" number of 25- to 44-year-olds and shortfall of younger workers will create major personnel and labor-relations problems, on whose effective resolution industrial peace in the 1980s may depend.

Shift No. 3. Increased Educational Attainment

The proportion of young persons going on to college but not to graduate school is likely to increase in the next decade, as the "shortage" of young persons improves starting opportunities for graduates and raises potential rates of return. Because of the increased education of older workers, however, the rate of increase in mean years of schooling and in the proportion with higher education in the work force as a whole will decline. If the BLS's projections of the occupational distribution of the work force are roughly on target, educated workers, particularly in the 25–44 age group, are likely to have great problems in obtaining jobs in the professional–managerial area in which graduates typically work. Still, the market for young graduates should improve relative to that of the 1970s, inducing more persons into college from the age group.

Shift No. 4. Increased Female Participation

The upward trend in female labor participation is expected to continue by all forecasts, and I see no reason for any marked slowing down or reversal in the pattern. The sectors of the economy which tend to hire relatively many women are likely to grow, creating demand pressures, while it is difficult to find any forces operating in the opposite direction. If the movement of women into previously male occupations, which began in the 1960s and 1970s, is maintained, the increased participation may be accompanied by an increased diffusion of women across the work force and convergence in the female share of various occupations and industries.

Shift No. 5. Distribution of Desirable Jobs

According to the preceding analysis, there is likely to be increased competition for "desirable" jobs among persons in the prime age brackets, 25–44, which may be intensified by the influx of women into traditional male areas. If equal-opportunity pressures are maintained, the increased number of highly qualified black and women workers will create new claimants for the prestigious jobs. One result of the increased number of eligible candidates will be a narrowing in the wage structure among experienced (but not young) workers. Another is a likely increase in the proportion of professional, managerial, and craft jobs held by minorities and women.

A more speculative possible shift, which perhaps should be added to the list, is for an increase in the work force of older persons, the result of potential loosening of Social Security restrictions, stronger age discrimination legislation, and mandatory weakening of retirement policies. Since no detailed study of this possibility has been made, it is best left as a speculative possibility, rather than a "likely" shift.

CONCLUSION

This chapter has examined past changes in the work force, considered economic models and explanations of changes, and sought, albeit with trepidation, to identify some major changes in the future work force. The analysis of changes found that the labor force had undergone major changes in the past that had not been accurately foreseen. The analysis of economic models pointed attention at some economic forces likely to affect labor-force behavior but found that, though economic factors could account for some changes, such as enhanced educational attainment, they explained only a small fraction of others, notably the increased participation of women. With respect to the future, the most important changes in the labor force are the coming shortage of youth and the bunching of the work force in the 25–44 age bracket, which will result from demographic factors whose effect will be difficult to ameliorate.

NOTES

1. U.S. Department of Labor, *Employment and Training Report of the President 1977* (Washington, D.C.: U.S. Government Printing Office, 1977), Table A-1, p. 135; Table A-3, p. 139. (Hereafter cited as *ETR.*)
2. *Ibid.,* Table B-9, p. 203.
3. *Ibid.,* Table A-15, p. 162.
4. U.S. Department of Labor, *Handbook of Labor Statistics 1976*, Bulletin 1905 (Washington, D.C.: U.S. Government Printing Office, 1976), Table 145, p. 297. (Hereafter cited as *Handbook.*)
5. *ETR*, Table A-30, pp. 181–2. These figures refer to voluntary part-time workers.
6. *Handbook,* Table 1, p. 22; Table 47, p. 100. Data are for 1974.
7. *Ibid.,* Table 48, p. 101, in which the South and Southwest include Regions IV, VI, and Arizona and Nevada but not California or Hawaii; Table 1, p. 22.
8. *ETR*, Table A-4, p. 142; Table A-3, p. 139. Of a total increase of 35 million persons, 22 million were women.
9. *Ibid.,* Table B-1, p. 189; Table B-4, p. 194.
10. *Ibid.,* Table B-14, p. 212.
11. *Ibid.,* Table A-3, p. 139; Table A-1, p. 143.
12. The relative employment numbers are from Freeman (1978, Table 1, p. 4); the relative income numbers from the same source, Table 2, p. 8, lines 6 and 8.
13. U.S. Department of Health, Education and Welfare, *The Condition of Education,* Volume 3, Part 1 (Washington, D.C.: U.S. Government Printing Office, 1977), Tables 3.14–3.16, pp. 186–7.
14. R. Freeman, *The Overeducated American* (New York: Academic Press, 1976), Table 1, p. 26; Figure 6, p. 35.
15. *ETR*, Table A-16, p. 164.
16. *Ibid.,* Table A-17, p. 165.
17. D. Sommers and A. Eck, "Occupational Mobility in the American Labor Force," *Monthly Labor Review* (January 1977).

18. R. Freeman and J. Medoff, "The Dwindling of Private Sector Unionism," in *What Do Unions Do?* (New York: Basic Books, in preparation).

19. This is a rough estimate based on discussion with Michael Piore.

20. Formally let a_i be the cross-section estimate of the impact of the ith variables on participation. Then the predicted change in participation would be $\Sigma a_u \Delta X_i$ where ΔX_i is the change in variable i.

21. See, for example, O. Ashenfelter and J. Heckman, "The Estimation of Income and Substitution Effects in a Model of Family Labor Supply," *Econometrica* 42 (January 1974): 73–86.

22. For a review of the time series literature, see J. Mincer, "Labor Force Participation of Married Women," in *Prosperity and Unemployment,* ed. R. Gordon (New York: Wiley, 1966).

23. J. Fields, "A Comparison of Intercity Differences in the Labor Force Participation Rates of Married Women in 1970 with 1940, 1950 and 1960," *Journal of Human Resources* (Fall 1976): 576.

24. The 1975 data were estimated by dividing current (1975) dollars of consumer durables of $497 billion as reported in the U.S. Bureau of the Census, *Statistical Abstract of the U.S., 1976*, p. 428, Table 695, by 71.1 million households (*ibid.*, p. xiii) with 1952 data for trend from U.S. Bureau of the Census, *Historical Statistics of the U.S., Colonial Times to 1970*, Part 1, p. 252, series F-373, and *Historical Statistics of the U.S., Colonial Times to 1957*, p. 15, series A242. The 1952 value was $2,079 (in 1958 dollars).

25. These data taken from Freeman (1976a, p. 168, Figure 29).

26. See Joseph Hebl, unpublished undergraduate thesis, Harvard College, 1978.

BIBLIOGRAPHY

Ashenfelter, O., and Heckman, J., "The Estimation of Income and Substitution Efforts in a Model of Family Labor Supply," *Econometrica* 42 (January 1974): 73–86.

Boskin, J., and Hurd, M., "The Effect of Social Security on Early Retirement," National Bureau of Economic Research, Working Paper No. 204, September 1977.

Cain, G., *Married Women in the Labor Force* (Chicago: University of Chicago, 1966).

Cain, G., and Watts, H., *Income Maintenance and Labor Supply* (Chicago: Markham, 1973).

Cartter, A., "Scientific Manpower Trends for 1970–1985," *Science* (April 1971): 132–40.

Dunlop, J., "The American Industrial Relations System in 1978," in *U.S. Industrial Relations: The Next Twenty Years,* ed. J. Steber (East Lansing: Michigan State University Press, 1958).

Fields, J., "A Comparison of Intercity Differences in the Labor Force Participation Rates of Married Women in 1970 with 1940, 1950 and 1960." *Journal of Human Resources* (Fall 1976): 568–76.

Freeman, R. *The Overeducated American* (New York: Academic Press, 1976a).

———, "The Depressed College Job Market: Issues and Implications," unpublished paper, January 1976b.

———, "Manpower Requirements and Substitution Analysis: A Synthesis," in *Research in Labor Economics,* ed. R. Ehrenberg (Greenwich, Conn.: Jai Press, Inc., 1977).

———, "The Effect of Demographic Factors on the Age–Earnings Profile in the U.S." (Cambridge, Mass.: Harvard Institute of Economic Research, 1978). Paper No. 643.

Freeman, R., and Medoff, J., "The Dwindling of Private Sector Unionism," in preparation.

Harris, S., *The Market for College Graduates* (Cambridge, Mass: Harvard University Press, 1949).

Hebl, J., A Look at the 20th Century Market for Public Elementary and Secondary School Teachers, Harvard College senior thesis, February 1978.

Lindblom, C., *Unions and Capitalism* (New Haven, Conn.: Yale University Press, 1949).

Mincer, J., "Labor Force Participation of Married Women," in *Aspects of Labor Economics: A Conference of the Universities* (Princeton, N.J.: National Bureau of Economic Research, 1962).

_____, "Labor Force Participation and Unemployment," in *Prosperity and Unemployment,* ed. R. Gordon (New York: Wiley, 1966).

National Academy of Sciences, National Research Council, *Doctorate Recipients from U.S. Universities, 1976* (Washington, D.C.: National Academy of Sciences, 1976).

National Science Foundation, *1969 and 1980 Science and Engineering Doctorate Supply and Utilization* (Washington, D.C.: National Science Foundation, 1971).

U.S. Bureau of the Census, *Statistical Abstract of the U.S.,1975* (Washington, D.C.: U.S. Government Printing Office, 1976).

_____, *Historical Statistics of the U.S.: Colonial Times to 1970* (Washington, D.C.: U.S. Government Printing Office, 1970).

_____, *Historical Statistics of the U.S.: Colonial Times to 1957* (Washington, D.C.: U.S. Government Printing Office, 1957).

U.S. Department of Health, Education and Welfare, *The Condition of Education (1977)* (Washington, D.C.: U.S. Government Printing Office, 1977).

U.S. Department of Labor, *Employment and Training Report of the President 1977* (Washington, D.C.: U.S. Government Printing Office, 1977).

_____, *Manpower Report of the President 1964* (Washington, D.C.: U.S. Government Printing Office, 1964).

_____, *Manpower Report of the President 1966* (Washington, D.C.: U.S. Government Printing Office, 1966).

_____, *Handbook of Labor Statistics 1976,* Bulletin 1905 (Washington, D.C.: U.S. Government Printing Office, 1976).

5.

Manpower Policy: A Look Ahead

ELI GINZBERG

A. Barton Hepburn Professor of Economics
Graduate School of Business, Columbia University
Chairman, National Commission for Employment Policy

Manpower* policy is sometimes viewed as an unnecessary extension of government into the economy, which results in the expenditure of large sums with little useful social output. Former Deputy Secretary of the Treasury Charls E. Walker, one of the foremost manpower critics in the early 1970s, insisted that the national unemployment rate had been reduced only a few tenths of one percent as a result of an expenditure of $40 billion. No knowledgeable person at that time was able to substantiate the $40 billion figure; the correct amount was probably closer to half that sum, or less. By the end of 1977, however, the cumulative expenditures for manpower since 1962, when the Manpower Development and Training Act was passed, were in the $70 billion range.

Although it is not unreasonable to use the changes in the unemployment rate as one criterion for assessing the success of manpower programs, sole reliance on this measure is questionable from the viewpoint of both economics and politics. A more sensible way to establish the framework for the present analysis is to describe the principal goals that Congress has sought to accomplish with the successive authorization and appropriations for manpower programs in the decade and a half between 1962 and 1977.

---

*The use of the term "manpower" reflects current usage. The commission which I chair, formerly named the National Commission for Manpower Policy, has been redesignated in accordance with congressional action the National Commission for Employment Policy. On its face, the terms "labor market," "work force," and similar expressions are not true synonyms for manpower. Accordingly, I use the term "manpower" not by preference but out of necessity.

These objectives can be quickly identified: the largest sum has been spent on public-service employment, which has provided work for the unemployed, the largest proportion of whom lost their jobs as a result of the severe recession in fall 1974, from which we still have not fully recovered.

Next in importance are the sums that have provided one or another type of work experience for large numbers of the hard-to-employ, many of whom have had little or no effective attachment to the labor force. Although the Neighborhood Youth Corps (NYC) could be classified under work experience or training, my own preference is not to use the latter category since it is difficult to find evidence of much serious training that is being carried out in this program. Many critics contend, with some justification, that a great many of the youth programs have been so poorly planned and supervised that they had a dysfunctional impact on young people, who have learned how to be paid for work which they have not performed.

Institutional and on-the-job training represent the third important category of manpower expenditures. Although some training programs have been well structured, well run, and have provided the trainees, upon completion, with useful and marketable skills—for example, in licensed practical nursing or in auto mechanics—most training has been of such short duration (four months) that the principal gains to the clients have been the allowances and the work orientation which they received.

The fourth category of expenditures is appropriations for labor-market services, particularly for operating the Federal–State Employment Service, which offers assistance to job seekers via testing, counseling, and, above all, placement services.

If Charls Walker's criterion for judging the efficacy of manpower programs is too restrictive, what alternative standards are suggested by this summary recapitulation of the objectives espoused by congressional legislation? The most simple measures would be income earned in public-sector jobs by previously unemployed persons, perhaps adjusted for the value of the output for which they are responsible and further adjusted for the reduction in transfer payments; income received by in-school and out-of-school youth who have participated in NYC, adjusted by the reduction in crime and delinquent acts which these youth have not engaged in as a direct result of the receipt of public monies; and income earned by participants in work-experience programs, often in lieu of other types of income transfers. For all of these groups, the degree of their attachment to the labor force as a result of program participation should also be considered. And finally, the improvements in employability and income that have resulted from newly acquired skills must be gauged.

One conclusion is certain. Manpower programs put a lot of money into the hands of the poor and the near-poor. There is evidence that also suggests that those who have had the opportunity to enter and complete a serious course of training have shown important gains in their later employment and income. Whether there has been much of a payoff for those in work-experience programs other than the income they received while in trainee status, is less clear. Some probably have been helped to become attached to the labor force.

The primitive state of evaluation studies does not justify, in my opinion, any firmer judgments than those sketched herein. A word of warning to the less informed reader: I have no reason to believe that expenditures for manpower would show a lower rate of productivity than increased governmental expenditures for education, health, or criminal justice. One can make a good case, due to the large amounts of transfer income going to individuals and families at the lower end of the distribution, that manpower expenditures have been more socially productive. But our interest here is with the future, not the past.

One way to gain perspective on the directions which manpower policy is likely to take in the decade ahead is to catalog its current uses. A further means is to identify potential commitments that are likely to make future demands on policy. And a final way is to analyze the scope and limits of manpower policy in terms of macroeconomic strategy, the budgetary outlook, and the pressures and constraints on social reform. The following sections are devoted to each of these approaches.

THE GOALS OF MANPOWER POLICY: PRESENT COMMITMENTS

The Comprehensive Employment and Training Act (CETA) calls for manpower programs to accomplish the following:

- To provide skill training for individuals who are encountering difficulties in securing employment, and, to a lesser extent, to offer opportunities for those who will be able to advance into better paying jobs and careers only if they can obtain additional training.
- To provide public-service employment for individuals from low-income families who have been on the welfare rolls. The hope is that

some or many of these individuals, after acquiring a work record and experience for a year or so, will then be able to make the transition to a regular job in the private or public sector.

• To offer residential and nonresidential training (Job Corps Centers) to selected groups of seriously disadvantaged young people who require remedial education, socialization, and skill training to improve their employability and to compete successfully for work.

• To implement a variety of manpower programs, other than those subsumed under the Job Corps Centers, directed to youth—in school and out of school, urban and rural—aimed at improving their employability and employment by providing training opportunities, part-time work, and full-time employment.

This outline of the principal titles of CETA legislation establishes several broad objectives:

• To provide opportunities for a wide range of individuals, not limited to low-income persons, to secure training that could improve their employability.

• To provide opportunities for persons unemployed because of cyclical contractions or structural conditions, and to allow persons on welfare to obtain a public-service job in the expectation that through such employment they will later be better able to obtain a regular job.

• To provide opportunities for targeted groups, such as American Indians, migrants, and youth, to obtain a range of manpower services to assist them in getting and holding a regular job.

These commitments indicate that a large disparity exists between the eligibility criteria that Congress has stipulated for participation in these programs and the sums which it has allocated to provide training and employment opportunities. A few figures will make this clear. The number of unemployed at any one point during the year is currently about 7 million, and the total number who are out of work during the course of the year exceeds 20 million. Adults on welfare who are presumably employable (receiving aid for dependent children and food stamps) number 2 million. The number of American Indians who are unemployed or underemployed added to the number of migrants who have need for manpower services exceeds one-half million. And the urban and rural youth and young adults between the ages of 16 and 22 who are unemployed, underemployed, or who could profit from additional training are in excess of 2 million.

In contrast to these substantial numbers of potential claimants, fiscal 1978 appropriations provide a total of only 725,000 public-service jobs and training opportunities (of six months' duration) for about 1.5 million. The one inescapable conclusion is that the impact of manpower programs on the eligible pool will be quite modest.

PROSPECTIVE COMMITMENTS

The Carter administration has signaled to Congress and the public that a major aspect of its projected welfare reform is to divide the present pool into two parts, the employables and the nonemployables, and to demand that the employables, under threat of losing benefits, accept jobs either full time or part time, depending on circumstances. Preferably, these jobs will be found for the employables in the private sector, but in the absence thereof, in the public sector. The welfare proposal asks that 1.4 million public-service jobs be made available to persons on the welfare rolls. For the most part, these public-service jobs will carry a wage at or close to the minimum, and those families that will continue to require supplementation will be better off if their wage-earning member gets a job in the private sector; this will encourage those in public-sector jobs to move off and find employment in the regular economy.

The final version of the Humphrey-Hawkins Bill passed in October 1978 reflects a great many compromises, including the growing national concern with inflation, the federal deficit, and the adverse balance of trade, as well as the continuing high levels of unemployment, particularly among youth and minorities. Small wonder, therefore, that in the final effort to obtain the required votes for passage, the bill contains not only a target figure for unemployment—4 percent by 1983—but also targets for inflation, balanced budget, and trade balance. The act stresses the new process for consultation among the Executive branch, the Federal Reserve Board, and the Congress in determining macroeconomic policies, but does not specify recommended actions to achieve the designated targets.

The 1977 Youth Employment and Demonstration Projects Act (YEDPA) is a third new commitment: the creation of several hundred thousand employment opportunities, largely in the not-for-profit sector (government and nonprofit institutions), aimed at absorbing large numbers of unemployed youth who reside in the inner cities. The legislation had been on the books for only a few months when some of the watchdogs of the federal budget, officials at the Office of Management and Budget, recommended that the new Youth Title of CETA be eliminated and that additional funding available for youth in the future be disbursed through other manpower programs. Although OMB was unsuccessful in eliminating the specific youth title, it succeeded in limiting the appropriation requested for 1979 to the preexisting levels, despite the president's acknowledgment in December 1977 that the issue of youth unemployment had predominated at the heads-of-state meeting in London the previous May. At the same time President Carter added that the challenge of reducing the unemployment rate for black youth continued to baffle him.

Given the continuing high rates of unemployment not only among black youth but also among black adults, and the often reported criticism by moderate black leaders of the inadequacies of the administration's urban policy, it is difficult to see how the leadership of the Democratic party will be able to avoid expanding the role of the federal government in job creation for unemployed and underemployed blacks.

A fourth likely expansion of federal effort in the years ahead is in manpower programs to assist workers who have been displaced through unfair trade practices. Conflict is becoming ever more severe between the long-established function of the United States as the leader in reducing trade barriers among nations and the growing number of employers and trade unions in this country that are pleading for a reversal of that policy on the grounds that imports from abroad are eroding both our jobs and our profits. Foreigners are capturing our markets with goods produced by workers whose pay is less than a quarter of our domestic wages; in many cases foreign governments are subsidizing their exporters to assist them in capturing our markets. Since 1962 we have had on the books the Trade Expansion Act (and later amendments), which stipulates that the federal government can assist employers and workers who suffer damage as a result of unfair trade practices. Included are various manpower programs providing access to training, and mobility allowances for workers who have lost their jobs.

The adjustment measures in the act do not come into play until a complex set of administrative determinations is made by different Washington agencies; from 1969 through 1975, the total number of workers assisted was relatively small, approximately 35,000, and the amount of assistance per worker was relatively modest.

The odds are strong, however, that if trade among the advanced industrial nations is not to become seriously constricted by a retreat to protectionism, the adjustment mechanism will have to be broadened and deepened. At minimum, one must anticipate that the federal government will grant workers adjudged to be injured by trade policy easier access to training and special consideration with respect to public-service employment.

A fifth likely area of greater commitment is the expansion of job-creation efforts directed toward easing the work and income problems facing hard-to-employ groups such as older persons, the disabled, released mental hospital patients, ex-drug addicts, and ex-offenders. "Operation Mainstream," dating back to 1963, is a program directed originally toward older unemployed coal miners in Kentucky who had little or no prospect of returning to the pits, but who, instead of drawing income transfers, were afforded an opportunity to be employed on publicly funded outdoor jobs. About four years ago several federal agencies, with the U.S. Department of Labor in the lead, underwrote, via a nonprofit organization—the Manpower Demonstration Research Corporation—a pioneer effort that goes under the name "Supported Work." It is a graded work program aimed at providing work and income for hard-to-employ persons as a first step to linking them to the regular labor market. Sheltered workshops, primarily under philanthropic auspices, have over many decades also provided employment opportunities for many small groups of disabled persons.

This review of potential commitments for the expansion of manpower programs has called attention to the following developments:

- The reform of the welfare system, strengthened by the Humphrey–Hawkins commitment, aimed at assuring that all employable persons (at least one per family) will be required to work in order to receive public assistance.
- The expanded use of manpower training and public job creation for minority youth and adults, particularly in large urban areas.
- A much stepped-up effort to expand and energize the trade-adjustment mechanisms now on the books and to add to the available services aimed at facilitating the reemployment of workers who lose their jobs as a result of trade policy.
- Expanded efforts to design large-scale programs based on older and more recent demonstration efforts directed toward improving the

employability and employment of hard-to-place groups, including, in particular, the disabled, the elderly, and formerly institutionalized persons.

THE SCOPE AND LIMITS OF MANPOWER POLICY

In the years that have passed since the passage of the Manpower Training and Development Act of 1962, the annual federal appropriations for work force programs have increased from around $52 million to approximately $13 billion in fiscal 1978, or by more than 250 times. The principal rationale for this steady expansion is that manpower training offers opportunities for different groups of disadvantaged citizens to improve their skills and thereby position themselves better to get and hold jobs that will enable them to support themselves and their families.

But one must note the training-related issues that remain unsettled, despite a federal effort dating back to 1962. In the face of a shortfall in job opportunities, how far can one go along the training route before one is simply changing the position of people in the queue? Those who receive the training are likely to move farther to the front of the line of job seekers.

But, assuming that good training in a reasonably balanced labor market can result in substantial gains in employment and income for those who go through the programs, who should be eligible to participate in such a costly public program? Congress has preferred to establish broad eligibility criteria, with the inevitable result that the operating agencies have sought to divide the limited funds over the largest number of eligibles, thereby ensuring that most people will receive little serious training and will therefore be less likely to enjoy significant posttraining benefits.

Other difficulties persist. Employers are clearly unable or unwilling to participate in on-the-job training during a period when they are forced to reduce their work force because of a falloff in business. And even in a strong labor market, those who go through institutional training often experience difficulties in finding a training-related job.

Still further difficulties in the design and implementation of an effective training component as part of a national manpower policy grow out of the inadequate educational preparation of many who are most in need of skill training. Until many poorly educated persons have an opportunity to bring their reading and calculating skills up to a minimum level, they are not likely to be able to enter into serious training. But such remedial efforts present serious problems from the vantage of both cost and motivation of potential trainees.

It is much easier to affirm that training offers a major opportunity to improve the operations of a modern labor market, to provide opportunities for disadvantaged persons, to improve their employability and income, and to contribute to the moderation of inflationary pressures by enlarging the pool of skills, than to design and implement such an effort in an economy characterized by cyclical fluctuations. Employers operate under trade-union contracts that affect hiring and firing, and congressmen, looking for public approval, seek to spread their limited appropriations over the largest possible number of voters.

Similar tensions exist between generalizations about the virtues of governmental job creation efforts and the implementation of several programs that could contribute significantly to easing the nation's unemployment problem. Most people, conservative and liberal alike, have a prejudice in favor of providing opportunities for the unemployed to work rather than having them rely on income transfers. Public-service employment (PSE) first appeared in 1971, and in 1978 reached its goal of 725,000 jobs (in an economy with more than 95 million jobs). This strikingly slow growth suggests that what appears clearly desirable at face value apparently presents serious difficulties when efforts are made to put the job-creation program into effect.

A short list of the difficulties includes the following: Who among the large number of potential claimants for jobs—from better educated youth to seriously disadvantaged adults with family responsibilities—should have priority claims on the positions which government creates? If such jobs are created, as they will be, in areas of substantial unemployment, what prospects are there to move these PSE workers into the regular economy at the end of one year or more on a public-service job? And if they cannot be moved into regular employment, does this imply that the federally supported jobs will have to be a permanent addition to the local government payroll? And if such continued financing is not available, what point is there in dropping the ex-PSE jobholder back into the pool of the unemployed?

Furthermore, what wages should be paid to those who hold PSE jobs? Currently the figure is considerably above the minimum wage—about 50 percent—but the administration's welfare reform package proposes a wage not much higher than the minimum. Many prime sponsors currently exercise their right to supplement the $10,000 ceiling for federal funds, which means that some PSE jobs carry an annual wage of up to $15,000, or higher.

If PSE job creation expands during cyclical downturns, as in 1974–1975, then there is conflict between the pressures on certain governmental units to cut back their work forces and the pressures on the federal government to allot funds to hire newly or chronically unemployed. And if the governmental units use the federal funds to ease their financial troubles and retain employees whom they might otherwise have fired, to what extent is this a substitution of federal for local tax money with no net job creation?

The complexities surrounding public-service employment include such additional matters as the value of the output produced by the jobholders; the amount of additional funding per position required to assure proper tools, materials, and supervision; the creation of a potential political bloc of PSE incumbents who will lobby against any cutback in the program (it took World War II to permit the liquidation of WPA); the lack of promise that public-service employment, without remedial education and skill training, holds for the seriously disadvantaged to be able to make the transition to a regular position; the opposition of municipal unions to the creation of two rates of pay for similar work (in the event that PSE jobs are paid below the regular Civil Service scale, as the administration proposes for employable welfare claimants); and still other troublesome questions.

A cautious reassessment is that the political forces pressuring for an expansion of manpower training and public-service employment are potent, but serious questions remain about the efficacy of government-sponsored training and job creation. This will not be the first nor the last time that the American public will be forced to make new and important decisions in the face of continuing uncertainty.

CONCLUDING OBSERVATIONS

No one who was present when manpower policy was born in the early 1960s would have been in a position to sketch its contours in the latter 1970s. This should be a warning that similar difficulties are faced by the investigator who seeks to discern the shape of things to come, even if a foreshortened future of the mid-1980s is used as the cutoff date.

In the belief that an intimate acquaintance with the evolution of manpower policy may provide the best, if admittedly a still inadequate, basis for guessing the contours and convolutions that lie ahead, I would speculate that these are the directions in which national manpower policy appears to be headed:

- A continuing, if moderate, rise in the level of federal financing for both manpower training and public-service employment.
- A basic reliance on the heavily decentralized present system for the delivery of manpower services through prime sponsors and their subcontractors, including community-based organizations.
- A heightened effort at both federal and local levels to engage large and small employers (and trade unions) in playing a more active role in the use of manpower funds, with the aim of linking training more closely to job placement in the private sector.
- An unwillingness of Congress to take radical action to target manpower funds more narrowly on the most seriously disadvantaged because it fears the loss of political support from its constituencies.
- A hesitance to reduce the flow of CETA funds to local governments under severe financial and economic pressure, such as the cities with eroding economies, high social costs, and sliding tax bases.
- A growing perception that much of the social output obtained from the employment of public-service workers, though beneficial, would not be able to command local tax dollars if federal financing were withdrawn.
- Substantial difficulties in establishing a two-tier wage system in the public sector, in which PSE workers would be paid considerably less than regularly employed civil servants for performing the same tasks.
- A growing recognition that the early enthusiasm of the supporters of a full-employment policy that uses public-service employment as the balancing wheel for shortfalls in regular jobs is not practical, given the continuing high rates of unemployment and the rachet effect of job expansion, which brings many new workers into the labor market.
- Growing concern with efforts to regulate the number of "illegal immigrants" who appear to have an elastic repsonse to the strengthening of the U.S. labor market.
- A growing appreciation of the considerable options, other than holding a regular job, that many people may take to obtain income. There are many sources of income transfer—the government, employer, family—as well as alternatives open in engaging in illegal

work. Since the total of such alternative sources equals about one out of every three dollars of earned income, it will prove not only difficult but probably impossible to divide the population into employables and nonemployables, as the welfare reform proposal contemplates.

In sum, manpower policy in the next decade must increasingly address the basic challenge on the employment front: broadening opportunities for disadvantaged groups to compete for the meaningful, good jobs in our economy. Granting access to any jobs, since income-transfer alternatives will continue to exist, will not be enough. And hopefully, manpower policy will be shaped increasingly to meet these claims for equity in the labor market.

6.

Minorities and Work: The Challenge for the Decade Ahead

BERNARD E. ANDERSON
Director of Social Sciences
The Rockefeller Foundation *

Some years ago, W. E. B. DuBois, the eminent black intellectual, observed that "the problem of the twentieth century is the color line." Since those words were written, many changes have occurred in the legal status of black and other racial minorities in American society. Twenty years of civil rights legislation, with varying degrees of enforcement, have abolished segregation and have virtually eliminated all forms of legally protected discrimination. But despite the broad advancement in legal protection of civil rights, substantial gaps continue to exist between the economic status of racial minorities and others in American society.

Much of the economic inequality is reflected in the disparities between minorities and others in the labor market. The rate of unemployment among blacks is now, and has been for many years, double the rate among whites. Conversely, the level of income of blacks and other nonwhites continues to fall below that of 60 percent of the majority population. The general measures of economic well-being may change in absolute value over time, but the relative position of minorities has remained largely unchanged.

One of the major challenges facing the nation in the decade ahead will be to reduce racial inequality in American life by enlarging the domain of

---

*At the time this chapter was written, Bernard E. Anderson was Associate Professor of Industry and Senior Research Associate, Industrial Research Unit, at The Wharton School, University of Pennsylvania.

opportunity for minority-group workers. This chapter discusses some of the necessary conditions for accomplishing that objective.

The task can be approached in several ways. One approach would be to review trends drawn from the recent past and to project future developments based largely on the continuation of the observed trends. The most likely developments can be assessed by gauging the relative strength and weakness of trends now observed and most likely to continue into the years ahead. A different approach would be to establish a set of desirable goals and objectives for economic equality and then identify the conditions necessary to achieve such goals. The probability that the necessary conditions will exist can be assessed in order to gauge the potential for reaching the desired goal.

Under the best circumstances, it would be difficult to project what the status of minorities will be in the world of work in the decade ahead. But developments in the years ahead will no doubt be influenced by past and present trends, as well as by conscious efforts to "invent the future."

The effects of some forces currently at work will be irreversible. For example, the number of minorities who will be employed ten years from now in the professions, such as medicine, law, engineering, and others, will be determined by the number of students now attending the professional schools and the number of preprofessional students who are now acquiring the academic preparation necessary to enter professional schools. Little can be done to reverse such trends immediately.

On the other hand, a conscious decision to enlarge the participation of minorities in the labor market and to equalize the distribution of economic opportunity could generate actions today that would produce attractive benefits for minorities and others in the years ahead. The future of minorities in the working world will be determined, in part, by economic and other developments affecting all workers, but also by policies and practices designed specifically to improve the relative position of minority groups.

Based on past experience, the relative status of minorities seems to depend on three major factors: (1) opportunity (the level and nature of demand for labor); (2) preparation (the education and training of minorities); and (3) access (the protection of equal job opportunity). Each factor has been a necessary ingredient in the mix of forces required to improve the minority work force's occupational position and level of income. No one factor alone has been sufficient to initiate and to sustain progress.

Equally important, past change in the status of minorities has been the product of changing American attitudes, values, and perceptions on race relations. And one of the key inducements to positive change in the environment for equal opportunity has been protest and agitation initiated by minorities who felt deprived of basic rights to participate in all sectors of American life.[1] The form and character of minority self-help activities has changed over time, but there is little doubt that without the persistent demands for equal opportunity enunciated by minorities and their allies, fewer progressive changes in the law and in the behavior of major American institutions would have occurred during the past several decades.

The following discussion will show how these factors have interacted with one another to influence the labor-market position of minorities. Because the same forces are likely to play a major role in future developments, it is useful to evaluate their most likely direction and strength in the decade ahead.

RECENT TRENDS IN THE LABOR FORCE, EMPLOYMENT, AND INCOME

During the past several decades, minorities have experienced uneven gains in the labor market.[2] The labor-force participation rate, a measure of a group's attachment to the world of work, has steadily declined among black men, whereas the rate among black women has remained stable. All age groups have shown a similar trend, but black men of middle age and above have dropped out of the labor force at rates significantly greater than that of whites of similar age.

Black women have long shown higher rates of labor-force participation than white women, but the gap between the two groups has narrowed in recent years as larger numbers of married white women have entered the job market. Indeed, the increased labor-force participation of white women has been perhaps the single most significant development in the labor force since 1960. Expanding female participation has increased job competition and contributed to the difficulties of reducing unemployment rates to satisfactory levels.

Among blacks in the work force, the share of employment increased during the 1960s. Of the total number of jobs created between 1961 and 1969, blacks obtained 12.8 percent. Within the black group, adult females received a relatively larger share of the expanded jobs than did black men. But black youths made almost no progress toward improving their relative employment position. This situation conflicted sharply with the trend among white youths, whose share of total employment rose from 5.6 to 7.0 percent during the decade.

Black Unemployment

Trends in unemployment reveal most clearly the difficulties faced by the black work force. Between 1961 and 1969 the number of unemployed blacks declined by 400,000, a reduction in line with the overall improvement in job opportunities associated with the expanding economic activity during the decade. The unemployment rate among blacks fell from 12.4 percent in 1961 to 6.4 percent in 1969. But since that time, unemployment among blacks has moved steadily upward.

From 1969 to 1974, black unemployment rose by 447,000, and during 1974–1975, 440,000 blacks were jobless. Thus, during the 1970s, though blacks account for 11 percent of the labor force, they account for almost 20 percent of the increase in unemployment. Since late 1976, the black unemployment rate has remained around 12 percent or above, whereas the unemployment rate among whites declined steadily from 7.1 to 5.2 percent in April 1978.

Black Youth in the Labor Market

Black youth have been especially disadvantaged in the labor market. During each of the past twenty years, the unemployment rate among black teenagers has exceeded 25 percent, whereas that among whites of similar age never rose above 15 percent. Further, an increasing number of black youth, especially young black men aged 16 to 19, have dropped out of the labor force. As a result, the measured rate of unemployment among these youth, 35.3 percent in April 1978, understates the full extent of joblessness within the group.

The unfavorable position of black youth is explained in part by general economic conditions, but also by serious structural imbalances in labor markets. A disproportionate number of black youth are concentrated in low-income sections of urban areas, where job opportunities have declined markedly in the past several decades. Such areas also display neighborhood deterioration reflecting high crime rates, poor social services, and inadequate public schools. The pathology of the inner city is reflected in the flight of many small businesses and other commercial establishments that in the past constituted a major source of jobs for youth,

including part-time jobs for youth attending school. Black youth unemployment is tied closely to the urban crisis, and a solution to one depends on efforts to deal with the other.

Occupational Trends

The occupational distribution of the black work force improved somewhat
during the 1960s, but the magnitude of change was insufficient to equalize
the job status of blacks and others in the labor market (Table 1). Blacks
have shown employment gains among white-collar workers, especially
professional, technical, and clerical workers. At the same time, blacks
have also experienced upgrading in the blue-collar fields; they have been
moving out of the unskilled labor and domestic-service fields; into semiskilled operative and skilled occupations.

Within the broad occupational categories, however, blacks tend to be
concentrated in the least prestigious and most poorly paid jobs.[3] Among
professionals, for example, blacks are disproportionately concentrated in
the teaching and social-service fields and have made only marginal gains
in fields such as engineering, sciences, and management. Moreover,
black occupational gains in the white-collar fields, especially management, have been concentrated in the public sector rather than in the private sector.[4]

Income Status

There are substantial differences between the incomes of black and white
Americans, differences that are based largely on their labor-market positions. In 1975, the median income of black families was $8,779, and that
of white families, $14,268 (Table 2). The ratio of black median income to
white median income was, thus, 0.615. Further, more than 27 percent of
black families were below the poverty income level in 1975, while less
than 8 percent of white families were in that category.

Black family income has increased relative to white family income during the past several decades, but the gains have been uneven. From the
early 1960s through 1969, the ratio of black median family income to
white median family income rose from about 52 to 61 percent. Since that
time, however, there has been virtually no change in the relative income
position of blacks.

The aggregate trends conceal some important developments among
specific sectors of the black community. For example, the rate of income

Table 1. Employed Persons 16 Years and Over by Occupation Group and Color: 1959, 1969, and 1974.

	1959					1969					1974				
	Total		Black			Total		Black			Total		Black		
Occupation	Number	Percent Dist.	Number	Percent Dist.	Percent of Total	Number	Percent Dist.	Number	Percent Dist.	Percent of Total	Number	Percent Dist.	Number	Percent Dist.	Percent of Total
Total employed	64,627	100.0	6,621	100.0	10.2	77,902	100.0	8,383	100.0	10.8	85,936	100.0	9,316	100.0	10.8
White-collar workers (total)	27,593	42.7	954	14.4	3.5	36,845	47.3	2,198	26.2	6.0	41,739	48.6	2,977	32.0	7.1
Professional and technical	7,140	11.1	304	4.6	4.3	10,769	13.8	695	8.3	6.5	12,338	14.4	970	10.4	7.9
Managers and administrators (ex. farm)	6,936	10.7	163	2.4	2.4	7,987	10.3	254	3.0	3.2	8,941	10.4	379	4.1	4.2
Sales workers	4,210	6.5	83	1.3	2.0	4,692	6.0	166	2.0	3.5	5,417	6.3	214	2.3	4.0
Clerical workers	9,307	14.4	404	6.1	4.3	13,397	17.2	1,083	12.9	8.1	15,043	17.5	1,414	15.2	5.4
Blue-collar workers (total)	23,993	37.1	2,728	41.2	11.4	28,237	36.2	3,590	42.9	12.7	29,776	34.7	3,748	40.2	12.6
Craftsmen	8,554	13.2	389	5.9	4.5	10,193	13.1	709	8.5	7.0	11,477	13.4	874	9.4	7.6
Operatives	11,816	18.3	1,321	20.0	11.2	14,372	18.4	2,004	23.9	13.9	13,919	16.2	2,041	21.9	14.7
Nonfarm laborers	3,623	5.6	1,018	15.3	28.1	3,672	4.7	877	10.5	23.9	4,380	5.1	833	8.9	19.0
Service workers (total)	7,697	11.9	2,109	31.9	27.4	9,528	12.2	2,239	26.7	23.5	11,373	13.2	2,337	25.1	20.5
Private household	1,948	3.0	973	14.7	49.9	1,631	2.1	714	8.5	43.8	1,228	1.4	474	5.1	38.6
Other service workers	5,749	8.9	1,136	17.2	19.8	7,897	10.1	1,525	18.2	19.3	10,145	11.8	1,863	20.0	18.4
Farm workers (total)	5,344	8.3	830	12.5	15.5	3,292	4.3	356	4.2	10.8	3,048	3.5	254	2.7	8.3
Farmers and farm managers	3,013	4.7	232	3.5	7.7	1,844	2.4	84	1.0	4.6	1,643	1.9	64	0.7	3.9
Farm laborers and supervisors	2,331	3.6	598	9.0	25.7	1,448	1.9	272	3.2	18.8	1,405	1.6	190	2.0	13.5

Source: U.S. Department of Labor, *Manpower Report of the President 1975*, Table A-15, p. 225, and Table A-16, p. 227.

Table 2.   Changes in Ratios of Nonwhite-to-White and Black-to-White Median Family Income, 1947–1975.

Year	Median Family Income (Dollars)			Ratio of Nonwhite to White	Ratio of Black to White
	Nonwhite	Black	White		
1947	1,614	NA	3,157	0.511	NA
1949	1,650	NA	3,232	0.511	NA
1954	2,416	NA	4,338	0.557	NA
1959	2,915	NA	5,643	0.517	NA
1964	3,838	NA	6,858	0.560	NA
1969	6,191	5,999	9,794	0.632	0.613
1974*	8,265	7,808	13,356	0.619	0.585
1974†	8,577	8,005	13,408	0.640	0.597
1975	9,321	8,779	14,268	0.653	0.615

NA = Not available.

*Unrevised 1974. This estimate should be compared to the earlier years.

† Revised 1974. Because of a change in estimation procedures by the Current Population Survey, the revised 1974 estimate should be compared to later years.

Source: U.S. Bureau of the Census, "Money Income in 1975 of Families and Persons in the United States," *Current Population Reports*, Series P-60, No. 105 (1977): Table 10.
Source

gain since 1965 has been more rapid among blacks in the South than in other sections of the nation. Over time, black income has also increased as a result of migration from low-income rural areas of the South to higher wage industrial areas of the North and the West. In other words, the improvement in black income has been the product of two developments related to locational considerations: (1) migration from low- to high-income areas prior to the 1960s, and (2) greater income gains in the South relative to other sections of the nation, stemming from the rapid industrialization of the South during the 1960s.

In addition, a close examination of income patterns shows a growing inequality of income distribution within the black community, whereas income inequality among whites has declined. This divergent trend may be due in part to the increasing inequality of earnings in general, and the fact that a larger share of black income than of white income consists of wage and salary earnings. The divergent trend may also reflect the greater gains of black professionals and others in better occupational positions relative to those in low-income jobs.

FACTORS AFFECTING PAST TRENDS

Of the many factors influencing the trends described herein, three seem most important: general economic conditions, improvements in education, and protection of equal job opportunity.

General Economic Conditions

A wealth of evidence accumulated over a long period of time shows clearly that black economic well-being is heavily dependent on the state of the economy. When economic activity is high and labor markets are tight, blacks find far more jobs at better wages than when labor markets are loose and unemployment is high.[5] This observation, simple as it may seem, is one of the most reliable predictors of the relative position of blacks under alternative economic conditions.

Evidence from the 1960s and 1970s illustrates the point. The most significant gains experienced by blacks occurred between 1965 and 1968, a period of long and uninterrupted economic growth.[6] During this period, the aggregate rate of unemployment was below 4.0 percent, and labor shortages were evident in many local labor markets. In that environment, many opportunities opened up to blacks who otherwise might not have gained a foothold in the labor market.

In contrast, the pause in economic activity during the 1969–1971 recession and the even more serious economic dislocations of 1974–1975 reversed many of the gains achieved by blacks during the previous decade. Upward mobility among black workers was arrested during the recessions of the 1970s, and the economic recovery since 1975 has not produced gains sufficient to restore blacks to the relative position they held in the late 1960s.

These trends suggest an important link between economic policy and the progress of minorities in the labor market. Different economic policies have differential effects on various sectors of the population. Economic policies designed to hasten the reduction in unemployment by accelerating economic growth are especially beneficial to minorities. Conversely, policies that retard growth, perhaps to minimize the fear of inflation or to accomplish other objectives, tend to perpetuate racial inequality in economic life. The relative position of minority groups in the labor market seems to improve only in an environment of expanding opportunity for all. For this reason, economic policies that sacrifice full employment for other goals are harmful to the economic interest of minorities.

Improvements in Education

Improvements in schooling among blacks have contributed to modest gains observed during the past decade. Increased high school enrollment by black teenagers, coupled with higher retention rates, has resulted in increased educational attainment as measured by the number of years of education completed. From 1970 to 1976, black enrollment in high school increased by 23.1 percent, whereas the gain among whites was only 3.9 percent.[7] Moreover, between 1970 and 1975, the proportion of students graduating from high school was significantly higher for blacks than for whites, thus narrowing the educational gap. By 1976, 80 percent of blacks 16 to 17 years of age and 89.1 percent of whites of the same age were enrolled in school.

But despite the larger number of blacks now enrolled in school, less progress has been made in improving the quality of education. In many urban public schools in which large numbers of blacks are enrolled, the quality of education is less than desirable. In some cases, achievement levels are several years below the average nationwide. The disparities in the quality of education reduce, but do not completely erase, the contribution that increased schooling has made toward an improvement in the labor-market position of blacks.

Also important are gains that blacks have registered in higher education. Between 1966 and 1976, college enrollment of blacks increased from 4.6 percent to 10.7 percent of total enrollment. Slightly more than 1 million blacks were enrolled in postsecondary schools during 1977, and 40 percent of that number were in four-year degree-granting institutions.

Data on career preparation in higher education show that black college students have broadened their occupational interests.[8] More are now entering the sciences, engineering, architecture, and other fields that relatively few black students entered in the past. Increased numbers have also selected law, medicine, and business management in recent years, although the proportion of blacks in such fields continues to be very low. These trends undoubtedly reflect the perception among black students that labor-market prospects will be more favorable than in the past.

Protection of Equal Job Opportunity

Efforts to promote equal job opportunity have influenced the labor-market status of minorities, but it is difficult to assign a specific value to this factor.[9] Black employment in firms reporting to the Equal Employment Opportunity Commission (EEOC) rose much faster than employment in the economy as a whole between 1966 and 1974. But the EEOC-reporting firms showed greater gains among black clerical and sales workers than among other white-collar employees. Indeed, among professional, technical, and managerial workers, the EEOC-reporting firms lagged behind the economy at large in expanding jobs for blacks.

Nonetheless, much anecdotal data suggest that, because of EEOC, blacks and other minorities have obtained jobs they might not have obtained otherwise. Increased pressures from the commission, as well as enforcement efforts by the Office of Federal Contract Compliance Programs and the Department of Justice, have created a climate of sensitivity to racial employment practices. It is hard to believe that these pressures have not resulted in job gains for minorities, even if proof of the relationship cannot be verified with precision.

A major contributing factor has been the changing concept of discrimination during the past decade. Prior to the mid-1960s, when the courts began to adjudicate disputes under Title VII of the Civil Rights Act of 1964, "discrimination" was viewed as overt acts by employers (and employment-related institutions such as trade unions and the U.S. Employment Service) to deny jobs to members of minority groups. But the judicial perception of discrimination that emerged during the past decade turned the focus from overt acts to seemingly neutral employment systems that had the effect of restricting the job opportunities of minorities. Increasingly, the courts drew a comparison between the proportion of minorities employed in a specific firm and their relative number in the population and, when a gross disparity was found, attributed the difference to discrimination. The remedies imposed by the courts to correct such "statistical discrimination" focused on placing minorities in jobs in which relatively few had been employed before.

The shift from the intent to discriminate to a focus on the consequences of employment policies resulted in large-scale examination of many employment practices that limited the job opportunities of minorities. Preemployment standards, such as testing, the requirement of high school graduation for entry-level jobs, automatic disqualification of persons with arrest records, and other commonly used devices, were carefully reviewed for their impact on minority employment. In many cases, these standards were changed when they were found to discriminate against minorities who, although unable to meet such standards, were capable of performing the job. It may be difficult to measure the impact of such changes in hiring policies on minority employment, but the emphasis on numbers employed rather than on conscious intent to discriminate has no doubt been highly significant.

FACTORS AFFECTING THE DECADE AHEAD

A review of past trends can be very useful for discussing the labor-market prospects for minorities in the decade ahead. Because the basic structure of the economy and attitudes and values concerning intergroup relations are not likely to change rapidly, the forces affecting opportunities for minorities in the 1980s may be very similar to those observed in the recent past. Opportunity, as reflected in the demand for labor, preparation for employment, and access to better jobs will be as important during the next decade as before. But there are several developments on the horizon that may influence the way these factors interact to affect minority employment. Specifically, an evaluation of the prospects for minorities in the decade ahead requires an assessment of likely trends in economic growth, the structure of labor markets, and government efforts to protect equal job opportunity.

Long-Term Economic Growth

In 1977, the Joint Economic Committee of the U.S. Congress released a report on economic growth prospects; the report represents a summary of the views of some of the nation's leading experts in the field.[10] The projection is for a slower rate of growth of the nation's potential GNP from its present rate of about 4 percent to about 3 percent by the late 1980s and to an even lower rate in the 1990s. Productivity gains, which since 1966 have proceeded more slowly than during the first twenty postwar years, are expected to accelerate again. Sources of mineral raw materials are expected to be adequate for demand, and investment funds should be readily available, barring a sustained investment boom extending into the 1980s. Most importantly, the experts believe that "social limits to growth" such as changing attitudes toward work and the growth ethic may be more important than the earth's physical limits in curbing the economy's development over the next several decades.

Labor Market Projections

Owing to the steady decline of birthrates in the United States since 1960, the annual labor-force growth is expected to fall to less than 1 percent by the late 1980s. The proportion of women who work is expected to continue its gradual rise, and the reduction in labor-force growth may be moderated somewhat by a rise in illegal immigration.

The minority group labor force is expected to grow more rapidly than the white labor force. From 1970 to 1980, for example, the black labor force is projected to increase by 26.9 percent, compared to an increase of 16.0 percent among whites. The widest gap in growth rates between the two groups, however, is observed among youth aged 16 to 24. The number of blacks in this age group is expected to increase by almost two fifths (39.5 percent), whereas whites of the same age will increase in number by slightly more than one tenth (13.4 percent).

The changing structure of employment observed in the recent past is expected to continue into the next decade with some modifications. Employment in manufacturing, transportation, and public utilities will grow more slowly than in trade, services, and the finance-related industries. Similarly, among occupations, laborers, semiskilled workers, and farm workers will experience modest growth, or even a reduction in employment, while professional and technical, clerical, and service workers will grow at rates exceeding the growth of the labor force at large.

SPECIAL LABOR-MARKET CONCERNS

Against the backdrop of these broad trends, several other developments should be noted. One is the continuing loss of domestic jobs in some industries associated with international trade. The volume of imports of apparel, textiles, electronic products, and basic goods, such as steel and automobiles, has increased markedly during the past decade and is expected to grow even more in the decade ahead. Although the impact of this development on the total number of U.S. jobs is questionable, there are clearly negative effects on some specific sectors of the work force. Workers have been displaced by import competition in some industries that have a sizable number of minorities. Continued pressures generated by import-related displacement will exacerbate the unemployment problem among blacks.

Another concern is the continued flow of undocumented workers into the United States. Estimates of the number of such workers vary from 4 to 12 million, but whatever the number, the continued influx of this labor supply could have a serious impact on job opportunities for domestic workers, especially minority workers in low-wage jobs. The implications of the undocumented immigration have been thoroughly aired by labor experts, and public policy prescriptions are now under consideration.[11] How this issue is resolved, and when, will surely influence minority labor-market opportunities during the coming decade.

Still another development has been the changing attitudes of American whites toward support of equal opportunity for minorities. A recent poll conducted under the auspices of *U.S. News and World Report* revealed that over two thirds of the respondents supported continued efforts by government to protect minorities and women against employment discrimination.[12] Broad public support for this objective is critical to a continuation of public policy measures designed to achieve equality of job opportunity. Attitudes have changed markedly during the past decade, and the evidence suggests that most Americans now expect continued progress in the economic status of minority groups.

ENERGY POLICY AND BLACK EMPLOYMENT

One of the major issues that will affect labor markets in the decade ahead is the availability and cost of energy resources. In an effort to examine the potential impact of energy policy on black employment, a study was conducted using the U.S. Bureau of Labor Statistics input–output matrix of the U.S. economy.[13] The simulated energy policy was one that would result in an average price of $9.00 per barrel of oil. The central questions were how a policy of that type would affect total employment, and how it would affect the employment of blacks. The following results are illustrative.

Total Employment Growth

Table 3 presents the occupational projections based on energy policy assumptions under the "basic energy scenario." Total employment, as covered by the Curent Population Survey, is projected to rise to 94.1 million by 1980, an increase of 19.7 percent above the level of employment in 1970.

Among broad occupational groups, rapid employment growth is expected for professional and technical workers (28.5 percent), clerical workers (29.9 percent), and skilled craftsmen (25.2 percent). Managerial and sales workers will increase at a rate comparable to total employment

Table 3.   **Employment Projections under a National Energy Policy, by Occupational Group and Race, 1980 and 1985 (Numbers in Thousands).**

	1980			1985		
		Black			Black	
	Total	Number	Percent	Total	Number	Percent
Professional, technical	14,318	1,216.6	8.5	15,967	1,434.0	9.0
Engineers	1,327	45.3	3.4	1,460	57.6	3.9
Chemical	57	2.7	4.7	62	3.9	6.3
Civil	199	9.2	4.6	225	11.2	5.0
Electrical	334	13.5	4.0	374	18.7	5.0
Mechanical	211	3.9	1.8	234	4.6	2.0
Registered nurses	1,008	79.4	7.9	1,190	100.3	8.4
Health technicians	499	78.3	15.7	614	99.3	16.2
Social scientists	209	20.6	9.9	242	25.7	10.6
Teachers	3,666	340.8	9.3	3,769	351.0	9.3
Accountants	911	59.4	6.5	995	70.5	7.1
Managers, officials	9,993	494.7	5.0	10,871	598.1	5.5
Sales workers	5,881	115.8	2.0	6,268	107.2	1.7
Clerical workers	17,813	1,825.7	10.2	20,122	2,220.7	11.0
Typists, stenographers	5,385	406.3	7.5	6,264	503.6	8.0
Office machine operators	697	101.1	14.5	725	108.0	14.9
Telephone operators	387	31.6	8.2	385	31.0	8.1
Craft and kindred workers	12,722	1,156.7	9.1	13,760	1,342.7	9.8
Carpenters	1,210	71.8	5.9	1,314	78.0	5.9
Brick-, stonemasons	193	24.5	12.7	211	31.4	14.9
Cement finishers	106	43.8	41.3	120	51.4	42.8
Electricians	653	33.0	5.1	731	40.4	5.5
Grading machine operators	355	22.6	6.4	420	26.6	6.3
Painters	486	35.2	7.2	502	35.1	7.0
Plumbers, pipe fitters	487	20.6	4.2	558	23.4	4.2
Boilermakers	52	6.4	12.3	62	8.4	13.5
Foremen	1,627	89.3	5.5	1,770	111.4	6.3
Machinists	470	16.1	3.4	487	18.7	3.8
Millwrights	106	5.4	5.1	115	6.4	5.6
Molders, metal	61	8.8	14.4	63	7.9	12.5
Rollers, finishers, metal	24	6.3	26.3	24	6.2	25.8
Sheetmetal workers	177	8.1	4.6	190	9.6	5.1
Crane operators	193	51.3	26.6	199	55.0	27.6
Operatives	14,606	2,123.8	14.5	15,178	2,287.7	15.1
Furnace tenders	83	20.9	25.1	86	21.5	25.0
Welders	738	79.2	10.7	814	89.8	11.0
Weavers	36	3.8	10.6	32	4.3	13.4
Checkers, examiners	874	125.2	14.3	172	153.4	15.8

Table 3.   (Continued)

| | 1980 | | | 1985 | | |
| | Total | Black | | Total | Black | |
		Number	Percent		Number	Percent
Packers (except meat)	700	114.7	16.4	720	119.9	16.7
Asbestos workers	41	1.4	3.4	50	1.8	3.6
Assemblers	1,254	251.6	20.1	1,350	283.2	21.0
Mine operatives	176	8.8	5.0	178	8.9	5.0
Painters, mfg. articles	185	29.4	15.6	187	30.1	16.1
Sawyers	137	29.7	21.7	140	30.3	21.6
Stationary firemen	87	10.2	11.7	85	10.1	11.9
Bus drivers	298	45.6	15.3	325	51.5	15.8
Conductors, urban transit	10	2.7	27.0	11	2.9	26.4
Delivery, route workers	622	65.3	10.5	645	68.9	10.7
Taxicab drivers	156	34.0	21.8	142	35.7	25.1
Truck drivers	1,832	258.3	14.1	1,900	268.1	14.1
Service Workers	13,112	1,941.1	14.8	14,562	2,062.4	14.2
Nonfarm Laborers	4,591	491.1	10.7	4,767	415.8	8.7
Carpenters' helpers	104	29.9	28.8	104	29.8	28.7
Longshore workers	52	22.9	44.0	50	21.6	43.2
Logging workers	73	17.3	23.7	63	12.9	20.5
Farm workers	1,100	144.5	13.1	848	53.5	6.3

Source: U.S. Department of Labor, Bureau of Labor Statistics.

growth (20.6 and 21.2 percent, respectively). But the most rapidly grow-ing occupational group will be service workers, whose numbers are pro-jected to expand by 35.0 percent above the 1970 level.

These projections reflect a continuation of trends in occupational growth observed during the past decade. Between 1960 and 1970, for example, white-collar jobs and service jobs expanded at much higher rates than semiskilled blue-collar jobs. Similarly, agricultural employ-ment has consistently declined for at least four decades.

Still, there are notable differences in the rate of occupational change and the differential pattern of growth among broad occupational groups based on assumptions regarding energy policy. For example, projections of employment in major occupational groups in 1980 and 1985, derived under methods that do not account for changes in energy policy, show somewhat less expansion in the number of service workers and skilled craftsmen than is reflected in the energy-influenced scenario. Conversely, total employment and employment in most occupational groups are projected to be higher under the status quo in energy policy than in the new energy scenario.

Occupational growth through 1985 shows the same pattern as the projections through 1980. Major gainers are expected to be professional, technical, and service workers, while laborers and semiskilled workers either decline in number or show only a modest growth above the 1980 level. Clerical and office workers display a notable expansion through 1985, increasing by about 13.0 percent above the 17.8 million projected for the group in 1980. Still, the patterns of change through 1985 under the energy-policy scenario are similar to changes projected to 1980 in comparison with the status quo policy.

These differences might reflect the impact of energy policy on the economy-wide growth rate. If higher energy costs, the key assumption of the "basic energy scenario," reduced the rate of economic growth, the impact on occupational growth would also be downward. Because of differences in the methodology underlying the energy and nonenergy projections, no firm conclusions regarding economic growth rates can be drawn. In fact, when the time frame is pushed up to 1985, the projections show higher employment under the energy policy in comparison with the status quo. The interoccupational growth comparison is a general guide rather than a highly reliable estimate of differential employment growth under a new energy environment compared with unchanged energy conditions.

Black Occupational Change

The projections for 1980 and 1985 show employment levels for fifty-six separate occupational groups. According to this projection, blacks will improve their position most significantly among professional and technical workers, managers and officials, clerical workers, and skilled craftsmen. The black participation rate is projected to decline among service workers and nonfarm laborers.

The projections for 1980 show a mixed picture of modest gains in the upper level jobs in each occupation group. For example, though blacks are projected to expand their proportion among skilled craftsmen by about one third, they are expected to rise to only 5.9 percent among carpenters, up from 5.5 percent in 1970. But among electricians, the participation rate is projected to rise from 3.1 to 5.1 percent, and among sheetmetal workers, 3.3 to 4.6 percent. At the same time, the projections show a decline in the black participation rate among brick- and stonemasons and machinists.

Among professional and technical workers, the projections show blacks making gains among engineers and accountants, while also expanding their numbers among registered nurses, health technicians, and schoolteachers. The projections show a continued decline in the proportion of blacks among service workers and laborers, two occupation groups in which the number of blacks has been diminishing for several decades.

The pattern of projected change to 1980 is expected to continue through 1985. But the degree of change, as measured by black participation rates in various occupations, may decline in comparison with the change projected for 1970 to 1980. Advancement into professional, technical, managerial, and craft jobs will increase the black participation rate in those fields. Similarly, the attrition of blacks in agriculture, nonfarm labor, and service work is expected to continue.

In comparison with the gains achieved by blacks through 1980, little penetration into the higher paying job classifications will occur by 1985 according to the projections. For example, although the black participation rate among skilled craftsmen is projected to increase from 9.1 to 9.8 percent between 1980 and 1985, the only occupational fields showing a sizable increase in the proportion of blacks are foremen and sheetmetal workers. These patterns of change cannot be extrapolated to draw implications about expected earnings trends because seniority and on-the-job advancement are often related to significant earnings gains within broad occupational groups. Thus, although the degree of occupational upgrading, as measured by black advancement into higher status job categories, is not widely evident in the projections, black workers might nonetheless experience an improvement in their income position.

On balance, the evidence of projected occupational progress for blacks leads to a modestly optimistic prognosis. Occupational upgrading observed in the past will continue, and further gains in the higher paying, more prestigious occupations will occur. Yet, no acceleration of upgrading is projected. In fact, in some of the skilled craft occupations, virtually no change is expected in the proportion of blacks between 1980 and 1985. This means that, although the occupational field is expected to grow during the five-year period, blacks at best might hold their own in competing for expanding job opportunities.

SUMMARY AND CONCLUSION

The prospects for minorities in the world of work in the next decade will be determined by much the same forces that have influenced minority status in past years. A vigorous and balanced economic growth environment is a necessary backdrop for minority labor-market gains. But in addition to economic growth, minority progress also must depend on special efforts to reduce economic inequality in American life. Continuing efforts to root out employment discrimination will be necessary for the status of blacks and other minorities to improve.

All indications suggest that minorities will continue to obtain more schooling, with increased numbers holding academic degrees in a variety of professional and technical fields. But labor-force projections also suggest an increasing degree of competition among college graduates for the relatively smaller number of jobs that this group typically holds. If the projections are correct, improvement in the relative position of minorities will not be assured.

In the past, labor-market gains among minorities have been uneven and unstable, although halting progress has been made. Given these projections of the most likely conditions in the national economy and the most likely set of attitudes and preferences among the population, it is difficult to conclude that the decade ahead will be very different from the recent past.

NOTES

1. Dorothy Newman, *Protest, Politics, and Prosperity: Black Americans and White Institutions, 1940–75* (New York: Pantheon Press, 1978).
2. For a comprehensive assessment of the economic status of blacks, see National Commission for Manpower Policy, *The Economic Position of Black Americans: 1976,* Special Report No. 9; and Congressional Budget Office, *Income Disparities between Black and White Americans* (Washington, D.C.: Congressional Budget Office, 1977). For an evaluation of black progress during the past decade, see Sar A. Levitan, William B. Johnston, and Robert Taggart, *Still a Dream: The Changing Status of Blacks Since 1960* (Cambridge, Mass.: Harvard University Press, 1975). On trends among black women, see Phyllis A. Wallace, *Black Women in the Labor Market*, unpublished manuscript.
3. Congressional Budget Office, *op. cit.,* pp. 82–83.
4. Levitan, Johnston, and Taggart, *op. cit.,* pp. 44–79.
5. Bernard E. Anderson, "Full Employment and Economic Equality," *The Annals of the American Academy of Political and Social Science* 418 (March 1975): 127–37.
6. Andrew F. Brimmer, "Economic Growth and Employment and Income Trends among

Blacks," in *Jobs For Americans,* ed. Eli Ginzberg (Englewood Cliffs, N.J.: Prentice-Hall, 1976), pp. 142–62.

7. U.S. Bureau of the Census, "School Enrollment: Social and Economic Characteristics of Students, October 1975," in *Current Population Reports,* Series P-20, No. 309 (Washington, D.C.: U.S. Government Printing Office, July 1977).

8. Institute for the Study of Educational Policy, *Higher Education and Equal Opportunity* (Washington, D.C.: Institute for Study of Educational Policy, Howard University, 1976).

9. Richard Butler and James Heckman, "The Government Impact on Labor Market Status of Black Americans," in *Equal Rights and Industrial Relations,* ed. Leonard H. Hausman et al. (Madison, Wis.: Industrial Relations Research Associates, 1977), pp. 235–67.

10. U.S. Joint Economic Committee, *U.S. Long-Term Economic Growth Prospects: Entering a New Era* (Washington, D.C.: U.S. Government Printing Office, 1977).

11. National Council on Employment Policy, *Illegal Aliens: An Assessment of the Issues* (Washington, D.C., National Council on Employment Policy, 1976).

12. "Who Rules America?" A survey conducted by *U.S. News and World Report,* April 17, 1978.

13. Bernard E. Anderson, "Energy Policy and Black Employment: A Preliminary Analysis," Industrial Research Unit Working Paper, November 1977. See also Stephen A. Schneider, *The Availability of Minorities and Women for Professional and Managerial Positions: 1970 to 1985* (Philadelphia: Industrial Research Unit, The Wharton School, University of Pennsylvania, 1977).

7.
Women and Work: Priorities for the Future

MARGARET S. GORDON
Associate Director
Carnegie Council on Policy Studies
in Higher Education

The large-scale movement of women into the labor force is one of the most dramatic social and economic changes of recent decades. It has occurred in all industrial societies and has played an important role in explaining rising real incomes for families throughout the industrialized world. It has also changed life-styles and patterns of family living, and these are having effects on patterns of demand that, in some respects, are only beginning to be felt. For example, families are eating out more; a working wife makes the ownership of two cars more feasible; and, as Eli Ginzberg has pointed out, professional couples without children are helping to revive the cities, for it is not as important to live in the suburbs if you are not going to have children.

In fact, we may thus far have seen only the tip of the iceberg in regard to changes in life-styles. The world of the future may be characterized by far more dramatic changes in life-styles, in the role of the family, and in the organization of work than any that we have already witnessed.

WOMEN IN THE LABOR FORCE

Although the percentage of women in the labor force has been rising throughout the present century, the movement was greatly accelerated beginning with World War II. The rush of women into jobs during the war did much to change old prejudices toward working women, as "Rosie the

111

riveter" and her co-workers helped the economy to achieve prodigious increases in production. Between 1900 and 1940, the proportion of women in the labor force rose from 20 to 26 percent, or about six percentage points.[1] Form 1940 to 1977—a slightly shorter span of years—the increase was from 26 to nearly 49 percent, or twenty-three percentage points.[2]

Traditionally, labor-force participation rates of women have been inversely related to their husbands' earnings—the lower the earnings of the chief breadwinner, the greater the likelihood that his wife would be working.[3] In other words, women tended to work out of economic necessity. Most of the jobs available to them were unattractive, ill paid, and socially demeaning. No wonder, then, that working-class men took pride when their wives did not have to work and that upper-class men would have considered a working wife a social disgrace.

If low incomes drove women to work, how, then, do we explain the upward trend in female labor-force participation in a period of rapidly rising real incomes? The answer lies chiefly in the growing availability of jobs that, at least in contrast with those of the past, are more attractive, better paid, and involve shorter standard hours of work, or can be held on a part-time basis. Women have responded by moving into the labor force in large numbers, especially in years when employment opportunities were rising sharply (Figure 1).[4] The many studies of women in the labor force since the early 1960s have tended to confirm the positive influence of favorable employment opportunities on movement of women into the labor force and the negative influence of recessions.[5]

Rising female earning rates are also a factor in attracting women into the labor force, but the influence of low family income is not as decisive as it used to be. In 1975 the percentage of wives with some earnings rose steadily with rising earnings of husbands up to the $8,000 to $10,000 range, but then dropped back (Figure 2). Thus, the wives of comparatively affluent husbands continue to be less likely to work than those whose husbands have moderate earnings. But this pattern is likely to change in the future, chiefly because of the rapidly rising educational levels of women, for educational attainment is positively related to the labor-force participation of married women, as the lower part of figure 2 shows, and college-educated women are likely to marry college-educated and generally more affluent men.

In the 1950s, the flow of women into jobs occurred chiefly among those aged 45 to 64 (Figure 3). Young women were marrying early and raising

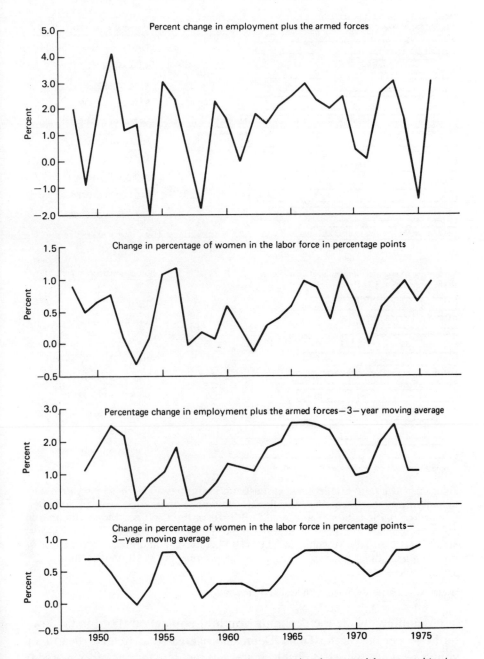

Figure 1.   Annual changes in civilian employment plus the armed forces and in the percentage of women in the labor force, 1947–1976. Source: Computed from date in *Employment and Training Report of the President, 1977,* Tables A-1, A-2, and A-3.

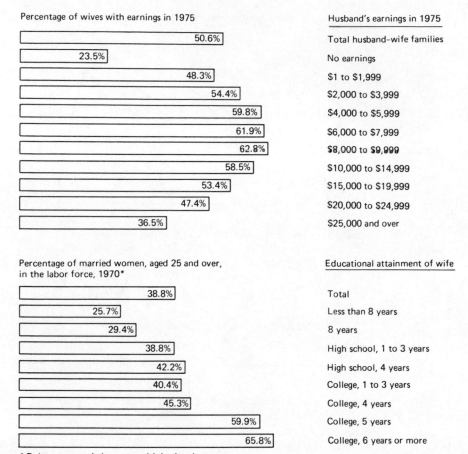

Percentage of wives with earnings in 1975 — Husband's earnings in 1975

Percentage of wives with earnings in 1975	Husband's earnings in 1975
50.6%	Total husband-wife families
23.5%	No earnings
48.3%	$1 to $1,999
54.4%	$2,000 to $3,999
59.8%	$4,000 to $5,999
61.9%	$6,000 to $7,999
62.8%	$8,000 to $9,999
58.5%	$10,000 to $14,999
53.4%	$15,000 to $19,999
47.4%	$20,000 to $24,999
36.5%	$25,000 and over

Percentage of married women, aged 25 and over, in the labor force, 1970* — Educational attainment of wife

Percentage of married women, aged 25 and over, in the labor force, 1970*	Educational attainment of wife
38.8%	Total
25.7%	Less than 8 years
29.4%	8 years
38.8%	High school, 1 to 3 years
42.2%	High school, 4 years
40.4%	College, 1 to 3 years
45.3%	College, 4 years
59.9%	College, 5 years
65.8%	College, 6 years or more

* Relates to married women with husband present.

Figure 2.   The relationship between husband's earnings and wife's labor-force participation and between the educational attainment of married women and their labor-force participation. Sources: U.S. Bureau of the Census, "Money Income in 1975 of Families and Persons in the United States," *Current Population Reports,* Series P-60, No. 105, Washington, D.C., 1977, Table 28; and *ibid., 1970 Census of Population,* Subject Reports, *Educational Attainment,* PC(2)-5B, Washington, D.C., 1973, Table 6.

[a]Relates to married women with husband present.

large families, while the declining youthful population (born in the low-birthrate period of the Great Depression) created a relative dearth of young workers, which probably increased the demand for older women. In the 1960s and 1970s, however, the situation changed dramatically. With later marriages and falling birthrates, the labor force participation

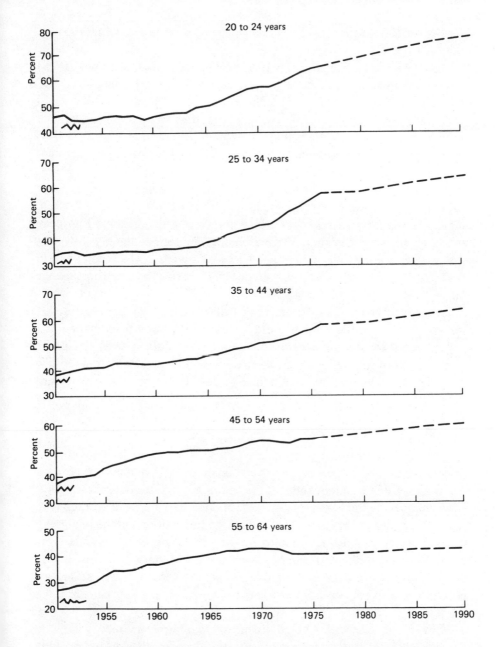

Figure 3. Annual changes in percentage of women in the labor force, by age, actual, 1950 to 1976, and projected, 1980 to 1990. Data for teenagers and women aged 65 and older are not included. Source: *Employment and Training Report of the President, 1977,* Tables A-2 and E-7.

rates of women in their twenties and thirties rose sharply, while those of older women leveled off.

The official projections of the U.S. Bureau of Labor Statistics (BLS) (Figure 3) show a continued rise to 1990, when the overall labor-force participation rate of women is expected to be about 51 percent, compared with nearly 49 percent in 1977. I suspect that these projections understate the probable rise in the percentage of women in the labor force, as BLS projections have tended to do in the past. The sharply rising educational levels of women, the erosion of old prejudices against working wives, and the probability that most young women will reenter the labor force quite promptly after bearing children (if they do have any children) suggest more pronounced future increases. Experience in some European countries also suggests more precipitate increases—notably Sweden, where 60 percent of all women aged 16 to 74 were in the labor force in 1976, compared with about 50 percent of American women in this age range.

Two developments, however, could alter the outlook appreciably. A slow rate of economic growth could discourage women from labor-force participation and might even lead to employer policies restricting the employment of married women, as in the Great Depression. A sharp rise in birthrates, which I consider unlikely, could also reverse the upward trend for young women.

OCCUPATIONAL CHANGES

In 1900 the most important single occupation for women workers, accounting for nearly three tenths of the total, was private household work. If we add semiskilled factory workers (operatives) and farm workers, we account for more than seven tenths of all women workers at the beginning of the century (Table 1). Since then, the upgrading of the female work force, as of the male work force, has proceeded more or less steadily. By 1976, only 16 percent of employed women were operatives, private household workers, or farm workers, whereas nearly 64 percent were white-collar workers.

Thus, if we paint with a broad brush, we find immense improvement in the occupational status of women over the decades. But when we look more closely, the picture becomes less appealing. Occupational segregation is still a conspicuous feature of the economic status of women, despite progress in certain respects. The great majority of women workers

Table 1. **Percentage Distribution of Women Workers by Major Occupation Group and Selected Occupations, 1900–1976.**

Occupation Group	Gainful Workers, 1900	Employed Workers			
		1940	1960	1970	1976
Total					
Number (in thousands)	5,319	10,965	21,894	28,591	34,609
Percentage	100.0	100.0	100.0	100.0	100.0
White-collar workers	17.9	46.1	55.3	61.0	63.6
Professional, technical, and kindred workers	8.2	13.6	12.3	15.5	16.2
Medical and other health workers	0.2*	3.2	3.5	3.8	4.5
Teachers, except college	6.0*	7.0	5.2	6.6	6.7
Other professional, technical, and kindred workers	2.0	3.4	3.6	5.1	5.0
Managers and administrators, except farm	1.4	3.6	5.0	4.5	5.7
Salaried	NA	NA	2.4	3.2	4.8
Self-employed	NA	NA	2.6	1.3	0.9
Sales workers	4.3	7.3	7.7	6.5	6.6
Clerical and kindred workers	4.0	21.6	30.3	34.5	35.1
Blue-collar workers	27.7	20.4	16.6	16.6	14.5
Craft and kindred workers	1.4	1.0	1.0	1.1	1.4
Operatives	23.7	18.5	15.2	15.1	12.0
Laborers, except farm	2.6	0.9	0.4	0.4	1.1
Service workers	35.4	29.2	23.7	21.0	21.0
Private household workers	28.7	18.0	9.5	4.7	3.2
Service workers, except private household	6.7	11.2	14.2	16.3	17.8
Farm workers	19.0	4.3	4.4	1.4	0.9

NA = Not available.

*Estimated.

Sources: Gertrude Bancroft, *The American Labor Force* (New York: Wiley, 1958), Tables D-2 and D-7; and U.S. Bureau of the Census, *Special Labor Force Reports,* selected issues.

are concentrated in traditionally female occupations, most of which are far from the upper echelons of the job hierarchy. In 1976, 70 percent of all women workers were in forty-eight occupations, all of which employed 100,000 or more women and in which women comprised more than 50 percent, and frequently more than 80 percent, of the workers.[6] The ten largest female occupations, in which about 40 percent of all women workers were concentrated, are indicated in Table 2, which also shows that these occupations are not becoming any less female-dominated than they have been in the past. In fact, in a number of them, the percentage of women has been increasing. Clearly, men are not moving into female occupations on any significant scale.

If we look at the other side of the coin, however, we find a rather different story. Women *are* moving into traditionally male occupations—in some cases in striking numbers. Some of the more significant examples are indicated in Figure 4. These range from lawyers and physicians to bus drivers, bartenders, and nonfarm laborers. The wide spectrum of occupations involved suggests a complex set of forces—changing attitudes of employers (including perhaps a search for less costly sources of labor supply in a period of rapidly rising wage rates), the influence of the women's liberation movement, and the impact of affirmative-action policies. The increased rate of enrollment of women in college and in advanced education is also an important factor, as much effect as cause, probably, of improved employment opportunities.

The employment data do not begin to tell the story of the movement of women into such professions as law and medicine because of the lengthy period of education involved before a woman shows up in employment statistics. Figures 5 and 6 show the increases in percentages of women among recipients of master's and advanced degrees. But even these data

Table 2.   Women as a Percentage of Employed Workers, Largest Female Occupations, 1960–1976 (Occupations Listed in Order of Number of Women Employed, 1976).

Occupation	1960 (%)	1970 (%)	1974 (%)	1976 (%)
Secretaries	97.1	97.6	99.2	99.0
Retail sales workers	63.3	64.6	69.4	70.7
Bookkeepers	83.4	82.0	89.2	90.0
Elementary school teachers	85.8	83.6	84.3	84.8
Waiters and waitresses	86.6	88.8	91.8	90.7
Cashiers	76.9	83.5	87.7	87.7
Private household workers	96.4	96.6	97.8	97.3
Registered nurses	97.5	97.3	98.0	96.6
Typists	95.1	94.2	96.2	96.7
Nursing aides, orderlies, and attendants	88.2	84.6	86.9	86.8

Sources: Barbara B. Reagan, "De Facto Job Segregation," in U.S. Congress, Joint Economic Committee, *American Women Workers in a Full Employment Economy,* Washington, D.C., 1977; and *Employment and Earnings,* January 1975 and January 1977.

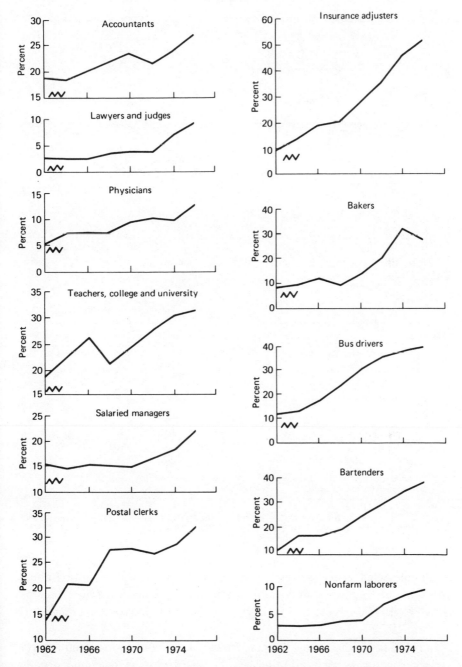

Figure 4.   Women as a percentage of employed workers in selected traditionally male occupations, biennial, 1962–1976. Sources: S. H. Garfinkle, "Occupations of Women and Black Workers, 1962–74," *Monthly Labor Review* 98 (November 1975); *Employment and Earnings* (January 1977).

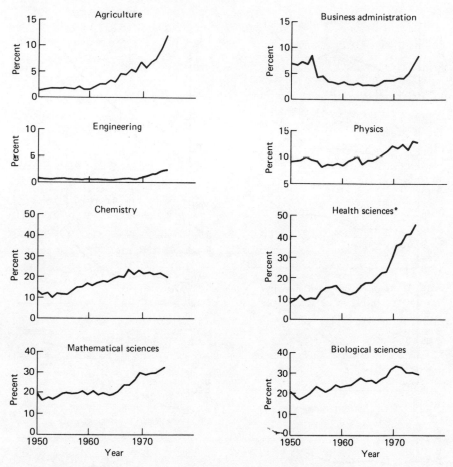

* Includes all health professions other than dentistry, medicine, nursing, physical therapy, and dental hygiene.

Figure 5.   Women as a percentage of persons receiving master's degrees in selected fields, 1950–1975. Source: U.S. Office of Education data adapted by D. L. Adkins.

understate what is happening. In medicine, for example, women comprised about 13 percent of employed physicians, 16 percent of the recipients of M.D. degrees, and nearly 25 percent of first-year medical students in 1976.[7]

In some fields, however, the percentage of women among doctorate recipients has barely returned to the level of the 1920s, if that. And women achieving advanced degrees in the sciences are much more likely to experience unemployment than are men.

The impact of affirmative action has been decisive in explaining the recent influx of women into salaried managerial positions. In the 1960s there was no appreciable change in the percentage of women among salaried managers, but a striking increase, from 15 to 22 percent, occurred from 1970 to 1976. Note that this increase related to managers of all ages. It would appear, then, that the movement of young women into these positions must have been very pronounced to have effected such a change in the overall percentage of women.

It was not until the 1970s that federal antidiscrimination and affirmative-action policies had a major impact on the employment of women in professional and managerial positions. The Equal Pay Act of 1963 did not apply to administrative and professional employees until 1972; Title VII of the Civil Rights Act of 1964 was extended to cover state and local governments and educational institutions under the 1972 amendments; and, most important, Executive Order 11246, banning employment discrimination under federal contracts (issued in 1965), was made effective against sex discrimination in October 1968, while the requirements for affirmative-action plans were applied to employment of women in December 1971.[8]

But will the women who have recently been hired in managerial positions be promoted to higher echelons of management? It is too soon to have much evidence, but the indications thus far are reasonably encouraging. Late in 1975 it was reported that about 5 percent of those in middle-management positions were women, a sizable rise in just a few years, and that women comprised about 1 percent of top management, a slight rise from the previous situation.[9] Meanwhile, there is a large and growing literature on what employers can do to enccourage the recruitment and promotion of women in management and how they can overcome the well-known sources of resistance, such as the reluctance of men to work under the supervision of women.[10]

The sudden success of women in managerial positions, however, has occurred in a period of serious deterioration in the job market for schoolteachers, which in recent decades has accounted for no less than one half of the jobs held by employed female college graduates. In fact, because the job market for college graduates of both sexes has been generally less favorable than in the 1960s, many graduates have had to accept jobs in clerical, sales, and blue-collar occupations.[11] But the extent of the slump has been overstated by some writers, who have contrasted the 1970s with the exceptionally favorable 1960s and have tended to ignore comparisons with the less favorable situation that prevailed in the 1950s.[12]

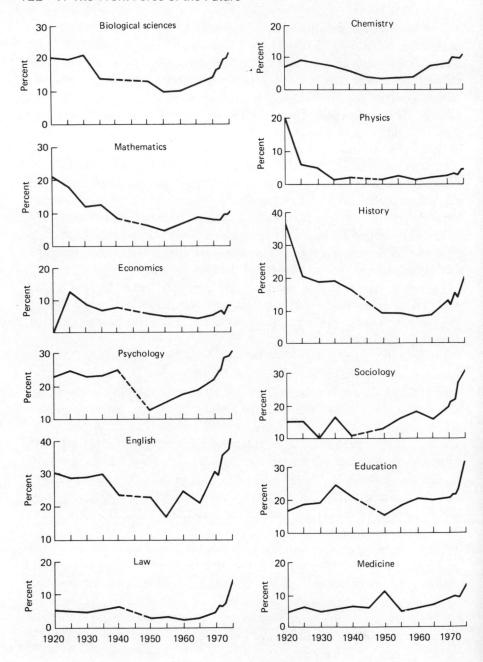

Figure 6.

Moreover, there is a tendency on the part of some writers to paint the outlook for college graduates as more or less permanently altered for the worse. In fact, if economic growth is reasonably satisfactory, the job market for college graduates is likely to become substantially more favorable around 1985, when the number of graduates will probably begin to fall, as those born in the period of declining birthrates reach the age of graduation.

What about nonwhite women? Their occupational status has improved very strikingly in the last several decades, but they still have a long way to go before their occupational situation equals that of white women. In 1960 nearly three fifths of all nonwhite employed women were either private household workers or service workers in settings other than private households. By 1976 that proportion was down to 36 percent, and the percentage of nonwhite women in white-collar jobs had increased markedly, though it was still below that of white women.[13]

EARNINGS DIFFERENTIALS

If occupational statistics show some movement of women into traditionally male occupations, the behavior of sex differentials in earnings is much less encouraging. In 1975 the median income of employed women was only 48 percent of that of employed men, but this comparison is misleading, because relatively more women than men are employed part time. Among year-round full-time workers the median income of women was 59 percent of that of men, approximately the percentage that has prevailed for a long time.

Sex differentials in earnings, however, vary enormously among occupations, though it is difficult to find statistics that are detailed enough to permit precise comparisons. Among the occupations listed in table 3, the differential varies from 0.93 at one end of the scale to 0.39 at the other. Although the pattern of variation is not entirely consistent, there is a ten-

Figure 6.   Women as a percentage of persons receiving doctorates and first professional degrees in selected fields, 1920–1975. Sources: L. R. Harmon and H. Soldz, *Doctorate Production in United States Universities, 1920–1962* (Washington, D.C.: National Academy of Sciences, National Research Council, 1963); D. L. Adkins, *The Great American Degree Machine* (Berkeley, Cal.: Carnegie Foundation for the Advancement of Teaching, 1975); and U.S. National Center for Education Statistics, *Digest of Education Statistics,* 1975 and 1976 editions (Washington, D.C.: U.S. National Center for Education Statistics, 1976 and 1977, respectively).

Table 3.   Ratios of Female to Male Median Earnings, Selected Occupations, Year-Round Full-Time Workers, 1975 (Arrayed in Order of Ratios).

Health workers, professional, other than physicians, dentists, and related practitioners	0.934
Health service workers, nonprofessional	0.898
Teachers, elementary and secondary	0.830
Teachers, college and university	0.781
Nonfarm laborers	0.765
Bookkeepers	0.753
Engineering and science technicians	0.675
Cleaning service workers	0.674
Personal service workers	0.645
Office machinery operators	0.639
Durable goods manufacturing operatives	0.621
Accountants	0.612
Food service workers	0.603
Cashiers	0.600
Craftsmen, foremen, and kindred workers	0.568
Salaried managerial workers	0.561
Self-employed managerial workers	0.539
Sales clerks, retail trade	0.529
Nondurable goods manufacturing operatives	0.521
Insurance, real estate, and stock agents and brokers	0.520
Nonmanufacturing operatives	0.475
Sales workers, total	0.389

Source: U.S. Bureau of the Census, "Money Income in 1975 of Families and Persons in the United States," *Current Population Reports,* Series P-60, No. 105, Washington, D.C., 1977, Table 52.

dency for ratios of female to male earnings to be relatively high in occupations in which (1) women have long been predominant, and (2) a certain amount of specialized education or training is usually required. The lowest ratios are found in occupations that have either been traditionally male or that require little previous training or specialized education. Within such occupation groups, men tend to be employed in the better paid job classifications. A particularly striking example of this is among sales workers, in which the ratio of female to male earnings tends to be much lower than in most other major occupation groups. In 1976 70 percent of male sales workers were employed in such relatively higher paid categories as insurance agents and brokers, real estate agents and brokers, and manufacturing sales representatives, whereas 68 percent of the women were in the lower paid retail sales clerks group.

In fact, in these days of equal-pay laws, women are apparently rarely paid less than men for precisely equal work, according to recent studies, but such discrimination as exists takes the form of assigning women to lower ranked jobs, even when the women are comparable in education and training to the men.[14] And, despite equal-pay policies, the overall ratio of female to male median incomes of year-round full-time workers declined somewhat from 1956 to 1975 (Figure 7). But the decline was largely attributable to a fairly steep drop in the ratio for clerical workers, which is by far the largest female major occupation group. The reasons for this drop are not readily apparent; certainly it did not reflect relatively

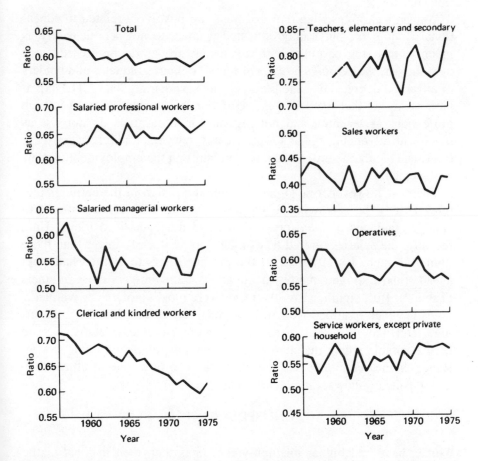

Figure 7.   Ratios of female-to-male median incomes, selected occupation groups, year-round full-time workers, 1956–1975. Source: U.S. Bureau of the Census, "Money Income of Families and Persons in the United States" (title varies), *Current Population Reports*, Series P-60, Washington, D.C. (annual).

pronounced employment increases in some of the male-dominated and better paid clerical occupations. My best guess is that it was explained by a comparatively sharp increase in the supply of women seeking clerical jobs, resulting from a combination of factors, including (1) the expansion of community colleges and other institutions offering low-cost stenographic training (in which men rarely enroll), and (2) the flow of women college graduates into clerical work in the 1970s. Probably another factor has been the increasing use of "Kelly girls," typists hired temporarily from specialist agencies, enabling employers with fluctuating needs for clerical workers to meet their peak requirements without permanent additions to staff.[15]

Women's earnings, like those of men, are positively related to educational attainment, but highly educated women do not benefit nearly as much from rising earnings with advancing age as do highly educated men. In fact, the earnings profiles of female college graduates and holders of advanced degrees over the life cycle are surprisingly flat.[16] The explanations are (1) that there is a concentration of educated women in such professions as teaching and nursing, in which earnings do not rise as much with advancing age as for physicians, lawyers, and business executives, and (2) that there is a lack of continuity in the employment of married women.

There is, however, one slightly encouraging sign in the earnings picture. That is the narrowing of the sex differential in salaries offered to college graduates in *some* professional and managerial positions. Until recently, the salaries offered to women were uniformly lower than those offered to men. By 1976–1977, the average offers to women had crept ahead of those to men in a few occupations and were very close in others (Table 4). But, significantly, the ratios were most favorable to women in fields in which qualified women were relatively scarce, that is, engineering, farm and resources management, and mathematics/statistics, and least favorable where the supply of women was relatively ample, for instance, home economics and library work. The influence of affirmative-action policies shows quite clearly here.

UNEMPLOYMENT

Women have had higher unemployment rates than men in most of the postwar years, and there has been some tendency for the difference to widen with the passage of time (Figure 8). Although the unemployment

Table 4. National Average Monthly Salary Offers to Bachelor's Degree Candidates, by Sex and Functional Area, 1976—1977.

Functional Area	Men (Dollars)	Women (Dollars)	Ratio— Women to Men
Accounting/auditing	1,065	1,060	0.995
Business administration	940	849	0.903
Communications	829	721	0.870
Community and service organizations work	747	702	0.940
EDP—programming/systems	1,115	1,090	0.978
Engineering	1,279	1,328	1.038
Farm and natural resources management	895	941	1.051
Finance and economics	936	927	0.990
Health (medical) services	937	864	0.922
Home economics and dietetics	853	685	0.803
Law enforcement services	933	798	0.855
Library and related work	742	598	0.806
Manufacturing and/or industrial operations	1,212	1,122	0.926
Marketing			
Consumer product–services	931	890	0.956
Industrial product–services	1,055	1,029	0.975
Mathematics/statistics	1,016	1,016	1.000
Merchandising/sales promotion	883	812	0.920
Personnel/employee relations	973	869	0.893
Public administration	879	762	0.867
Research			
Nonscientific	990	789	0.797
Scientific	1,119	1,062	0.949
Rotational training			
Technical	1,241	1,195	0.963
Nontechnical	911	866	0.951

Source: College Placement Council, *CPC Salary Survey: A Study of 1976–77 Beginning Offers,* Final Report, Bethlehem, Pa., July 1977. "CPC Salary Survey: A Study of Beginning Offers." The beginning salary data reported are based on offers (not acceptances) to graduating students in selected curricula and graduate programs during the normal college recruiting period, September to June. The Survey covers job openings in a broad range of functional areas, *except* teaching, within employing organizations in business, industry, and government. The data are submitted by a representative group of colleges throughout the United States.

rate of women varies cyclically much as the rate of men does, the *ratio* of the female to the male rate varies countercyclically, rising in upswings and declining in downswings of the business cycle. This occurs because men are more likely to be employed in cyclically sensitive industries, in which unemployment rises sharply in recessions, *and* because women

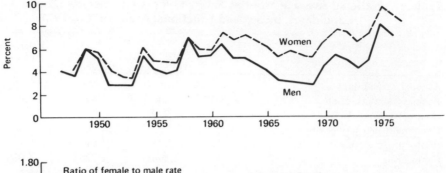

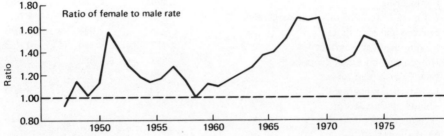

Figure 8.   Unemployment rates of men and women, 1947–1976 (annual averages).
Source: *Employment and Training Report of the President, 1977*, Table A-19.

tend to flock into the labor force in periods of rising employment opportunities, as we have seen, often experiencing a period of unemployment
before finding a job.

In fact, about 40 percent of unemployed women, compared with
slightly less than 20 percent of unemployed men, were jobless in 1976
because they were reentering the labor force or had never worked before.
And, of these, the great majority were reentrants rather than new entrants.
Men, on the other hand, were considerably more likely than women to be
unemployed because of having lost a job. In view of these differing
reasons for unemployment, it is not surprising that women tend to be unemployed for shorter periods than men, although the difference is not very
great.[17]

PRIORITIES FOR THE FUTURE

The phenomenon of working wives has clearly become a permanent feature of our society; in the coming decades I believe that the great majority
of wives will work over the greater part of their adult lives. True, in the

last few years we have witnessed the growth of an antifeminist movement of significant proportions, manifesting itself especially in efforts to defeat ratification of the Equal Rights Amendment, but I do not believe that this movement represents the "wave of the future." Girls reaching adulthood in the coming decades are far more likely to seek the freedom and independence to pursue a career that is so important a part of the philosophy of the women's movement than revert to older attitudes of female dependence.

In discussing priorities for the future, I propose to be very selective. It is impossible in a brief chapter to do justice to all the employment issues that women are raising, and thus I prefer to concentrate on a few that I consider especially important.

As a society, we have permitted the influx of married women into the labor force to occur without displaying serious concern for the adaptation of social policies that so important a change in the roles of women demands.[18] It is true that antidiscrimination and affirmative-action policies have been stressed at both the federal and state levels, though generally without adequate or carefully integrated policies of enforcement, but in many other respects we have failed to develop social policies that accommodate and encourage careers for women while at the same time protecting the welfare of the family.

In the United States, at least until very recently, there has been little discussion of a "family policy," and we lag behind other industrial countries, especially France, Sweden, and Israel, in the development of such a policy. The philosophy of a family policy was comprehensively spelled out in Alva Myrdal's path-breaking book, *Nation and Family*.[19] The need for a family policy in the United States has recently been emphasized in a report of the Carnegie Council on Children, with major emphasis on the central importance of effective full-employment policies and an adequate income-maintenance policy, while at the same time improving and expanding the services available to families and children.[20]

I strongly agree with the central importance of full-employment and income-maintenance policies, but would like to call attention to certain features of family policies in other countries that have not received adequate attention in the United States. These include maternity benefits, family allowances, and social provisions for child care.

Most other industrial countries provide maternity benefits as part of a national sickness cash benefit scheme. Virtually all other industrial countries have a universal family allowance or children's allowance program, although the amounts paid for each child vary greatly and have tended to be most generous in France and Belgium.[21] And a number of countries, especially France, Sweden, and Israel, have quite extensive programs of provision for child care.[22] Our major program of child support is the Aid to Families of Dependent Children (AFDC), which has a number of flaws, among them a provision offering incentives for a husband to desert his family, because payments are available only if a parent is incapacitated or absent from the home. Proposals for reform have, of course, been submitted to Congress from time to time.

The Urgency of the Child-Care Issue

Among the three major aspects of the family policy mentioned earlier, I should like to emphasize the urgency of the child-care issue, because at the moment it seems to be falling into neglect. I consider it urgent for two main reasons: (1) Lack of continuity in employment is a major factor in perpetuating occupational segregation and low earnings of women, and (2) there is evidence that, at least to some degree, problems of absenteeism in the schools, juvenile delinquency, and alcoholism and drug usage among teenagers may be associated with a lack of adequate child care and parental supervision in the early teens.

As Mary Keyserling, who has long been concerned with this problem, recently put it: "Our record, as a country, with respect to meeting day-care needs, is shockingly inadequate compared with most other industrialized nations."[23] Nationwide surveys conducted in October 1974 and February 1975 provide the most comprehensive data that have been gathered in recent years on child-care arrangements of working mothers. Among children of working mothers in the 3 to 6 age group, the great majority were cared for by the mother, father, or some other relative, whereas only 1.4 percent were in a day-care center and only 6.7 percent received care by a nonrelative in someone else's home (in some cases, this latter type of care was given by someone licensed to care for several children in her home). Children aged 7 to 13 generally need care before and after school, and some publicly operated day-care centers, such as those associated with the school system in California, do provide such part-day care. However, among children in this age group, only 3.9 percent received care in either a day-care center or a nonrelative's home, while a shocking 13 percent were left to care for themselves.[24]

Although employers and unions may not consider child care a matter of direct concern to them, surely they have an interest in policies that would minimize the need for women workers to be absent from work, and they are in a position to influence national policies on the question.

I have found, in the course of many discussions of this issue, that women are far more convinced of the need for adequate provision of child-care centers than are men. There is a tendency for men to feel they must make a moral judgment on whether or not it is right for a mother of a young child to work. As I stated some years ago on this issue:

> In my view, there is no single answer to this question that is the right answer for all mothers. Many mothers of young children, whether in one-parent or two-parent families, have skills and training which they could use to good advantage . . ., but they are prevented from doing so by the high cost of private child care in the home—and . . . by the absolute unavailability of competent domestic help in some areas. . . . These mothers and their children would in many cases be better off if the mother could satisfy her desire to use or acquire skills and make a significant contribution to the family income, rather than endure the frustration of being forced to stay at home with children. In other cases, mothers much prefer to be at home with their children, and they and their children both benefit from this arrangement.[25]

I do not advocate social provision of free child care regardless of parental means—care should be completely subsidized only for the poor, but the nonpoor should be required to contribute on a sliding scale in relation to income. The important point is that in too many cases a mother is forced to stop working because child-care arrangements have broken down. And research on the AFDC program has shown that the majority of AFDC mothers expect and want work, but that pregnancy, illness, child-care problems, and the termination of a job are the most frequent reasons their employment is interrupted.[26] The administration proposals for welfare reform place emphasis on the provision of jobs but not on child care, except as some public-service jobs may go to child-care workers.

No doubt many antifeminists blame juvenile delinquency and the shocking problem of absenteeism from junior and senior high schools on working mothers. But here we must be very careful. A number of sociological studies have examined these relationships, and, so far as I know, none has established a clear-cut relationship between juvenile delinquency and whether or not a mother is employed. But it has been shown that inadequate supervision tends to encourage delinquency, and some studies, though not all, have indicated that employed mothers are less likely to provide adequate supervision. Moreover, the link between broken homes and delinquency is well known—a finding that brings us back to the urgency of welfare reform.[27] In any case, it is the possible, indeed probable, link between inadequate supervision of children of school age and the onset of juvenile delinquency that I find a matter of particularly serious concern.

More adequate public spending for child-care programs would, of course, be costly, but I strongly suspect that, on a social cost–benefit basis, making adequate allowance for savings in the costs of welfare and juvenile delinquency and for the contribution of the mothers' earnings to the Gross National Product, the social costs would be minimal or perhaps even negative. And many school districts, faced with overstaffing problems, could sponsor child-care programs using existing buildings and teachers.

Changing Patterns of Work

In the long run, the problem of social provision for child care may become less urgent than it is today, if patterns of organization and hours of work change as much as some of the more imaginative writers on future social changes anticipate. In fact, some of the changes are already occurring, but on a small scale.

In this world of the future, child rearing will become a joint responsibility, shared equally, between the parents. This will probably be most feasible if both parents work on a part-time basis, alternating responsibilities for child care, but other arrangements, such as alternating periods of full-time work, are conceivable. There is growing interest in "flexible hours" or "flexitime," in which employees have considerable voice in selecting their working hours. The idea was first promoted by a German economist and management consultant, Christel Kaemmerev, in 1956. Flexible hours are now used by 6,000 European companies and have been adopted by several hundred larger American concerns. There is evidence that when flexible hours are adopted with genuine management support, productivity and morale improve and turnover, absenteeism, and overtime decline.[28]

Widespread adoption of more opportunities for part-time work or "flexitime" will often require extensive and sometimes difficult efforts on the part of employers, frequently requiring union cooperation. The benefits envisaged are, however, extensive. The effects on the quality of family life and on parent–child relationships would almost certainly be beneficial. And such changes would encourage the more flexible patterns of participation in education and in lifelong learning that are now being encouraged in one way or another in most industrial countries.

The chief factor that makes more part-time work or much shorter hours feasible is the steady rise in real per capita income. Two cannot live as cheaply as one, but two part-time incomes in many lines of work today will provide a reasonable level of living for a couple, and even for one with several children. Moreover, concern for the environment and for the need for energy conservation, among other influences, is creating a greater appreciation of relatively simple styles of living. In addition, a drastically reduced workweek might be the answer in some industries, such as the automobile industry, to an increasing problem of absenteeism.

Whether or not employers and unions currently see that such changes as these are desirable, the changes may well be forced on our economy by a gradual increase in the desire for leisure, already manifest in many ways, made possible by the rise in productivity. But whether the busy industrial or government executive, the physician, the lawyer, or the innovative researcher, all of whom tend to work much longer hours than the average worker, will be much affected by the changes is doubtful. And this will complicate matters for their wives, and for women in such occupations.

Who Has What Responsibilities?

If the changes that are needed are to come about, I see the following responsibilities for employers and unions:

1. *Support the ratification of ERA in those states that have not done so.* If the Equal Rights Amendment is not ratified, the political power of the forces that are fighting the emancipation of women would be strengthened. This would be particularly significant in the South, where the majority of states that have not ratified the amendment are found, where laws banning discrimination on the basis of sex (or on any other basis) have not been enacted, and where the relative absence of unions means that both men and women are likely to be found working under poor conditions and with low pay.

Ratification of ERA would have the opposite effect, strengthening the political power of those who are striving to improve the situation of women in the economy and in the social area. Much legislation will have to be enacted, especially at the state level, before the full implications of the amendment are spelled out in specific laws, but the impetus toward such action would be greatly enhanced with ERA embodied in the constitution.

2. *Support, through collective bargaining and otherwise, employment policies that will provide for more flexible hours of work and break down occupational segregation.* The union record of bringing women into positions of leadership, especially at the top, has been abysmal. Statistics show unequivocally that the world of union leadership is a man's world, even to a considerable extent in those unions with predominantly female membership.

American unions have also lagged behind European unions in pressing for paid educational-leave programs, for reasons that I understand (we do not yet have national health insurance, for example, whereas that particular battle has long since been won by European unions). But the time will come when American unions will push for paid educational leave—quite possibly the rapidly growing public-sector unions will be in the vanguard of this movement—and it will be of great importance for women who want to rise in the occupational hierarchy.

To both employers and unions, let me add that the movement of women into men's occupations is changing the world of work in ways that are probably only beginning to be felt. When women were absent from management, and from many of the occupations that were almost exclusively male, it was possible to ignore their view, but that is not what the world of the future is going to be like.

What should government leaders do?

1. *Support ratification of ERA.*
2. *Support the Carter administration proposals for welfare reform.* They are the best we have seen yet, and, although not perfect, they would help to stop the dangerous drift toward what Senator Daniel P. Moynihan and Andrew F. Brimmer have called the "deepening schism"—that is, the growing gap in the black population, and among certain other disadvantaged minorities, between those who

are experiencing impressive upward social and occupational mobility and those who are sliding more and more hopelessly into a dead-end slum existence. The family-splitting effects of our present welfare system must be given part of the blame for this distressing situation.

3. *Encourage through federal, state, and local action the development of more extensive and effective arrangements for child care.*

4. *Encourage more effective and more integrated enforcement of antidiscrimination and affirmative-action policies.* There are enough laws on the books—probably too many, except at the state level in the South—but their enforcement has been hampered by inadequate enforcement staffs, on the one hand, and by overlapping and duplication of the responsibilities and activities of federal and state agencies on the other.[29]

In the last analysis, many of the barriers to more equal participation of women in economic and social life are psychological. They stem from man's age-old need to feel superior, on the one hand, and from woman's age-old need to feed man's superiority complex, so well described in the writing of Matina Horner, on the other. Are we ever going to get out of that box?

ACKNOWLEDGMENT

I wish to express my gratitude for the able assistance provided by Dr. Charlotte Alhadeff and Ruth Goto of the Carnegie Council staff in the preparation of this chapter.

NOTES

1. G. Bancroft, *The American Labor Force* (New York: Wiley, 1958), Table D-1a.

2. The 1976 figure is from *Employment and Training Report of the President, 1977*, Table A-2. The earlier and later figures are not precisely comparable, partly because the earlier figures include girls aged 14 to 15.

3. For extensive historical evidence, see C. D. Long, *The Labor Force under Changing Income and Employment* (Princeton, N.J.: Princeton University Press, 1958).

4. We use civilian employment plus the number of persons in the armed forces in figure 1 as a more appropriate measure of the demand of the economy for labor rather than using civilian employment alone. The relationships are revealed somewhat more clearly in the form of three-year moving averages, which even out irregular fluctuations.

5. It has also been shown that in a recession some women withdraw from the labor force because

of poor job opportunities (the discouraged-worker effect), while others enter because husband or other family members are unemployed (the added-worker effect), but withdrawals tend to be more important than entrances. See especially, J. Mincer, "Labor-Force Participation and Un-employment: A Review of Recent Evidence," in *Prosperity and Unemployment*, ed. R. A. Gordon and M. S. Gordon (New York: Wiley, 1966); G. G. Cain, *Married Women in the Labor Force: An Economic Analysis* (Chicago: University of Chicago Press, 1966); and W. G. Bowen and T. A. Finegan, *The Economics of Labor Force Participation* (Princeton, N.J.: Princeton University Press, 1969).

6. Computed from *Employment and Earnings,* January 1977, Table 1. See also M. Blaxall and B. Reagan, eds., *Women and the Workplace: The Implications of Occupational Segregation* (Chicago: University of Chicago Press, 1976).

7. Computed from *Employment and Earnings*, January 1977, Table 1; *Journal of the American Medical Association* 236 (December 27, 1976): 3066; and *Journal of Medical Education* 52 (February 1977): 165.

8. See P. A. Wallace, "Impact of Equal Employment Opportunity Laws," in *Women and the American Economy*, ed. J. M. Kreps (Englewood Cliffs, N.J.: Prentice-Hall, 1976).

9. The data are based on estimates made by executive recruiters and other corporate officials in *Business Week*, November 24, 1976.

10. See, for example, E. Ginzberg and A. M. Yohalem, eds., *Corporate Lib: Women's Challenge to Management* (Baltimore: Johns Hopkins Press, 1973); and F. E. Gordon and M. H. Strober, eds., *Bringing Women into Management* (New York: McGraw-Hill, 1975).

11. See Carnegie Commission on Higher Education, *College Graduates and Jobs* (New York: McGraw-Hill, 1973); and M. S. Gordon, ed., *Higher Education and the Labor Market* (New York: McGraw-Hill, 1974).

12. See, for example, R. G. Freeman, *The Overeducated American* (New York: Academic Press, 1976); and S. P. Dresch, "Educational Saturation: A Demographic–Economic Model," *AAUP Bulletin* (Autumn 1975): 239–47.

13. See U.S. Bureau of Labor Statistics, *Special Labor Force Reports*, selected issues; and S. H. Garfinkle, "Occupations of Women and Black Workers, 1962–74," *Monthly Labor Review* 98 (November 1975).

14. See, for example, B. G. Malkiel and J. A. Malkiel, "Male–Female Pay Differentials in Profes-sional Employment," *American Economic Review* 63 (September 1973).

15. Kelly girls are not likely to be included in income data for year-round full-time workers, but their competition probably holds down earnings of year-round full-time female clerical work-ers.

16. See, for example, the chart in *Economic Report of the President 1973*, p. 105.

17. See *Employment and Training Report of the President 1977*, Table A-25; and *Employment and Earnings,* July 1977, Tables A-13 and A-14. As might be expected in a period of economic recovery, the proportion of unemployed women who were reentrants to the labor force in-creased between June 1976 and June 1977.

18. For a thoughtful and comprehensive expression of a similar theme, see A. Pifer, "Women Working: Toward a New Society," in *Annual Report of the Carnegie Corporation of New York*, 1976.

19. A. Myrdal, *Nation and Family: The Swedish Experiment in Democratic Family and Population Policy* (London: Kegan Paul, Trench, Trubner and Co., second printing, 1947; first published in Sweden in 1940).

20. K. Keniston and the Carnegie Council on Children, *All Our Children: The American Family under Pressure* (New York: Harcourt, 1977).

21. See U.S. Social Security Administration, *Social Security Programs Throughout the World, 1975* (Washington, D.C.: U.S. Government Printing Office, 1976).

22. See A. J. Kahn and S. B. Kamerman, *Child-Care Programs in Nine Countries*, a report pre-

pared for the OECD Working Party on the Role of Women in the Economy (Washington, D.C.: U.S. Department of Health, Education and Welfare, 1976).

23. M. D. Keyserling, "The Economic Status of Women in the United States," Papers and Proceedings of the 88th Annual Meeting of the American Economic Association, *American Economic Review* 66 (May 1976): 205–12. See also M. H. Strober, "Formal Extrafamily Child Care—Some Economic Observations," in *Sex Discrimination and the Division of Labor*, ed. C. B. Lloyd (New York: Columbia University Press, 1975), pp. 346–75.

24. U.S. Bureau of the Census, "Daytime Care of Children: October 1974 and February 1975," *Current Population Reports*, Series P-20, No. 298 (Washington, D.C.: U.S. Government Printing Office, 1976).

25. M. S. Gordon, supplementary statement in *Poverty Amid Plenty,* Report of the President's Commission on Income Maintenance Programs, 1969, p. 69.

26. G. W. Carter, "The Employment Potential of AFDC Mothers," *Welfare in Review* 6 (July–August 1968): 1–11.

27. For a good recent summary of the sociological research on working mothers, see L. W. Hoffman and F. I. Nye, *Working Mothers* (San Francisco: Jossey-Bass, 1974).

28. See K. Keniston and the Carnegie Council on Children, *op. cit.,* p. 124.

29. For a more extensive discussion of problems and needed changes, especially as they affect higher education, see Carnegie Council on Higher Education, *Making Affirmative Action Work in Higher Education* (San Francisco: Jossey-Bass, 1975).

8.
Child Rearing, Parenthood, and the World of Work

MONCRIEFF M. COCHRAN
Assistant Professor of
Child Development and Child Care
Cornell University

and

URIE BRONFENBRENNER
Professor of Human
Development and Family Studies
Cornell University

Who cares whether parents are good workers, or workers good parents? Is anyone interested in where all those fathers and mothers go when they leave home at 8 A.M. every weekday morning, or where all those workers go when they leave work at 5 P.M.? Most people will reply in the affirmative, for these questions relate to a sizable portion of the population. This polite show of interest, however, is nothing more than that.

Let us look at the record. The American employer apparently does not care about parents, for only in rare instances are maternity leaves, flexible working hours, and day care considered as practical options.

The disinterest shown by employers is, perhaps, exceeded only by that manifested in the university setting, where those who seek an understanding of family life have virtually ignored the interface between the workplace and the rearing of the young. On the one hand, changes in the American family are being documented and analyzed by increasing numbers of social scientists. They point to the fact that divorces are taking place at an unprecedented rate and that family violence is surfacing as a major American epidemic. They remind us that women are entering the work force in growing numbers and that fatherhood increasingly involves more than just bringing home the monthly paycheck. Each of these changes might both affect and be affected by the world of work, but their relationship to jobs and conditions on the job is rarely recognized by family researchers.

On the other hand, industrial sociologists have been studying worker performance for decades with virtually no mention of workers as parents. They look at how businesses and factories are organized, and how jobs are defined and structured, but, from most accounts, one could as easily assume that the workers live in barracks attached to the plant. Families simply are not mentioned.

The thesis of this chapter is that the institution with the greatest influence over the future of the American family in its child-rearing role is the world of work. Underlying this thesis is the contention that employers have great influence upon workers *as parents,* for better or for worse. If true, then social policies that strengthen families must include, and even begin with, changes in the world of work. This does not imply that employers alone can create conditions of work that are ideal for family life. On the contrary, to achieve the objective of strengthening families, social policy will also have to provide supports and incentives for employers to effect the needed changes in conditions of employment. As the foregoing statement indicates, neither the issues nor the solutions are simple ones. To deal with them effectively, we must first learn why, in today's society, increasing numbers of parents work outside the home and are even more likely to do so in the future. Next we explore the effects of unemployment upon the care provided children by their parents and review what is known about the effects of parental employment and day care on the development of children. The chapter culminates with the presentation of six policy-related issues that employers and the society at large must address if they are to improve the fit between the roles of parent and worker, and so contribute to the strengthening of the family and to the quality of succeeding generations of Americans.

WHY PARENTS WORK

In order to understand the impact of the workplace upon child rearing, it is necessary, first, to understand why parents go to work. Before answering that question, let us consider the numbers of workers shown in Table 1.

Table 1.   Workers with Children, by Family Type*

	Two Parents		One Parent† Working	Total
	One Parent Working	Both Working		
Number of workers	12,613,000	22,714,000	3,352,000	38,678,000
Percentage of total work force	13	24	4	41

*Includes at least one child under age 18, and excludes military families.
†Excludes one-parent families headed by men.

Source: H. Hayghe, "Special Labor Force Reports—Summaries: Marital and Family Characteristics of Workers, March 1977," *Monthly Labor Review* (February 1978): 51–54.

Over 38 million workers, more than 40 percent of our entire work force, have at least one dependent child. If we are to understand the motives driving this vast number of parents into the work force, the various types of working families represented in this table must be distinguished.

The single parent is almost always a woman and poor. Women are the sole wage earners in at least 3 million American families with children under the age of 18. They constitute 62 percent of all single-parent families. These women work outside the home because they must take a job to earn a living and "keep off welfare." Some argue that such women would be better parents if they remained at home with the children, on public assistance, instead of working outside the home. Such persons do not understand either the American work ethic or the American tradition of "rugged individualism." These values are reflected in such common expressions as "You can't get something for nothing," and "Dependence is degrading." Income supports from the public coffers, disbursed as they now are by departments of social welfare, implement this orientation by requiring that clients constantly reiterate their helplessness and worthlessness in order to qualify for aid. Such degradation is, of course, felt by parents, who can neither put up with it themselves nor keep it from infecting their children. Thus the "stay at home" alternative becomes unacceptable for most single parents, some of whom keep jobs otherwise intolerable in order to remain independent of a repressive and family-weakening system of public assistance.

In families in which there are two wage earners (a category that constitutes 45 percent of all intact families with children), it might at first appear that a shift back to one parent at home might be a viable alternative. But consider the economic realities of child rearing. Conservative estimates put a $40,000 price tag on the support of a child through high school.[1] This financial burden is difficult to bear on a single salary; it should, therefore, come as no surprise that the number of families with two working parents is on the rise. Total family income increases at least 25 percent when both parents work outside the home.[2] This increase is so important that the wife will work for pay outside the home despite the fact that her husband almost never makes an equal commitment to household tasks.

Some observers note that where two-earner families are in the higher income brackets, they have a choice as to whether one of them will stay home with the children. "One of them" generally means the mother, of course. It is important to point out, in this connection, that two relatively recent demographic changes in the American family are related to the changing attitudes of women toward work. First, parents are having fewer children, and thus full-time child rearing is increasingly seen as a short-term occupation rather than as a lifetime career. Thus, increasing numbers of women are preparing themselves for work roles outside the home, and attitudes are changing accordingly. The second demographic change is in the frequency of divorce. Faced with the possibility of having to support themselves and their children someday, more and more women are acquiring skills and experience to ensure their employability before they venture into parenthood. As a matter of fact, salaried work for both partners, which leads to the development and maintenance of an equalitarian spouse relationship, may actually prevent divorce. Thus, American values of work and independence, previously limited in practice only to men, are now being responded to by women who can "afford" to make the choice of staying at home or entering the job market.

The "traditional" family, in which one parent (usually the man) works while the other (usually the woman) takes care of the children, is no longer the major family–work arrangement in American society (see Table 1). Its relative decline as an economic and social response to child rearing may indicate that it has now become an all too vulnerable alternative. That vulnerability stems from a combination of the pressures already described: (1) the high cost of rearing children, and (2) the movement to equality of opportunity for *both* sexes. For a working man, the press is increasingly likely to come from two directions within the family—costly children and a wife convinced that there is more to life than "raising the kids."

The preceding analysis leads to the conclusion that the overriding reason that parents work is to provide, through earned income, some degree of independence for themselves and their families. Several other reasons for working require mention. Parents work outside the home because such work often brings with it regular and frequent social contact. Workmates sometimes become friends and, even as acquaintances, are resources to whom one can turn for information and advice. Studies of work inside the home (housework), on the other hand, indicate that adults doing such work (overwhelmingly women) often feel isolated and lonely.[3]

Finally, there are parents who work because they receive a good deal of intrinsic satisfaction from the job. Whether the work is with hands or head, with people or things, there are those who find pleasure in their work that is provided by the nature of the tasks themselves. Although there is great fulfillment to be found in child-rearing activities, and in some aspects of housework, such as cooking, much of the variety and complexity that contribute to the intrinsic pleasures of work are to be found outside one's own home.

UNEMPLOYMENT AND CHILD CARE

Income, however, remains the overriding factor leading parents to enter the job market. Supporting a family is expensive, and American families are "on their own" in their search for the means to provide such support. What happens when support is not found? How does unemployment affect child care?

The inability to find a paying job has two kinds of impact upon children. One impact is that of poverty. Very little money is available for the needs of children in families with no wage-earning member. The second and less visible effect of unemployment is related to the behavior of the unemployed adults, whether or not the family is destitute.

JOBLESSNESS AND POVERTY

Most estimates indicate that "between a quarter and a third of all American children are born into families with financial strains so great that the children will suffer basic deprivation."[4] The Carnegie Council on Children reported in 1977 that these children are two thirds more likely than nonpoor children to die in the first year of life, four times more likely to have "fair to poor" health, and one fifth as likely to attend college, regardless of intellectual ability. Although seemingly self-evident, the statistics remind us that child care is basic to the survival of the species. Poverty inhibits the care of children to the point at which that very survival is threatened. The Carnegie report goes on to state:

> Parenthood is deeply rewarding, but it is not easy and it is not cheap. We believe that those who choose to bear children must be expected to support and care for them, barring unexpected catastrophes. Today, far too many parents are unable to accept the full responsibilities of parenthood because there are no jobs or support for them, or jobs they can find do not pay a living wage.[5]

Unemployment is, perhaps, most devastating when it involves young people. Finding and holding a job is a fundamental prerequisite for entrance into the adult world. Yet over 20 percent of the young people between the ages of 16 and 20 who are looking for work cannot find it. Among blacks 16 to 20 years old that unemployment rate is almost one in two. A recent article in the *New York Times* magazine section refers to "a fundamental and systematic failure to bring the new generation of inner-city youth into the adult world of jobs and families."[6] Pointing to the fact that such young people are ten times as likely to have criminal records as youth with jobs, the writers go on to state that

> if lawlessness is a symptom of the state of emergency of inner-city youth, the emergency itself is joblessness. . . . For minority youth, these are the years of the great depression, far worse in its impact on them than any depression the country as a whole has ever encountered.[7]

Within the context of the present welfare system, joblessness has a direct and devastating impact upon the young parent, because he or she cannot marry, especially if there is a child in the picture. As the *Times* points out, the father

> . . . cannot marry because he cannot earn nearly as much as the amount that the welfare system and associated poverty benefits grant to a woman and child, and most of those benefits are lost if he is reported as a working spouse. If he doesn't marry, on the other hand, his woman can keep all her benefits and he can retain his earnings.[8]

The emerging picture is one in which joblessness, psychologically and economically debilitating in its own right, pushes young parents into a welfare system that operates to separate them even farther from the adult world by penalizing those spouses who acknowledge their responsibilities to each other and their child by sharing the same household.

Young people denied access to the job market are likely to become involved in criminal activities, and, as parents, to become dependent on a welfare system that encourages them to avoid acceptance of responsibility for the needs of their spouses and children. This is the danger for one group of jobless families, the "never-employed parents." What about the more visible victims of the unemployment picture, those parents who had a job, but were laid off when work became scarce? How does that kind of unemployment affect child care?

Unemployment and Violence

In a study of families in the process of divorce, O'Brien (1971) found that when violent behavior by a parent was reported, either toward a spouse or a child, that behavior was strongly related to work and earning capacity. In O'Brien's words, "The men in the violent subgroup of families apparently were not fulfilling the obligations connected with the work/earner role."[9] O'Brien found a high incidence of family violence in what was essentially a middle-class sample; none of the families was from the "lower-lower" class, and none lived in an urban ghetto. He proposes dissatisfaction with the work situation as the "trigger" for the violence that occurred. Gelles (1974) cites O'Brien's work as lending support for the proposition that unemployment of the husband is a contributing factor in intrafamily violence.[10] As additional corroboration, he points to the finding of Gill (1971) that nearly half of the fathers of abused children were not employed during the year preceding the abusive act and 12 percent were jobless at the time of the incident.[11] Galston (1964) also found that in abusive families the father was more often unemployed or worked part time.[12]

None of the foregoing researchers meant to focus on conditions of unemployment as a potential influence on family interaction. In each case, the investigator initiated research in a different problem area (divorce, violence, child abuse) and then stumbled across the link to unemployment. One research study carried out by the United Auto Workers in Flint, Michigan, did begin with an examination of unemployment. In 1975, 20 percent of the labor force in that city was out of work. The investigators found that, during that year, alcoholism increased 150 percent and the incidence of verified child abuse doubled.[13] At a more general level, Dr. Harvey Brenner at Johns Hopkins University conducted an analysis of economic trends between 1940 and 1974 and found that periods of depressed economy and high unemployment were accompanied by significant increases in infant mortality, mental disorders, homicide, heart disease, and alcoholism.[14]

It is obvious that intrafamily violence and alcoholism are related to child rearing and that alcoholics and the beaters of spouses and children are not healthy, productive parents. To the extent that unemployment contributes to such circumstances, and our economic system contributes to unemployment, this pattern constitutes a causal chain for producing family instability and unhealthy child-rearing practices in American society.

WORKING PARENTS AND CHILD CARE

When the subject of the working parent is associated with child care, the typical American reflex is to think "mothers." We shall shortly adduce evidence that the relation of the father to the world of work may be even more critical for family life and the process of child rearing than the mother's job situation. First, however, the few available studies on the effect of a mother's working on the development of her child are reviewed here. Hoffman and Nye (1974) summarize the results of their study by stating that the mother's working outside the home appears to have no negative impact on the child, and, in the case in which the mother is sole support for the family, appears to be beneficial.[15] Evidence gathered in an interview study by Colletta (1977) indicates that economic stability and increased self-esteem, which often accompany successful job performance, strengthen mothers in their parental roles and outweigh the difficulties of finding reliable day-care services and providing time each day for activities with the children.[16] Viewed within the context of the status given work by society and the economic necessity of income for family survival and stability, these findings are hardly surprising.

The other body of data related to the effects of working parents on child care has emerged from research on day care. Many investigations of alternative care arrangements turn out to be work-related, because the parent would be providing that care personally were he or she not employed outside the home. Once again, reviews of this research (Ricciuti 1976; Bronfenbrenner et al. 1976) indicate that reliance upon nonparental child care while the mother is employed outside the home is not harmful to the children involved.[17] It is clear from the evidence that parents remain the most important adults in the lives of their children regardless of the child-care arrangements used by a family. It is also apparent that children develop normally within any day-care arrangement utilizing a stable, stimulating environment provided by warm, loving adults.

EFFECTS OF THE FATHER'S WORK ON FAMILIES AND CHILDREN

In sum, maternal employment appears to have little enduring impact upon the child, except when the mother is the only wage earner in the family, and then the effects are positive. But what about paternal employment? How does it influence family life and the development of the child? The evidence we have reviewed on the consequences of the father's inability to find work suggests that not only the fact but also the conditions of employment might turn out to be significant in affecting the course of family life. In modern industrialized societies, work requirements have moved primary wage earners farther and farther from their families, both physically and psychologically; and in the United States, these wage earners have most often been men. The impact on children of the increased alienation of fathers from family activities has gone unexamined, perhaps because the appropriateness of full-time and even overtime employment has never been questioned in our society, regardless of the demands of the job vis-a-vis family life. But the growing movement of mothers into jobs outside the home has provoked a new look at the role of fathers in family life. We propose that this reexamination must include attention to the interface between the father's workplace and the home.

A search of the published literature revealed no systematic investigations in this area, but results from a recently completed pilot study of our own raise some provocative questions. The study was carried out in connection with a five-nation project on the impact of formal and informal support systems on family functioning and the development of the child. The data emerged from the pretest of an interview designed to identify and assess aspects of the environment experienced by parents as assisting or impairing their child-rearing efforts. The pretest was conducted with a sample of seventy families with young children, stratified by social class (three levels), family structure (one versus two parents), and mother's job status (not working, working part time, working full time).[18]

The results of the pilot study revealed that, along with financial worries, the conditions of the husband's work constituted the principal source of stress for two-parent families with young children. The problems in the father's job situation obtained whether or not the mother was also employed. Indeed, even in the families with working mothers (comprising 56 percent of the two-parent households in our sample), both mothers and fathers saw more difficulties from a parent's viewpoint in the husband's job than in the wife's.

Mentioned most frequently as sources of strain were the father's working hours, averaging forty-nine hours per week for the group studied. As might be expected under these circumstances, both parents viewed as a particular source of strain the husband's working overtime and on weekends, or having to make trips out of town.

Parents also described work features that made child rearing easier, such as flexible schedules, convenient job location, and an opportunity to have the child visit at work. In the case of the father, however, the job stresses tended to outweigh the supports. Understandably, aspects of the work situation viewed as beneficial to family life were more likely to be recognized by the jobholder than by the spouse, who tended to be more sensitive to the problems of the job. On balance, however, the husband's work situation was described as much more stressful and offering somewhat fewer supports to family life than the wife's.

Some indication of the impact on the family of the varying conditions of work as experienced by husbands and wives is provided by the reports of parents in the study sample. These parents saw their jobs as affecting both their sense of personal well-being and their capacity to function as parents. In general, the mother's employment was perceived as having more positive than negative effects, whereas for fathers the impact of the job situation was reversed—the effects were slightly more negative than positive. Mothers were also more likely to see these negative consequences of the father's job situation than were the husbands themselves.

To what extent are the stresses of the job situation relieved when the mother stays home instead of working, or works part time rather than full time? A mother's not working was indeed seen as an advantage for parenthood by those mothers who stayed home, but this view was not shared by the fathers.

Context and perspective become even more salient for understanding the differences in perceived stress associated with the mother's working part time rather than full time. Upon first glance, it would appear that part-time as against full-time employment for the mothers resulted in greater stress both at work and in family life. Paradoxically, however, these marked negative consequences were associated not with the mother's own job, but with the father's. When the mother worked part time rather than full time, both parents, and especially the mother, described the father's job as not paying well, affording fewer opportunities for advancement, demanding longer hours, and resulting in problems within the family for both parents and children. In contrast, the mother's own part-time job was viewed by both parents as considerably less stressful and disruptive to family life than the father's. It appears likely that mothers who take part-time jobs often do so because the husband's job does not provide sufficiently for the family's needs. But when this occurs, the task of parenthood is not made any easier.

Because of the small size and the ad hoc character of our sample, the foregoing results must be viewed with caution. Even if reliable, they may be valid only for situations found in predominantly professional communities. Nevertheless, the data point to one consistent trend: In the experience of the parents in our sample, it was the conditions of work for the husband, rather than for the wife, that were mainly seen as frustrating the parents' ability to care for and bring up their young children in the way they thought best.

This finding is consistent with the line of evidence and argument adduced in this chapter. In terms of social policy, it argues for adaptations in the world of work to enable and assist families, and especially fathers, to function effectively, not only as workers on the job, but also as family members engaged in a task that is equally critical for any society—the process of making human beings human.

HOW EMPLOYERS CAN HELP FAMILIES

Most businessmen will agree that the family is the backbone of American society, and that as our society goes, so goes American business. Families are changing in both structural and functional terms. Whether they continue to be able to fulfill one of their most fundamental responsibilities, the rearing of the young, depends in good measure on the nature and availability of work for pay. Because most salaried work is no longer family-based, the availability and characteristics of jobs are increasingly beyond the control of individual parents. So the survival of American families is dependent in good measure on the farsightedness of employers. To be sure, as we have already emphasized, employers have limited power to provide job opportunities. But our analysis points clearly to the need for incentives for the creation of additional jobs, whether in the public or private sector. In our view, the prime source of expert advice about the kinds of incentives that might work best for employers should be the employers themselves. Yet little attempt has been made, to our knowledge, to gather ideas and proposals from that group of experts. This use of employers as a reservoir of talent and energy committed to the maintenance of family life would provide the resources needed for a major initiative on behalf of the working parent. This initiative could be carried out by major employers themselves and should be encouraged and appropriately supported by the federal government. The goals of the undertaking would be educational, with a format to consist of regional conferences followed by action workshops of two different kinds and subsequent follow-up activities. The process is presented in the accompanying outline.

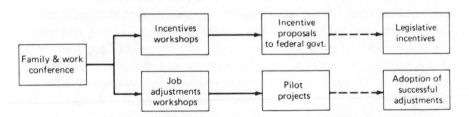

The overall process should be overseen by an advisory group made up of major private- and public-sector employers from across a given state or region. The kickoff conference would focus on the interface between the roles of parent and worker, using information gathered from employees who are parents, at all occupational levels, as a data base for the thoughtful presentation of the challenges faced by parents who are working or looking for work.

As shown in the diagram, the initial conference would be followed by two courses of action, each aimed at the development of family-strengthening public policies. Let us examine each course of action separately.

Workshops would be designed to make maximum use of employers as expert informants on the subject of how to develop the incentives needed to create the additional jobs that mean so much for families with children.

Underlying the search for such incentives would be the mounting evidence that unemployment debilitates families by undermining the self-confidence and social attitudes of parents who are seeking work. Resultant anger and frustration are, in turn, related to alcoholism, child abuse, and spouse battering. Included in these workshop discussions might be a reexamination of the relationships between work and welfare and ideas for ensuring continuity in the establishment of new jobs. Particular attention should be focused on incentives for the hiring of young people, who must develop the work habits which will sustain them for a lifetime.

Out of these workshops would come job-creation-incentive proposals for federal and state governments, and other workshops designed to stimulate policy-oriented discussions between employers and public officials. The employer advisory groups could oversee these subsequent discussions and then monitor the progress of any legislative initiatives growing out of them.

The second and simultaneous course of action would begin with workshops designed to examine and discuss innovative work practices already in existence in the world of work that have potential for improving the fit between the roles of parent and worker. Emphasis would be on presentations given by employers and candid discussions of the pros and cons in each approach. These discussions might, in turn, lead to government- or industry-supported pilot projects, carefully monitored to provide employers with information about job performance and parental satisfaction. Five major work-related arenas deserve special attention in these action workshops. A rationale for each domain is presented in the following paragraphs, beginning with modifications in jobs themselves and then moving to arenas one step removed from the work site which affect the ability of parents to perform competently on the job.

Hours of Work

This domain includes the issues of flexible working hours, compressed time (forty hours per week in less than five days), part-time jobs or work sharing, and mandatory overtime. At issue is the meshing of the parental and work roles, with our data indicating that fathers deserve special attention in this regard. A flexible work schedule, for instance, permits variation in work start-up and completion times from day to day. This flexibility makes it possible for a parent to fit in a morning visit to the nursery school, or to leave early on Wednesday to do the weekly food shopping.

Splitting jobs (two people for one job) can free parents in similar fashion. Mandatory overtime, on the other hand, may place a tremendous burden on the scheduling of a parent's life, leaving virtually no time for the children after working, eating, and sleeping.

Benefits

Serious consideration of part-time jobs as a means of supporting families requires careful examination of the benefits question. Health insurance, retirement and pension plans, and vacation time need to be geared to the part-time employee in an equitable fashion. A national health insurance program should be examined by employers as one way to equitably distribute that benefit to part-time workers.

Maternity/paternity leaves permit workers to be full-time parents during the early months of a child's life and to make long-term child-care arrangements carefully. Fathers deserve as much opportunity as mothers to play a central role in the care of the child during infancy.

Transfer Policies

The movement of workers from one area of the country to another for reasons of employment is a widespread phenomenon in American family life. A substantial amount of this movement is involuntary, including workers in the private sector who are moved from one part of a large corporation to another and those in the military or foreign-service segments of the public sector who are shifted from one duty station to another. The social and psychological uprooting associated with such moves is common knowledge, although not well documented in the research literature. Children give up their friends and their familiarity with the neighborhood, and those of school age must readjust to school expectations that often deviate markedly from one locale to the next. The educational and employment opportunities of spouses are often sacrificed to the moves, creating resentment and disillusionment within the family. These family-weakening forces, associated with repeated transfers, combine to produce a family unit at high risk of dissolution. Existing transfer policies should be reassessed in light of the effects of these policies upon workers' families, with particular attention to the possibility that long-term rootedness in neighborhood and community strengthens family life, and with it commitment to the job and job performance.

Day Care

Thirty-four percent of mothers with children under the age of 6 were in the work force in 1977. That percentage will increase over the next five to ten years. There are more and more two-percent families in which both parents work, as noted earlier, ant the costs of rearing children continue to rise. Fathers are increasingly expected to become more involved in child-care activities as their wives enter or reenter the job market.

Second only to the availability of the job itself for relieving the pressure on the family, is access to high-quality day-care options for working parents. American parents recognize and accept the fact that they have the primary responsibility for rearing their children. They will, therefore, make every effort to retain that responsibility as they select people to assist them with child care while they work. A pilot study recently conducted at Cornell University documents the critical role played by child-care arrangements in regard to the stresses and supports experienced by working parents. The study found that a mother's satisfaction with her child's care, whether it is performed by herself or someone else, at home or by a substitute in another home or center, determines in large measure how satisfied she is with her work, with herself as a parent, and with her child. Dissatisfaction with the child-care arrangement brought unhappiness with the work situation, disappointment with the parental role, and an increased feeling that the child was difficult to bring up.

Employers can be reassured by the fact that they need not, in most instances, provide child care at the work site. The majority of parents prefer care arrangements close to home and neighborhood rather than on the job. Workshops should be designed to explore ways that employers could best endorse and encourage publicly supported day-care programs that are of high quality and that provide several options to working parents. Contributions to the public coffers, which help finance such family supports, will pay large dividends to employers in the form of worker satisfaction and productivity.

Transportation

Especially in rural America, total reliance on the automobile for transportation has prevented a significant number of job seekers from taking advantage of available employment opportunities. Even when a family can afford a car, use of it by one wage earner completely immobilizes the rest of the family, isolating them from social contact and community services. The escalating costs of automobile purchase and maintenance have made public transportation attractive to an increasing number of Americans, and especially to families with children. Employers might wish to examine the benefits associated with more actively supporting the development and expansion of such transportation options.

SUMMARY

This chapter began with a presentation of the thesis that child rearing cannot be understood without reference to jobs and the world of work. Support for this thesis is predicated on an understanding of why parents work. Three principal reasons for the presence of parents in the work force were outlined and the need for income identified as the overriding cause. The importance of work in relation to how parents behave toward their children was underscored by the devastating impacts of unemployment emerging from studies of child abuse, spouse battering, and general family violence. In contrast to that evidence are studies of children who have working mothers and are in day care; these studies show no clear evidence of deleterious effects and give indication, in some circumstances, of positive outcomes. Data from our own research indicate that the conditions of work for the husband rather than for the wife were perceived as interfering with the ability of parents to care for their young children in the way they thought best. Finally, the focus is shifted to the employer in the role of family strengthener, and two major and complementary courses of action are sketched out for these, providing leadership in both the public and private sectors of the world of work. Thus, the care of children and the nature and availability of productive work become inextricably entwined, and the neglected role of the employer as a support for families with children is given the attention it deserves.

Since families are the reservoir from which workers draw the energies needed for good performance on the job, work performance cannot be separated from the rest of family life. It is time now for employers to take a leadership role in the development of work-related social policies that strengthen families. That investment is in their long-term interest, because a commitment to jobs that strengthens the capacity of parents to rear their children as responsible citizens is an investment in the next generation of American workers.

NOTES

1. Personal communication to authors from Department of Consumer Economics and Housing, Cornell University.
2. L. Hoffman and F. Nye, *Working Mothers* (San Francisco: Jossey-Bass, 1974), p. 28.
3. A. Oakley, *The Sociology of Housework* (New York: Pantheon Press, 1974), p. 182.
4. K. Kenniston and the Carnegie Council on Children, *All Our Children: The American Family under Pressure* (New York: Harcourt, 1977).
5. *Ibid.,* p. 77.
6. "To Be Young, Black, and Out of Work," *New York Times Magazine,* October 23, 1977, pp. 38–61.
7. *Ibid.*
8. *Ibid.*
9. J. O'Brien, "Violence in Divorce-Prone Families," *Journal of Marriage and the Family* 33 (November 1971): 692–8.
10. R. Gelles, "Child Abuse as Psychopathology: A Sociological Critique and Reformulation," in *Violence in the Family,* ed. S. Steinmetz and M. Strauss (New York: Dodd Mead, 1974), pp. 190–204.
11. D. Gill, "Violence against Children," *Journal of Marriage and the Family* 33 (November 1971): 637–57.
12. R. Galston, "Observations of Children Who Have Been Physically Abused by Their Parents," *American Journal of Psychiatry* 122 (April 1964): 440–3.
13. N. Raussell, unpublished report, The Mott Foundation, Flint, Michigan, 1976.
14. M. H. Brenner, "Estimating the Social Cost of National Economic Policy: Implications for Mental and Physical Health and Criminal Aggression," paper No. 5, Joint Economic Committee, Congress of the United States, October 26, 1976 (Washington, D.C.: U.S. Government Printing Office, 1976).
15. Hoffman and Hye, *op. cit.* pp. 126–66.
16. N. Colletta, "Divorced Mothers at Two Income Levels: Stress, Support, and Childrearing Practices," unpublished dissertation, Department of Human Development and Family Studies, Cornell University, 1977.
17. H. Ricciuti, "Effects of Infant Day-Care Experience on Behavior and Development: Research and Implications for Social Policy," and U. Bronfenbrenner, J. Belsky, and L. Steinberg, "Day Care in Context: An Ecological Perspective on Research and Public Policy." Both reviews prepared for the Office of Assistant Secretary for Planning and Evaluation, U.S. Department of Health, Education and Welfare, Fall 1976 (Washington, D.C.: Department of Health, Education and Welfare, 1976).
18. Because the sample was small (seventy families) and selection of families was not random, caution should be used when generalizing these results to other populations of families. The interviews were carried out in or close to a small city without an urban slum and dominated by a large university. Day-care and public-health services are widely available in this community, and the sample was heavily weighted with families having access to such facilities.

II.
THE EMERGING WORK ENVIRONMENT

9.

Quality-of-Work-Life Issues for the 1980s

JEROME M. ROSOW
President, Work in America Institute, Inc.

Factors contributing to, or influencing, the quality of working life in America over the next decade will be far greater in number, as well as significance, than during any other period in the nation's history. This chapter considers some of the economic, sociological, technological, and psychological factors influencing the shape of work in America during the 1980s. The intention is to provoke thoughtful consideration of the issues, stimulate planning to cope with the new work environment, and encourage earlier attention and involvement by decision makers in management, labor, and government in policy actions that will influence the course of productivity and quality of working life over the next decade.

It would be difficult, within the scope of this chapter, and even of this volume, to define all aspects of the quality of working life, discuss each in depth, and project the characteristics of the working environment envisioned for the 1980s. From the perspective of the late 1970s, however, seven critical factors have been selected that, to a greater extent than any others, will affect the quality of working life, and with it productivity, in the years ahead.

Each of these issues is important in and of itself. Considered collectively, they represent economic rewards for work, psychic rewards, and sociological needs associated with work.

The focus of the discussion is on emerging trends and their probable impact on productivity and the quality of working life during the decade of the 1980s. As identified by the Work in America Institute, Inc., the critical issues most important to track include:

- Pay
- Employee benefits

- Job security
- Alternative work schedules
- Occupational stress
- Participation
- Democracy in the workplace

The Work in America Institute was founded in 1975 to advance productivity and the quality of working life in the United States, drawing on experience and successful practices and policies in the worldwide work environment. In addressing the fundamental issues just listed, the institute has examined ways to enhance and improve the transition from the educational world to the workplace, labor–management relationships, and national work force policy.

Although the role that these issues have historically played in the work environment has long been recognized, it is increasingly evident that they will play an even more significant role in the years ahead. One important aspect of the institute's research has concentrated on forecasts of that emergent role. The emphasis upon future needs, problems, and opportunities is offered to challenge employers, unions, and the government to earlier and more effective development of programs in human resource management.

PAY

Pay ranks high on any list of employee expectations, as reflected in a survey in which 77 percent of the workers cited "good wages" as the most important aspect of the job. (In contrast, medical benefits, which ranked second, were cited by only 43 percent.) Both management and workers remain keenly aware of the importance of pay. Quality of working life must be built upon a base of adequate and fair pay if the program is to succeed in the external labor market and is to survive in the internal organization.

Although the basic nature of pay in our system of economic motivation is well accepted, problems prevail. These relate to changes in the external economy and to the constant search for effective methods of "performance pay" that can differentiate rewards to individuals or groups without distorting the equity system.

Pay policies in the future will continue to be squeezed by inflation and taxation, corrosive external elements that can erode an incentive system.

Employers will face a steadily rising cost of from 6 to 8 percent annual wage inflation, while employees will face the problem of conserving a share of their gross pay gains as meaningful take-home pay. Four factors will tend to weaken the incentive value of pay raises:

- The inflated costs of goods and services, especially housing, education, energy, and health care.
- The growing Social Security tax, which will triple the maximum tax by 1987.
- The steady rise in federal and state income taxes linked to progressive tax brackets.
- Rising property and sales taxes.

The issue of financial motivation for the average worker in the 1980s will be one of maintaining direct cash take-home pay incentives, while employers will require a heightened sensitivity to the maintenance of meaningful cash incentives.

Economic Participation

The growing desire for economic participation in the overall economic performance of the firm will move up on the agenda of the 1980s. More and more employees will expect a "piece of the action" over and above direct pay and benefits. The forms of economic participation extended to executives and middle management, such as stock options, stock appreciation rights, bonuses, and deferred compensation, are not available today to most other employees. The question is, then, what form will broad-based participation take? Profit sharing, cost-reduction sharing (e.g., Scanlon Plans), employee stock ownership, or other new forms? Of course, any new broad-based program must have a sound economic rationale, so that it reinforces rather than weakens the goals of the enterprise and sustains itself over time.

Considering the importance of teamwork and group cooperation within the workplace and then adding the rich talent pool characteristic of today's educated work force, it follows that plant-wide and company-wide reward systems add a valuable incentive for improved performance. Innovative executives will look ahead and anticipate this employee desire in terms of business self-interest and will experiment with new forms of economic participation that meet these dual objectives.

The Future of Pay Policies

Among the predictable developments in the area of compensation, the following stand out:

1. An increase in the number of pay systems that reward and differentiate groups over and above basic, adequate, and fair pay to individuals and that are based on job responsibility and performance. These may take the form of group bonuses or other incentive-based distributions, including deferred stock. They will be designed to reinforce and maintain group cooperation, sustained effort, and teamwork.
2. Conversion of wage-and-hour pay systems to annual salary plans in order to eliminate economic class differences, confirm the continuity of income, reduce periodic variations in pay, and underline the economic security provided by the pay plan.
3. Increased experimentation with the "executive type" incentives for middle management and professional personnel, including stock appreciation rights, performance bonuses, deferred pay, stock awards, and other extra incentives that are tailored to individual performance and motivation with year-to-year discretion. These provide flexibility and high opportunity for individual selectivity. They are one-time payments, impose no benefit-plan costs, and provide greater management involvement in the decision process.
4. Pay policymakers will devote more critical attention to take-home pay results to assure the validity of incentives and to take early corrective measures to counter an undue erosion by factors not under the employer's control, such as inflation and taxes.
5. Pay determination outside of collective bargaining will remain the prerogative of top management and is unlikely to become a pawn in the process of increased participation.
6. Broad-based company-wide forms of economic participation will grow in popularity and will be offered in preference to sharing power. Monetary motivation has worked, but the real problem ahead is whether conventional incentives alone will continue to motivate the new breed of employees in the next decade.
7. Company-sponsored thrift and savings plans will grow in popularity, since they combine a number of attractive multipurpose features at low cost. These features include voluntary participation; tax-

sheltered income; long-term employee savings encouraged by employer-matching formulas; investment options, including company stock; withdrawal and loan provisions to finance education, housing, and the capital needs of workers; and the long-term achievement of a second layer of pension protection resulting from these savings. The federal government should provide tax incentives to encourage the growth of such plans.

EMPLOYEE BENEFITS

American workers have raised their expectations and now feel "entitled" to benefits that were once considered a part of the bargaining process. Employees increasingly view adequate health-care coverage and pension protection as entitlements. Whereas only one out of two in the public expected health-care coverage in 1968, today the view is held by two out of three. The demand for adequate retirement income has grown from one out of two in 1968 to more than three out of four by the mid-1970s. These expectations will place increasing pressures upon small- and medium-sized employers who have provided minimum benefit protection in order to limit labor costs.

The intense attention to the benefit area reflects the great danger of facing illness and old age today without adequate coverage. For example, with medical care inflating at least twice as fast as all other consumer costs, the individual worker is hard pressed to share premium costs with the employer, much less pay the entire cost of medical care out of pocket.

Employee benefits are provided in substantial variety and generous measure by only one segment of the private sector, major employers, who provide the better world of pay and benefits for a total package that is most attractive. By contrast, a great number of companies, especially small- and medium-sized labor-intensive employers who are nonunionized and marginally efficient, provide as few benefits as possible, with a rather grudging attitude at that.

This two-world reality should not escape our attention, since we tend to look at the Fortune 500 corporations and cite the substantial payroll costs of employee benefits as a representative condition today. The fact is that over 50 percent of all American workers remain without employee private pension coverage. Many of those with coverage may never draw a dollar in benefits due to lack of vesting and high turnover.

Future employee benefits will be affected by the competing demands of workers and the pressures on management to control costs. Thus, the challenge ahead in the next decade is not so much one of innovation as it is the attainment of an effective balance of cost and program results within a concept of total-package compensation. At the same time, the most critical questions will concern the relationship of private employer benefit programs to the rapid changes in federal social programs which embrace all American workers.

Two major areas merit our attention: pensions and health-care insurance.

Pensions

The most radical and far-reaching impact on American private employer pensions occurred in December 1977, when Congress revised Social Security taxes. As a result, the Social Security wage base will jump from $16,500 to $42,600 by 1987, and the tax rate will rise from 5.85 percent to 7.15 percent for both employee and employer.* This means the maximum tax per year will more than triple from $965.25 to $3,045.90. The combined tax maximum will rise to $6,091.80.

Although this forecasts a tremendous boost to the funding of Social Security, it also has serious side effects. First, it means a reduction in direct take-home pay for all Americans and is probably the largest peacetime tax increase ever enacted. In fact, many workers will pay more Social Security tax than federal income tax. Second, it imposes a major cost on workers and employers (although the employers deduct their costs as a business expense). These costs will be passed along in price increases as inflation or lead to some reduction of employment to offset costs. Third, it must lead to an adjustment of Social Security benefits, if not fully proportionate to tax payments, at least moving toward that ultimate goal. Thus, those who pay three times as much may expect to benefit accordingly. Taking a simplified approach, the maximum Social Security benefit in 1977 for a married couple was $655.70 per month. Assuming a tripling of benefits at the $42,600 salary level, the monthly benefit would be $1,967.10 in 1977 dollars. It is conceivable, of course, that Congress will scale down the benefits so that they are not directly propor-

---

*Although efforts in Congress to revise the tax schedule downward were unsuccessful in 1978, the issue will most certainly reappear at a later date.

tionate to the escalating taxation, but there will be limits to its ability to withstand pressure for equity from employers and employees who are funding the program.

Based on the estimates of the Social Security Administration, by 1987 92 percent of the work force will be earning salaries less than or equal to the $42,600 wage base provided by the revised tax. This means that the entire earned income of these workers will be insured under the Social Security Act and that, under present cost-of-living escalation provisions, benefits will maintain their real purchasing power.

What then is the future outlook for private pensions? It is reasonable to anticipate that the revised Social Security tax could play havoc with the private pension world and create serious disincentives for new pension plans and even overwhelm existing well-established plan coverage for the great majority of workers. Private pensions may become a benefit limited to the elite few, that is, the 8 percent minority with earned income above the taxable Social Security wage base.

The Future of Pension Programs

1. Since pensions represent one of the major benefits, employers will be forced to reexamine pension planning and financial costs to consider the most effective cost–benefit integration with Social Security benefits.
2. Programs permitting retirement for the military, policemen, and firemen after twenty years of service, regardless of age, require review. These systems are imposing heavy costs on the defense budget and on local government. Recent proposals to establish age 55 as the minimum retirement age for the military represent one effective measure. Similar reforms for policemen and firemen require legislative review to restore a reasonable balance between the risks of these occupations and the costs and benefits to society.
3. The development of IRA (Individual Retirement Accounts) growing out of ERISA legislation will mean greater economic security for many workers and for the self-employed. It also points to increased pension portability as middle managers and executives capitalize their pension rights and pyramid the capital values of two or more careers to create a layered pension fund.
4. Before the next decade it will become urgent to reexamine the existence of multiple pension rights, where a relative few receive pensions from two or three sources, including Social Security. This

issue in itself may create great pressures to nationalize most pension rights under the federal government and buy out existing commitments on a one-time basis.

Health-Care Insurance

Despite public interest and union legislative efforts in national health insurance, it seems unlikely that the government will enact such a law before the mid-1980s.

The greatest single deterrent is the rapid rise in health-care costs. Other obstacles include the glut of social legislation, especially jobs and welfare; the high cost overruns and financial scandals in Medicare and Medicaid; the lack of voter pressures on Congress; and the failure of Congress to deal with difficult health legislation.

Although health-care costs are likely to hit $180 billion in 1978, only one third of all personal health bills are out-of-pocket to consumers. The remainder are met through private health insurance and federal programs.

The Future of Health Care

1. Employers, even those who basically oppose national health insurance, will be required to take an increased responsibility for the provision of employee health insurance programs.
2. The coverage of health insurance will continue to expand to embrace psychological, dental, vision, and other comprehensive services. Employees and unions will press for lower contributions to premium costs (or no contribution at all) at the same time that such costs will continue to inflate at a fast pace. These costs may challenge or exceed pension costs.
3. Employers and unions will turn greater attention to insurance costs and may well become a powerful force to achieve some reasonable restraints upon the relentless rise in medical and hospital costs. These will include more competitive measures in contracting for insurance and more direct involvement of private-sector executives in health and hospital affairs.
4. The government will be forced to design effective incentive systems for financing health care and to create a competitive and cost-conscious environment in the medical profession and in hospitals as a means of restoring a measure of consumer power to the individual.

5. Since the health industry has become one of the nation's major employers, opportunities for improved quality of health services and improved hospital productivity must attract new interest and positive results in the 1980s.

6. In order to reduce absenteeism, increase productivity, control health-care costs, and pay for time not worked, employers will increase their efforts to respond to stress by providing in-house services and stronger links to community-based programs that deal with alcoholism; drug addiction; family stress related to marital problems, divorce, and difficulties with children; and work-related stress, either occupational or resulting from poor supervision or working climate.

7. In order to maintain the free-market employment system whereby millions of workers change jobs each year, it will be necessary to establish medical care catastrophe insurance "umbrellas" to protect workers for periods up to one year while they undergo employment shifts.

JOB SECURITY

Employment without security places the burden of survival on the individual worker instead of on the enterprise or on society. This is an unequal burden. It cannot be borne lightly. Naturally, therefore, the average worker is insecure and constantly fearful of job loss. Concerned about an insecure and uncertain future, the employee is less likely to produce at the optimum level in day-to-day employment. The position itself seems transitory, the attachment to a career nebulous, and the investment of loyalty to the employer often unrewarding.

Job security is fundamental to quality of working life for the individual employee. In fact, security of employment ranks above higher pay for many workers. The American worker, manager, or executive, regardless of status or income level, wants a reasonable degree of security. The employer also prefers stable and loyal employees who have a healthy attachment to their work and to the organization. However, the employer also fears contractual job security, since he seeks to preserve maximum business flexibility in relation to changing economic circumstances and fluctuating labor needs.

Tenured employment patterns through education and civil service career rules have provided maximum job security within large systems of what has been called "meritocracy." Yet new questions have arisen regarding the productivity and motivation of employees in these relatively secure work environments. In fact, leaders in both government and education are under increasing financial and performance pressures to temper job and career security with a stronger degree of managerial flexibility to censure or, ultimately, to dismiss the poor performer. This issue is joined, but the outcome is unclear, thereby weakening efforts in the private sector to extend more job security.

General Situation

The great majority of American employees (excluding those in education, civil service, the military, and the church) have a minimum degree of job security. Although union members are often protected by labor contracts that provide seniority protection, most American workers can literally be dismissed on a moment's notice with little, if any, recourse.

During the automation scare of the 1960s, attrition clauses attracted attention as a means of minimizing separation of employees. But as of late 1974 an AFL–CIO analysis of 102 agreements directly affecting about 3.5 million employees showed that only five of the agreements included attrition clauses and that two of these five were ambiguous. In a 1972 survey of contracts covering 1,000 or more workers, the Bureau of Labor Statistics found that 0.5 percent contained attrition clauses.[1]

Advance notice provisions in collective bargaining agreements covering 1,000 or more employees are applicable to fewer than 1.2 million workers, or 17 percent of those covered by the agreements. We are a long way from providing early warnings to workers regarding the impact of technological change, economic displacement, business plan changes, or internal organizational restructuring.

Contrast with Japan

By contrast, the lifetime security system in Japan has a relatively brief history but a high rate of success. The remarkable productivity growth, the spectacular industrialization, and the cooperative spirit of Japanese workers are linked to lifetime employment. Although this employment philosophy is undergoing an apparent reevaluation in some Japanese firms, the fact remains that Japanese workers welcome and cooperate with change and encourage higher productivity in an environment of lifetime job security. Ironically, however, Japanese management may be tempted to forego these advantages in order to follow American-style personnel practices.

Human Resource Planning

Human resource planning has grown in popularity as a concept in personnel management. Aided by computer technology, many employers have mechanized personnel records and can produce a great deal of useful factual data. Information systems are not decision systems, however, so the link between human resource information and planning still needs to be forged. Although these technologically sophisticated systems could be employed as management plans to avoid layoffs, they rarely are. This is the crux of the problem. Job security can be increased without added labor cost, but only if work force strategy is an inherent part of overall corporate strategy.

The Future of Job Security

Within the next decade major employers in America must become more adept in the management of human resources so as to protect both the organization and the individual worker from the full burden of change. Policies that reduce insecurity are compatible with employer objectives of efficiency and productivity and will serve to reinforce the goals of product and service quality and higher profitability.

For this reason, as expectations for increased job security grow, the workplace will be expected to respond with acceptable conditions. Job security for minorities, women, and older workers (over age 40) represents one critical aspect of equal-employment opportunity. In response to worker expectations for increased security we can anticipate increased restrictions and restraints upon the powers of employers under civil rights and equal-employment laws. The trick for the private sector is to convert these restrictions into management advantages through their potential to reduce worker insecurity.

The combination of economic incentive and legal penalties should serve to reinforce employer programs to strengthen job security, while at the same time retaining for the employer the right to require adequate performance on the job. Thus, employers may address this two-pronged problem as a basic goal for the 1980s. Some of the needs to be considered include:

1. Formal recognition of past service and performance as factors in job security.
2. Published policies and rules regarding retention, layoffs, removals, and recall rights.

3. Early warning systems to integrate labor force changes within business planning and to anticipate the impact of economic changes on the work forces as early as possible. Thus, normal attrition can remove the first layer of potential labor surplus on a voluntary basis; coupled with tight limits on new employment, it can help the organization through a difficult economic period.
4. Maximum use of and opportunity for worker retention or reassignment within individual work locations or through transfer to other locations.
5. Both advance notification and severance pay graduated with service, to reduce economic shock and to create incentives for better business planning.
6. Integration of programs with federal income transfer systems, including unemployment insurance and Social Security. This should also include private initiatives to increase the use of major public financial resources for education, retraining, and income, in combination with company programs.
7. Early full-pension vesting and, ultimately, pension portability to ensure long-term economic shelters against cyclical unemployment. Pension portability will become an asset for management, since employees can volunteer to leave dead-end, nonproductive roles and seek new careers.
8. Recognition of the fact that job security can reinforce general morale, enhance productivity, advance career personnel management, reduce turnover, and strengthen the continuity of the organization, provided that job security is balanced with an obligation for good performance on the job.

ALTERNATIVE WORK SCHEDULES

Despite a number of experiments to change the standard work schedule, the five-day, forty-hour "standard" workweek has remained a fixture in American industry for almost four decades. Since 1940, the basic workweek has been relatively stable, despite a growing feeling that we are in a postindustrial society and that the American people derive much satisfaction from the increase in leisure.

Since the beginning of the seventies, however, industry and government have become increasingly interested in experimenting with new kinds of work schedules. This is both a response to the changing nature of the labor force and an attempt to achieve improved productivity, job satisfaction, and reduced absenteeism. Rearranging work schedules in a more innovative and responsive design offers one of the new opportunities for the 1980s.

Alternatives to the standard work schedule vary considerably in their degree of flexibility and their rationale. Generally, they are intended to meet the needs of working women, give employees some control over their work schedules, provide for greater efficiency and service, and ease the strain on resources and the environment. Some objections made to alternative schedules are that they may adversely affect productivity or employee cohesiveness and morale, require workers to learn a greater variety of tasks, and require unions to be more flexible in bargaining.

Among the alternatives available are the following: flexitime, staggered hours, part-time employment, and the reduced workweek, including the four-day week.

Flexitime means that the working day is composed of core time (for instance, 10:00 A.M. to 3:00 P.M.), during which all employees must be present, plus flexible time. For example, the workday may extend from 6:30 A.M. to 6:00 P.M., but the daily schedule for individuals or groups will follow a flexible band of time in the hours preceding and following the core time. Thus, one individual may work from 9:30 A.M. to 6:00 P.M., while another may work from 6:30 A.M. to 3:00 P.M., both eight-hour days, plus a half hour for lunch.

Flexitime, a European innovation, is now practiced in over 6,000 European companies in a great variety of industries. About one tenth as many blue-collar as white-collar workers have been placed on flexitime programs in Europe. In the United States, by contrast, flexitime has been adopted by only a few hundred companies and includes fewer than 1 million workers (about 2½ percent of the labor force). Legislation has been enacted to authorize a three-year experiment with flexitime in the federal government, to build on the highly successful program of the U.S. Social Security Administration in Baltimore, Maryland, involving 4,500 of its 9,000 employees. Organizations that have used the plan have reported substantial benefits in terms of reduced absence, increased service to the public, less tardiness, sharing of skills, uninterrupted time for planning work assignments, reduced travel time and costs, and additional employee participation in nonwork activities. Some problems have been encountered with employee supervision, increased overhead costs, and pay differentials between employees who have flexitime and those who do not.

Union experience with flexitime is limited, and concern has been expressed regarding pay, especially overtime premium pay, once the traditional eight-hour work period has been extended to ten or twelve hours. Other union concerns relate to health and safety. By contrast, the greatest single obstacle on the part of management is the concern of supervisors who fear loss of control and who face the necessity for new forms of scheduling tailored to operational needs.

Staggered hours, involving adoption of daily hours different from the normal nine-to-five schedule for all workers at a given location, is being tried extensively. A survey of 100 firms in lower Manhattan using staggered hours showed that employees had a favorable reaction in terms of morale and better transportation options. For the most part, the firms saw no change in areas such as productivity, communications, and management control. Staggered hours are sometimes recommended as a shift that can be made quickly and at little cost and as a bridge toward the later adoption of flexible hours.

Part-time employment, now including more than 13 million workers, constitutes one of the fastest growing segments of the American work force. Part-time employment accounts for nearly 18 percent of the working labor force. It is likely to increase in the future, since 20 percent of all unemployed workers today are seeking part-time rather than full-time employment, compared with only 5 percent of those seeking work in 1950. Two thirds of all part-timers are adult women, most of whom are married and working to supplement family income or to pursue interests outside their homes. The next largest component, 25 percent, are teenagers, and the balance are men, with a growing number of older workers seeking part-time jobs. Part-time employment is therefore especially prevalent among women and workers under 20 or over 65 years of age.

The advantage to employers is primarily flexibility in scheduling, a feature that has considerable appeal to retail trade and service organizations. Retail trade concerns are extensive users of part-timers. For example, 90 percent of the 250,000 employees at McDonald's fast-food restaurant chain are part-timers. Insurance companies, banks, computer firms, pharmaceutical manufacturers, and a great number of other companies have increased their use of part-time workers and have developed "minishifts" to supplement their regular clerical personnel. One company, Control Data Corporation, has created a total organization of part-time workers, with welfare mothers working the morning shift, and high-school students, the afternoon shift.

One clear-cut advantage of using part-time rather than full-time workers is the avoidance of overtime payments to regular full-time workers. In addition, part-timers are generally paid less in wages than full-time workers, averaging $4.21 per hour, compared to $5.16 per hour for full-time workers nationally in 1977. The nation's unions are not altogether happy with the accelerating trend toward part-time workers, since relatively few become union members. However, the Retail Clerks International Association has stepped up efforts to organize part-timers, and says that half of its 700,000 members are part-time workers in whose behalf it has been able to win pro rata fringe benefits (such as health insurance and pensions) not usually provided for part-time workers. Still, equity remains a troublesome problem in the growing use of part-time employees.

Research on the use of part-time workers points increasingly to satisfactory work performance. Many companies have reported that part-timers offer higher productivity, positive attitudes toward work (especially when the supervisors favor part-time workers), greater scheduling flexibility, lower personnel costs, and easier attainment of equal-opportunity goals.

The Reduced Workweek

The four-day week has attracted considerable attention, but the interest in this development has not been justified by the results. As of May 1976, only about 750,000 workers were on four-day schedules, about the same number as a year earlier and about 100,000 more than in May 1974. The proportion of workers on the four-day week has ranged between 1.0 and 1.3 percent over the past four years, according to the Bureau of Labor Statistics. At present, an estimated 10,000 firms use the four-day workweek for at least some of their employees.

From the point of view of workers, the four-day week means three days of leisure in every week, the elimination of one day's commuting, and the option to use extra time for moonlighting. The price is a change from five eight-hour days to four ten-hour days, without overtime pay for the extra hours per day.

From the standpoint of the employer, the benefits can be measured in terms of productivity, job satisfaction, and reduced absenteeism, although the findings here are not universally favorable. Nor does the four-day work schedule appear to have had an appreciable impact on turnover rates, according to current research. The spread of moonlighting, which could reduce efficiency on the primary job, is a distinct disadvantage so far as employers are concerned.

For society as a whole, a significant increase in the adoption of the shortened workweek would change many accepted patterns. It would affect consumer spending habits, educational schedules, and family relationships. The implications for housing patterns and recreational and leisure activities are particularly significant.

The most important question, and a key factor in union support, is whether the shorter workweek actually will lead to an increase in jobs at a time when America is struggling with lingering high levels of unemployment. However, if the four-day workweek results only in the substitution of four ten-hour days for five eight-hour days, it is difficult to see how the number of jobs will be increased. Some critics also point out that a shorter workweek enables workers to take second jobs, which may offset the expansion of work opportunities.

The Future of Alternative Work Schedules

During the 1980s, we can anticipate increased applications of alternative work schedules in the American workplace. The fastest growing phenomenon will continue to be the part-time job. It is responsive to the needs of three major special groups: young people, women, and older workers. It is also more compatible with the changing nature of the labor market. Its growth and effectiveness will accelerate as employers find solutions to the problem of equity between full- and part-time workers.

Staggered hours represent more of a community-wide approach to work scheduling. With the increased attention to problems of urbanization and the basic reliance on private auto transportation, combined with energy costs and shortages, the incentives for staggered work hours are becoming more obvious and more appealing. The nine-to-five pattern of the past must give way to a more flexible and diverse pattern so that the many individual work forces within an entire metropolitan labor market can adopt a variety of daily schedules in order to reduce commuting time, increase punctuality, and save energy. This involves limited planning, no extra cost, and a minimum change in managerial and supervisory attitudes. The adoption of staggered hours requires strong leadership, such as that provided by the Port Authority of New York and New Jersey, an example that the mayors of big cities may want to emulate in proposing staggered hours for businesses in their localities.

The concept of flexitime, one of the more exciting options, has opened new horizons for employee–employer accommodation to the realities of the new life-style, urbanization, and the growing role of working mothers in the labor force. Indications are that it will grow at a phenomenal rate over the next decade, since it provides an adaptation to change with a minimum of risk and effort and a relatively high payout in flexibility and adaptability of the organization to the labor market.

The four-day workweek is an interesting and important variation of the work pattern and will continue to be valuable for a small segment of the labor force. However, because ten-hour days are not practical for the majority of workers, and because adoption of this pattern of work does not appear to result at present in a greater number of jobs, extensive adoption of the four-day workweek would seem to hinge on a substantial shortening of the workweek to thirty-two hours. This does not seem to be a likely possibility for the 1980s. Nevertheless, in the face of high unemployment, the nation must take a hard look at the issue of adjusting hours to increase jobs. This is a much more important question than the attraction of the four-day week as an accommodation to a leisure society.

OCCUPATIONAL STRESS

Occupational mental-health programs to deal with stress are beginning to emerge as a new and important aspect of working life. Thirty thousand Americans die each year by their own hand. Hundreds of thousands are incapacitated or killed by serious accidents, many in the world of work, as a result of stress. Millions suffer from alchohism, drug abuse, heart disease, hypertension, ulcers, emotional disturbances, migraine headaches, and serious personal or financial problems.

There are significant relationships between the kinds of work people do and psychological disorders that develop. Yet two factors must interact with causes of occupational stress to create disabling symptoms. First is the context in which the individual functions—at home, at work, in the community, and in the society. Second is the ever-changing individual vulnerability, including genetic and hereditary factors modified by early developmental experience. Thus occupational mental health is a complex problem that requires attention. One of the most promising and effective places to offer assistance is the workplace, according to Dr. Alan McLean, who heads the Center for Occupational Health at New York Hospital, Cornell Medical Center, White Plains, New York.

Why the Workplace?

Mental-health services recast the workplace. They signal that the employer cares and desires to promote individual self-esteem. They further indicate that the problems can be dealt with in a nonthreatening manner.

Employees are being drawn increasingly into the area of mental-health services for both economic and legal reasons. These directly affect the bottom line of profitability. From the legal point of view, three important areas exist: workmen's compensation, which now covers mental disorders; Occupational Health and Safety Administration (OSHA), which fixes standards for occupational health and safety; and the Rehabilitation Act, which requires affirmative action programs for handicapped employees, including those with psychiatric disabilities.

Economic motives are also intensifying. Experts estimate that between 10 and 20 percent of the labor force will make use of mental-health services in any one year. About 70 percent of the problems are in the areas of behavior and social adjustment, with the remaining 30 percent in legal aid, housing, credit assistance, and related areas. Of the behavioral and social problems, half the cases relate to problems reflected in work.

These are troubled workers. They have increased grievances, are four times more accident prone, use three times the usual extended sick-leave benefits, and have the worst absenteeism records.

Alcoholism costs industry between 12 and 25 billion dollars per year. These dollars are spent without any formal treatment programs. The end result is usually destructive since the alcoholic worker without some help at work—referral, diagnosis, treatment, rehabilitation, and support on the job—usually ends up losing family, financial security, job, and even life.

The costs of ignoring occupational behavioral-medical problems are reflected in absenteeism, excessive use of sickness and accident benefits, on-the-job accidents, low productivity, high medical insurance premiums, and other more subtle symptoms. Of course employees bring human problems to work—marital and family strains, middle-life stress, depression, and debt. It is impossible to separate the problems of life from life at work. And, of course, the physical, emotional, and mental causes of stress at work in turn affect the family and life patterns away from work.

Obstacles to Mental-Health Care

Many working-class people are unable or unwilling to avail themselves of community services. They cannot afford time away from work to solve problems that are causing poor performance on the job. And, despite growing attention to psychiatry and human psychology, a stigma still attaches to mental-health problems. Most people believe they should solve their own problems. Thus, there is no referral system in our society, no linkages between the individual and the community. Finally, the existing care system is not responsive. It treats the poor and the upper middle class and is generally not geared to the majority of blue-collar and office workers.

Even within a workplace where medical facilities are available, concerns over privacy, job security, and the future act as serious barriers to access.

Dr. Sheila H. Akabas of Columbia University's Industrial Social Welfare Center describes an effective company program as having four roles. The first is to train people who already help employees or could learn to do so, such as foremen, shop stewards, supervisors, and other union and management representatives.

The second role is to offer direct services to enhance and maintain the health and productivity of each individual employee. This program should be as comprehensive as possible. It should be anchored in a broad definition of health, not just as an absence of disease, but as the prevention, elimination, or control of physical, emotional, behavioral, and social maladjustments that affect well-being and impair effective work performance.

The third role is to act as a linkage with community facilities. This is a double role: not only to make referrals, but also to make demands on the community facilities to include working-class needs. The fourth role is to serve as the ombudsman for any employee who needs mental-health care and needs representation in the workplace to obtain services or benefits or to take advantage of community resources.

Future of Occupational Mental-Health Programs

There is growing evidence of progress in occupational mental-health programs at the workplace. Major employers are increasing their activities, and major unions have undertaken programs in cooperation with employees and independently.

Since the complexity of both urban and industrial life shows no signs of diminishing, the worker and the professional alike will continue to face increasing stress on and off the job. The employer frequently pays the bill in several ways: health-care insurance, pay for time not worked, and lost productivity on the job.

Thus, the greater involvement of employers in the entire arena of occupational health will be propelled by economic considerations. However, the slowness of action characteristic of our industrial society should dispel excessive optimism about a major breakthrough by the 1980s.

PARTICIPATION

In a 1977 survey, 54 percent of the American public stated that they feel they have a right to take part in decisions affecting their jobs. Among younger workers, 62 percent expressed this view, compared with 53 percent as recently as 1973.[3]

These attitudes reflect important changes in work values in America and a clear demand for more participation in the decision-making process at the workplace. Certainly this represents a positive goal at the same time that it poses a threat to conventional decision making in authoritarian-structured activities.

This claim to a legitimate and meaningful role in decisions is much more difficult to satisfy than are the direct economic demands for pay and benefits. The latter are tangible, with few emotional overtones. The former are subtle and represent a novel management style foreign to the experience and managerial style of most American executives today.

Thus, the "participation" demand will prove to be a most thorny issue. The goal itself is broad and implies a reversal of the conventional flow of power in the modern organization. In a sense it is akin to reversing the decision process to flow upstream.

Contrast with Western Europe

Participation in decision making on the shop floor, in the office, and in the boardroom has attracted a great deal of attention in Western Europe. In Norway, Sweden, France, the Netherlands, West Germany, and the United Kingdom remarkable advances have been made. Considering the relative similarity in industrial progress and the parallel nature of political democracy, one would anticipate similar developments in the United States. Are these European trends a harbinger of the future from which we can anticipate similar or even greater progress here?

The answer is no, certainly not in the European image. The reasons are largely related to cultural and institutional differences that tend to distort the very meaning of the concept of "participation." Causal factors in Europe include:

- Higher rates of unionization in all occupations.
- Strong political affiliations of unions.
- The anticapitalistic philosophy of the more radical union leaders.
- Centralization of collective bargaining, with the virtual absence of company-level participation.
- Relative occupational and social immobility of the labor forces.
- Greater role of government in social policy and in the outcome of collective bargaining.

These European conditions represent differences in the structure of power and the exercise of authority, most of which tend to reduce the level of participation at the company or plant level. Recent trends toward enterprise-level activity are evident but are not widespread enough to change the overall picture. In fact, many Europeans consider American-style collective bargaining at the plant level one of the most advanced forms of participation.

Obstacles to Participation

In addition to the less receptive environment in this nation, America faces internal obstacles to the widespread application of the more advanced concepts of "participation" within the workplace. These obstacles are deep-seated and represent a combination of historical, psychological, and economic factors. The following are among the more serious obstacles:

- Managerial philosophy generally considers worker participation of limited value at any level in the organization. The predominant belief is that the costs outweigh the benefits.
- Because the art of participative management is new, top executives lack experience and know-how in dealing with it.
- The concept is viewed by executives, managers, and supervisors as a threat in terms of conventional power and authority. The problems of managing an increased conflict of ideas and sharing power are frightening to many.
- Impatience to achieve short-term economic gains while dealing with a sensitive new process that requires long-term commitments forecasts at best an uneven pathway to meaningful results.
- Unions are suspicious of the process and fear that it will weaken the adversary relationship, complicate the current problems of collective bargaining, and impose new problems for their memberships.

- There is a shortage of talented third parties who can engender the necessary trust and provide the required know-how to introduce and maintain a participative style of working.
- Broad-based participation threatens the framework of conventional, hierarchical organizations and is seen as topsy-turvy management, which may substitute consensus decision making for one-man rule.

The Future of Participation

American industrial relations are quite different from those of Western Europe. Certain elements of participation already exist here but, by and large, genuine broad-based and advanced ideas for participation in decision making are present in only a handful of organizations. The level of experimentation is growing; especially noteworthy are the major efforts by General Motors, where conditions are among the most difficult.

On balance, when one considers the obstacles that lie ahead, it is difficult to be optimistic and forecast a virtual revolution in managerial styles, with new power-sharing ideas and a new generation of organizations that have adapted themselves to participation as a way of life.

However, we cannot realistically ignore the growing necessity for a greater degree of openness and participation in progressive organizations in the 1980s. There exists a clear danger that employees will continue to respond to "nonparticipation" in a variety of negative ways that are counterproductive to the goals of the enterprise and of society itself.

Opinion Research Corporation has measured employee attitudes since the 1950s among 175,000 managerial, clerical, and hourly employees in 159 firms in eighteen different industries. Its findings indicate that more nonmanagement employees are unhappy with their jobs now than at any other time in the past twenty-five years. Hourly and clerical workers, in particular, have become increasingly dissatisfied with their companies as places in which to work, with the work they do, and with the way they are treated as individuals. In particular, younger and better educated workers with higher expectations are mounting new pressures for greater participation in the industrial decision-making process.

A number of significant economic and sociological factors observable today point to the necessity for greater involvement and participation at work in the future:

1. The permissive society has fostered a change in authority roles. Employees have higher expectations and place intelligent limits on the exercise of authority over their lives.

2. The decline in confidence in business, government, education, and other major institutions has affected employees who are members of such organizations. The relative decline in trust and confidence weakens performance on the job.
3. Changing attitudes toward religion and work reflect the values of a postreligious society, which no longer views work as a punishment that will be rewarded in the afterlife.
4. Less commitment to the work ethic and greater public cynicism have spread to all classes of workers: blue-collar, white-collar, professional, managerial, and executive.
5. The era of rising entitlements has created a widespread feeling that jobs, income, employee benefits, and a higher standard of life are no longer privileges, but rights.
6. Employee expectations for participation in decisions affecting their jobs have reached the point at which a majority consider this a right. Among younger workers, 62 percent expressed this view in 1977.
7. Significant changes in Japan and Western Europe teach us that young American workers are not a peculiar breed and that, for the first time, work must compete with other personal values.
8. The rising educational level of workers, combined with higher cost per employee, creates an economic necessity to secure a better return on the human investment.
9. Growing automation and advanced technology in both office and factory increase the complexity of the interaction between man and machine.
10. Changes in American social values, mores, and folkways have been rapid and penetrating over the past decade. By contrast, large organizations are slow to change. Thus, the institutional lag persists and must be corrected over the decade ahead to bring organizational life into a more harmonious balance with society and its values.

Work is under competitive pressure from other life-styles and interests. The high cost of an educated work force combined with lagging productivity presents a clear necessity to address the new sociology of work and to achieve the goal of greater participation and more active involvement of the work force. This is the most difficult and most important challenge of the future.

DEMOCRACY AT WORK

The modern organization is a total society in microcosm in which employees hold voluntary membership. Living within a free and open democratic political system, the American worker expects conditions within the workplace to be compatible with political and social conditions in other aspects of life.

Current Trends

Let us examine some of the prevailing conditions revealed by a series of polls of American workers taken at selected intervals over more than twenty-five years, beginning prior to 1960, and concluding in 1977. [4]

- Relatively few (17 percent) clerical and hourly workers felt, as of 1977, that they were treated fairly. This was a dramatic drop compared to statistics prior to 1960, when one third of hourly workers and two thirds of clerical employees considered they were treated fairly.
- In the period 1975–1977 about one third of all hourly employees and only about one half of all clerical employees surveyed felt that they were "treated with respect as individuals."
- Managers' attitudes also reflect a sharp decline. Eighty-four percent felt they were treated fairly prior to 1960, a figure that had dropped to 45 percent in 1977—almost a 50 percent decline.
- In 1977 less than one third of hourly employees and only 38 percent of clerical employees felt that their companies were willing to listen to their problems and complaints. Even among managers, only about half appeared to be satisfied in this regard.
- In terms of perceived inequity, as of 1977, about one in five hourly and clerical employees and only half the managers believed that their company selected the best person for the job.

Employee Expectations

Employees are citizens who now are eligible to vote at age 18. They are products of a permissive and affluent society. Their expectations and sense of entitlement have risen faster than the performance of most work institutions. Increasingly, they question authority, believe in the right to dissent, and expect a more open and interactive workplace environment that resembles their life-styles in other areas.

These proper expectations include the right to free speech, the right to privacy, the right to dissent, the right to fair and equitable treatment, and the right to due process in all work-related activities.

Democracy in the workplace does not mean the right of employees to elect supervisors, managers, or executives, for they cannot effectively do so. The "one man, one vote" concept is unworkable in an economic environment in which management and control are confined to the few who have the executive authority and hold the responsibility for the destiny of the entire enterprise. There are those who would carry the concept of industrial democracy to such extremes, but this presupposes an undesirable change in the present laws regarding private property and the capitalist system. This should not be at issue.

The Future of Democracy at Work

During the 1980s American organizations must advance the process of accommodation between economic and political institutions. They cannot grow and thus outdistance the free-world competition for ideas and products if they repress human needs and expectations within their own internal social and political spheres of influence. Such organizations may survive, but they will not thrive.

Leadership within the corporation must elevate its own sights. It must open its ears and its eyes to the internal sounds and sights of the corporate citizens who are voluntary members of the organization. It must engage the ideas and the motivations of its own employees, and it must tap its existing reservoir of talent.

New strategies and new policies are needed to bring the modern enterprise into the 1980s with a clearer vision of the importance of employees and an unequivocal acceptance of their democratic rights and responsibilities. This requires considerable management training, a new style of supervision, less autocracy, the skill to manage dissent, and the patience and confidence to expose power to criticism without unreasonable fear of loss of control.

American workers cannot live a double life—flexibility in the community and rigidity in the workplace. Their reactions may well include withdrawal on the job, resentment, lower performance, dissaffection, and, ultimately, resignation or early retirement. Thus, although the costs to the organization are often concealed, they are, nonetheless, real.

In the final analysis, a response by external political forces may be called for, whereby the federal government continues to expand its role as arbitrator in shaping private employer–employee relations to correspond more closely to public expectations and to the level of democratic values in the society at large.

CONCLUSION

Obstacles to Changes in the Quality of Working Life

The decade of the 1980s will be more susceptible to change in the environment of work than any preceding period. At the same time, these changes will be uneven and continue to lag behind the social changes in society at large, with many obstacles to changing human relationships in the workplace slowing, if not blocking, progress. Since its inception, the Work in America Institute has tracked contemporary trends that reflect management's ability to utilize human resources more effectively and that may be expected to continue to do so during the 1980s. Among the more significant of these trends are the following:

1. Slow economic growth in the mid-1970s has combined with inflation to reduce profit margins and reduce the incentives for capital investment. Major employers, as a result, are preoccupied with decisions concerning capital formation and investment and applications of technology. In such a restrictive economic climate, particularly one in which strong foreign competition is also a major factor, improved work force productivity should not remain a secondary concern. Individual and organizational slack can, in fact, be reduced by tapping individual productivity.
2. Industry has a growing apprehension over government regulation and enforcement of labor and civil-rights legislation. The federal government, in particular, has become a major force with regard to civil rights in the workplace. Personnel policies relating to minorities, women, older workers, veterans, and disabled and handicapped persons are all under increasing government surveillance. Within the past decade, occupational health and safety, pensions, environmental protection, age discrimination, and equal-employment enforcement have all emerged as major issues. In some instances, this legislation has created a "fortress" mentality on the part of management, growing out of their resentment of the bur-

geoning role of government. In other cases it has resulted in confrontation, class-action suits, legal penalties, and bad public relations for the employers involved.

These negative reactions have not been universal, however. Many progressive employers have responded to social and political changes with new programs designed to improve the quality of working life in accordance with the changing spirit of the times.

3. The governance of the corporation is under intensifying public attack. Corporate ethics have become a major issue in the face of revelations of illegal political contributions by more than 400 large corporations. As the debate is mounted, pressure grows to change the composition of the corporate board of directors, most significantly by increased reliance on outside directors. Proposals in Congress would require federal chartering of corporations and appointment of one or more public directors. SEC Chairman Harold Williams has proposed limiting inside full-time directors to one member. A related emerging issue concerns the appointment of worker-directors. At present, neither management nor most labor unions in the United States favor this approach. Yet, the growing popularity of worker-directors in Europe (now a practice in seven nations) is generating considerable uneasiness in American management. We may witness a few experiments here by the mid-1980s.

4. Business organizations are caught in the economic and political crosscurrents of high unemployment, a major slowdown in the rate of productivity growth (to about half of the long-term secular trend), and a growing demand from employees for interesting, productive jobs. Youth, women, and older workers are anxious to enter or remain in the work force, except for those who have strong pensions. This runs counter to the theory that an oversupply of labor produces more cooperative and productive behavior on the part of those who are currently employed. However, educated workers under the pervasive influence of an affluent and permissive society have produced new challenges to authority and developed more subtle expectations. Thus, employers have the problem of managing a new work force, but continue to rely mainly on old methods that reflect old values. If this lag persists through the decade ahead, it will be adverse to both human values and economic performance.

5. Employers are concerned over rising wages, salaries, and benefits.

Although inflation alone has pushed these costs up tremendously, an enriched occupational and skill mix in the work force has also contributed to the upward pressure on overall personnel costs. Thus, the organization focuses more on the economics of work rather than on its psychosocial aspects. This natural preoccupation with the economics of work tends to detract from quality-of-work-life issues which in the long run may prove to offer a more permanent solution to the problem of increasing labor costs.

Effective Programs in the United States

In order to broaden its base of knowledge the Work in America Institute initiated a complete search of the literature for the four-year period 1971–1975, to review U.S. experimentation with worker productivity. This study resulted in the book *A Guide to Worker Productivity Experiments in the United States, 1971–75* by Raymond A. Katzell, Penney Bienstock, and Paul Faerstein.[5] It consists of summaries of 103 experiments aimed at improving productivity. The survey findings bear repeating.

In eighty-five of the experiments favorable effects on one or more aspects of productivity were reported. This indicates that improvement of worker performance, a result that should benefit all segments of society, is attainable through strategies already within our grasp. What kinds of programs had the greatest success? In terms of popularity, of the fourteen categories classified, an old standby, training, was the most frequently cited, followed closely by the more recent strategy of redesigning jobs to increase worker motivation. Evaluating these techniques, the study noted the following:

- Behavioral analysis, identifying for the worker what effective work behavior is, providing occasions to enact it, furnishing prompt and frequent feedback regarding results, and giving material or symbolic rewards contingent on effective performance, appears to be particularly valuable.
- Setting clear and difficult but attainable goals for performance— "Management-by-Objectives" or similar programs—has produced useful results. Like behavioral analysis, goal setting typically requires frequent and prompt feedback.
- Redesign of jobs, either those of individuals or of work teams, often has beneficial effects, but fails in a significant proportion of instances.

Apparently, it is likely to fail unless there is a commitment on the part of all concerned to make it work, unless the program "meshes" with other elements in the system—kinds of workers, technology, labor relations, and so on.

• Compensation continues to have a major influence on worker productivity, particularly when creative ways are devised to make remuneration contingent on performance.

• Wider sharing of responsibility and control for job content among rank-and-file workers usually is found to have positive results in terms of enhanced productivity and quality of working life.

• In this context, organizational structures that integrate functions and decentralize authority show promise.

• Plans to maintain or improve productivity should be approached in terms of all the interrelated psychological, social, technological, economic, and cultural factors that must be balanced if the system is to be effective over the long haul. Productivity programs that work in some situations may fail in others. Therefore, achieving major improvements in productivity requires that each new step be compatible with existing programs.

These findings, of course, are based on a relatively small number of productivity experiments, though they are perhaps the most significant such experiments undertaken during the early 1970s. One important obstacle is that many experiments, successes and failures alike, are not reported in scientific or professional publications. Publicity may be particularly lacking in regard to programs that give the organization a presumed competitive advantage, or where there are other reasons (such as risking a delicate union–management balance) for maintaining a "low profile."

Keys to Successful Programs

In an effort to uncover these unreported experiments, the Work in America Institute's monthly newsletter, *World of Work Report,* has investigated and published, with the cooperation of employers, dozens of outstanding case histories that have generated tangible results for these innovative organizations. Based on these case histories and the institute's experience in quality-of-work-life and productivity programs, the following have been found to be the primary components of successful programs:

1. Improvements in quality of working life that are an integral part of a sound, long-term employee-relations policy, tailored to individual plants or offices.
2. Reform or innovation that does not require substantial capital investment or excessive start-up costs.
3. Changes that are relatively gradual, present limited risks, and can be controlled (or reversed) without major consequences.
4. Cooperative programs that engage the mutual interests of management, unions, and employees and ultimately produce shared economic or other benefits.
5. Increased participation and involvement of employees, without radical surgery on existing production technology.
6. Programs that have top-level direction, an economic motivation, and strong support, based on the premise that in the productivity equation people "count," and that their effectiveness requires constant reinforcement.
7. Changes in the quality of working life that are compatible with the American philosophy of management, but that are also cognizant of and responsive to government regulation and the changing expectations and aspirations of the employed work force.
8. Plants that combine participation, measurement, and openness to maximize the mutual interest of employees and management to increase the effectiveness of the organization.

A Look Ahead

The 1980s promise excitement, challenge, and increased complexity in managing people. The twin goals of productivity and an enhanced quality of working life are attainable, but only for those managers who make the effort.

An accommodation between the organization's goals and the employee's expectations will be more difficult. People will bring a more complex and varied set of needs to the workplace. The workplace itself will impose technological and information demands upon its internal human resources. The aging of the population, the growing role of women, the increased pressures for equality of opportunity, and the rising personal expectations for decent, satisfying, and challenging jobs will all demand an effective response.

Management, labor, and government will each place greater demands on the workplace and these will not always be harmonious. Thus, those who are most imaginative and innovative stand to gain the most in the new environment, whereas those who resist change at every turn are more likely to suffer problems and disappointments.

We have good cause to be optimistic. The nation is rich in its supply of human talent. The political system is open and democratic, constantly buffeted by change, yet constantly adapting to new economic and social conditions. Our economic system is strong and resilient too; it will accommodate to the energy problem and go on providing an improved standard of life. And our work institutions, which have contributed so much to the advancement of the national welfare, will continue to be a source of productive achievement. In the decade ahead, one of the nation's greatest challenges will be to advance the quality of working life, while at the same time nurturing a healthy work ethic and using human resources productively.

NOTES

1. *Productivity and Job Security: Attrition—Benefits and Problems* (Washington, D.C.: National Center for Productivity and Quality of Working Life, 1977), p. 5.
2. *Adjusting Hours to Increase Jobs,* National Commission for Manpower Policy, Special Report No. 15 (Washington, D.C.: U.S. Government Printing Office, 1977).
3. Yankelovich, Skelly and White, Inc., Corporate Priorities, "The New Worker," *Briefings for Management* (November 16, 1977).
4. Opinion Research Corporation, *Public Opinion Index* 35 (mid-September 1977).
5. Raymond A. Katzell, Penney Bienstock, and Paul H. Faerstein, *A Guide to Worker Productivity Experiments in the United States: 1971–75*, Work in America Institute, Inc. (New York: New York University Press, 1977).

10.
Productivity Trends and Prospects

JEROME A. MARK
Assistant Commissioner For Productivity and Technology
Bureau of Labor Statistics
Washington, D.C.

Over the last three decades, productivity, as measured by output per hour of all persons, grew slightly less than 3 percent per year for the private-business sector of the economy. During the last ten years, however, the rate has fallen dramatically, and the question of whether this falloff reflects a new pattern of productivity growth for the U.S. economy or a temporary phenomenon is of great importance in assessing the prospects for the future growth of the economy.

Productivity growth has accounted for over half the growth in real output and has contributed to the realization by the American people of improved living standards, better medical care, longer schooling, and a strong national defense. It has also been important in providing a source for wage increases and other costs to companies, such as benefits, to temper the effect of the increase in prices. As such, productivity improvement plays a key role in stabilizing the economy. It is useful, therefore, to try to assess what the outlook for productivity growth will be. In keeping with the frame of reference of this volume, this discussion centers on the next decade.

Trends in productivity reflect, among other things, changes in technology, changes in the quality and composition of the labor force, changes in the rate and kind of capital investment, and changes in the industrial composition of employment and output. Another important element is the impact of short-term cyclical influences such as changes in the degree of capacity utilization. The complexity of these factors and their interactions, as well as the limitations of the data concerning them, creates uncertainties about any set of productivity projections. Any assessment of the outlook for productivity growth involves examining current and historical movements of these factors and their impact, attempting to separate the transitory factors from the more permanent ones, and evaluating future prospects for the long-term factors in order to make some judgments on future changes in productivity.

This chapter analyzes current and longer term movements of productivity, particularly labor productivity; examines some of the factors associated with the productivity trends; and explores the outlook for these factors and their possible impact on productivity growth over the next decade.

The conclusions drawn with regard to productivity trends are that there has been a slowdown in productivity growth over the last decade, which, in part, was the result of cyclical factors. However, longer term factors were operative, some of which contributed to the slowdown, such as changes in the composition of the work force and changes in the industrial composition of the private sector. On the other hand, several factors often cited as sources of the slowdown, such as the shift to services and changes in the capital intensity of the economy, in my view, have not played a large role.

I believe that over the next decade productivity will increase at a somewhat lower rate than it has during the past thirty years, but at a substantially higher rate than it has in the most recent decade. Some of the factors reflected in the continued slowdown are the end of the shift in employment from the farm to the nonfarm sector and, initially at least, the impact of additional investment set aside for pollution and safety and health requirements and the need to invest in energy-saving or conversion facilities because of higher energy costs. Some of the factors contributing to accelerated growth are an expected increase in the importance of more experienced age groups in the labor force and further improvements in the capital–labor ratio in the private sector.

In making these assessments, certain assumptions are implicit concerning the political and economic climate during this period. In general, it is assumed that the institutional framework of the American economy will not change radically and that no major cataclysm, such as war, which would disrupt, destroy, or radically alter institutional arrangements, will take place. It is also assumed that current economic and social trends will continue, including values placed on work, education, income, and leisure. Much has been written about a changing work ethic and its impact on productivity, but it is almost impossible to ascertain the extent to which this tendency has permeated society, and it is hazardous to attempt to place quantitative judgments on the impact on overall productivity growth.

HISTORICAL MOVEMENTS

As mentioned earlier, labor productivity as measured by output per hour of all persons in the private-business sector[1] rose from 1947 (the first full year largely free of the immediate post-World War II adjustments) through 1977 at a rate of 2.8 percent per year. However, this average reflects a much sharper rate of gain during the first two decades than during the last. From 1947 to 1967 the rate was 3.2 percent per year, but from 1967 to 1977 the rate dropped by one half to 1.6 percent per year, a very substantial decline. During the latter period, the economy experienced two recessions, one complete recovery, and one almost complete recovery, so that the decline in productivity growth is partly attributable to cyclical functions.

Although by 1977 productivity had surpassed its record in the peak year of 1975, it had not sufficiently recovered from the sharp decline which occurred during the 1974 recession to reach the level that would have been attained had even the low 1966–1973 growth rate (2.0 percent) continued, let alone the longer-term secular rate.

The major sectors that comprise the private-business economy experienced widely varied rates of productivity growth. The farm sector had an extraordinarily high rate of productivity growth over the three-decade period (5.4 percent), more than twice the growth rate of the nonfarm sector as a whole (2.4 percent). In addition, the falloff in farm productivity growth since 1967 (to 4.8 percent) was not as substantial as that of the rest of the economy. Nonfarm business productivity growth fell from a rate of 2.6 percent in the 1947–1967 period to 1.4 percent per year since 1967.

Within the nonfarm sector, communications and transportation industries experienced higher than average growth rates; business and personal services had lower than average growth rates.

The pervasiveness of the slackening in productivity growth since 1967, however, is apparent from Table 1. More than two thirds of the specific industries for which productivity measures are currently available had lower rates of productivity gain in the latter period.

TABLE 1.   Average Annual Rates of Change in Output per Employee-Hour for Selected Industries, 1947–1966 and 1966–1976 .

Industry	1947–1966	1966–1976
Mining		
Iron mining, usable ore	3.8	0.8
Copper mining, recoverable metal	3.6	−0.2
Coal mining	6.6	−3.5
Bituminous coal and lignite mining	6.8	−3.6
Nonmetallic minerals	4.1[a]	2.3
Crushed and broken stone	3.9[b]	3.6
Manufacturing		
Canning and preserving	2.7	3.2
Grain mill products	4.0[c]	2.9[d]
Flour and other grain mill products	4.0	2.0
Cereal breakfast foods	2.0[c]	1.2[d]
Rice milling	8.5[c]	1.3[d]
Blended and prepared flour	4.7[c]	1.4[d]
Wet corn milling	2.1[c]	5.3[d]
Prepared feeds for animals and fowls	4.1[c]	3.4[d]
Bakery products	2.0	1.8
Sugar	4.6	1.5
Candy and confectionery products	3.5	4.7
Malt beverages	4.3	6.7
Bottled and canned soft drinks	2.2[b]	3.2
Tobacco products—total	3.7	1.7
Cigarettes, chewing and smoking tobacco	1.4	1.3
Cigars	6.6	2.7
Hosiery	4.8	8.7
Sawmills and planing mills, general	3.5[b]	2.1
Paper, paperboard, and pulp mills	3.9	3.5
Corrugated and solid-fiber boxes	3.2[b]	4.5
Synthetic fibers	4.1[e]	8.1
Pharmaceutical preparations	5.0[c]	4.8
Paints and allied products	3.7[b]	2.5
Petroleum refining	5.9	3.1
Tires and inner tubes	4.2	2.3
Footwear	1.9	0.4
Glass containers	1.3	2.2
Hydraulic cement	4.7	1.7
Structural clay	3.3[b]	3.5
Clay construction products	3.1[b]	3.5
Clay refractories	4.0[b]	3.3
Concrete products	3.2	1.9[d]
Ready-mixed concrete	2.3[b]	1.4[d]
Steel	1.7	1.8

Table 1.   (Continued)

Industry	1947–1966	1966–1976
Gray iron foundries	2.4[a]	2.6
Steel foundries	1.8[a]	1.9
Primary copper, lead, and zinc	2.6	2.3
Primary aluminum	5.3	1.2
Copper rolling and drawing	6.7[b]	−0.5
Aluminum rolling and drawing	6.6[b]	5.8
Metal cans	2.5	1.7
Major household appliances	6.8[b]	4.6
Radio and television receiving sets	6.1[b]	3.2
Motor vehicles and equipment	4.8[e]	3.4
Other		
Railroads, revenue traffic	4.6	3.4
Intercity trucking	2.8[a]	2.3[d]
Intercity trucking (general freight)	2.4[a]	2.0[f]
Air transportation	7.9	4.4
Petroleum pipelines	9.6[b]	6.0
Telephone communications	7.2[g]	5.6
Gas and electric utilities	7.3	3.6
Retail food stores	3.1[b]	0.8
Franchised new-car dealers	2.5[b]	2.5
Gasoline service stations	2.8[b]	4.3
Eating and drinking places	0.9[b]	0.5
Hotels and motels	2.7[b]	1.3

Source: Bureau of Labor Statistics.

[a]1954–1966.
[b]1958–1966.
[c]1963–1966.
[d]1966–1975.
[e]1957–1966.
[f]1966–1974.
[g]1951–1966.

REASONS FOR THE SLOWDOWN AND PROSPECTS FOR THE FUTURE

Much attention has been focused on the reduction in productivity growth in recent years. A number of economists have advanced explanations that include the effects of shifts in the industrial composition of the economy; changes in the composition of the labor force; an apparent slowdown in improvements in the capital–labor ratio in American industry; the leveling off of research and development expenditures in the early 1960s; the diversion of investment to pollution-abatement expenditures; the maturation of many industries with little new technology; and changes in attitudes toward work, toward employers, and toward society.

There is no simple explanation for the decline, and there is no general agreement as to the quantitative impact of these various factors. Indeed, if they were aggregated in some fashion, they might "overexplain" the slowdown. Moreover, it is difficult to separate the effects of these longer term factors from those of the short-term cyclical factors that took place during the same period.

Productivity growth has not yet recovered sufficiently to reach the extrapolated 1973 level. The movements since that year have been dominated by short-term cyclical forces.[2] In trying to assess the direction of productivity growth over the future, some allowance must be made for the continued recovery from 1973 when longer term factors were more dominant.

Changes in the Quality and Composition of the Work Force

Over the long term, one of the important sources of growth in output per hour has been the changes that have occurred in the average quality of the work force as indicated by changes in education. Educational background affects the type of work an individual is able to perform and his or her proficiency in that type of work. Therefore, changes in the average educational level of the work force can affect the productivity of the economy. An upward shift in the educational background of the U.S. work force has contributed greatly to the increase in productivity over the last three decades. Various attempts have been made to assess the impact of educational upgrading on productivity, using earnings differentials to reflect productivity differences. Most estimates have shown a strong positive effect. For example, Denison has estimated that the increase in education has contributed as much as 0.5 percentage point per year to the growth in nonresidential business national income per person from 1948 to 1969.[3] He also concludes that within that period there was no decrease in the contribution of education to productivity. From 1948 to 1964 Denison estimates that education contributed 0.48 percentage point and from 1964 to 1969, 0.53 percentage point.

In recent years, however, there has been some concern as to whether or not the increase in education can continue and further aid productivity growth. There are a few indications that a decline in the contribution of increased education to productivity growth has already set in. For example, the greater difficulties experienced by college graduates in locating positions in recent years and an apparently reduced differential in earnings and implied marginal productivity would support that conclusion. However, there is great difficulty in separating permanent secular changes from short-term fluctuations in relationships associated with cyclical changes in demand. At present, insufficient data are available to substantiate the conclusion that there has been a reduced impact of educational changes on productivity growth. In fact, after examining the limited data from the *Current Population Survey* from 1967 through 1974 on mean earnings of men by education and age, Denison has concluded that virtually no narrowing of earnings differential and, hence, reduced impact on productivity, has occurred. [4]

Undoubtedly, education cannot continue to increase and contribute to productivity growth indefinitely as it has in the past, but I would be inclined to agree with Denison, who feels the decline will be very gradual with a reduced impact amounting to 0.1 percentage point over the next decade.

Changes in the age–sex composition of the work force, however, have been substantial in the period from 1966 to 1976, and many researchers have attributed much of the decline in productivity growth to this shift. [5] The rate of growth in the labor force rose substantially in the late 1960s, and the proportion of young people rose very sharply as persons born during the baby-boom era of the early post-World War II period began to enter the labor force. Also, labor-force participation by women rose significantly after 1966 and abruptly in more recent years. New entrants typically are less productive because they lack experience, and women, at least traditionally, are less productive because they are concentrated in less productive occupations. Depending on the assumptions made and estimating techniques followed, measures of the effects of combined age–sex compositional changes vary somewhat, but the results indicate a significant contribution to the deceleration of productivity. In general, estimates of the incremental effect of these changes on reducing productivity growth average from 0.2 to 0.3 percentage point per year—approximately 12 to 18 percent of the decline in the productivity growth rate.

Over the next decade, the expected changes in the composition of the labor force should have a positive influence on productivity growth. First,

the postwar baby-boom cohort will have been almost completely absorbed. Bureau of Labor Statistics projections of the growth and composition of the labor force are that it should grow at an annual rate of 1.9
percent in the latter half of the 1970s and only 1.3 percent during the
1980s.[6] This is in sharp contrast to the rate of increase of 2.2 percent during the last half of the 1960s and first half of the 1970s. Behind this slowdown is a sharp drop in the birthrate of the 1960s, which means that there
will be fewer youths reaching working age in the 1980s. On the other
hand, the prime age group, composed of persons aged 25–44, should
grow more rapidly over the next decade—2.2 percent per year during the
late 1970s and 2.5 percent in the first half of the 1980s. The proportion of
the labor force accounted for by prime workers is expected to increase
from 61 percent in 1975 to 65 percent in 1985. As a greater proportion of
workers enter the more experienced and more productive higher age
groups, productivity may be expected to rise.

Another reason for the positive effects of the expected shift in the composition of the work force is that, although the increase in the participation rate of women will continue, it will also be primarily in the central
age groups. Moreover, the proportion of women entering semiskilled,
skilled, and professional occupations is expected to increase as entrance
barriers are reduced over the next decade.

Shifts in Industrial Composition

The overall trend of productivity for the private sector reflects both
changes in the productivity of component sectors and industries and shifts
in the relative importance of sectors with different levels of output per
hour. Thus, even if there is no change in productivity in any industry, the
overall productivity rate can still change if there is a shift in resources
from areas of low productivity to areas of high productivity.

Over much of the last three decades, there has been a marked shift of
labor from the farm to the nonfarm sector. Since the level of output per
hour was much lower in agriculture than in most nonfarm industries, this
shift contributed to the overall rise in productivity. Most of this shift occurred before 1966. From 1947 to 1966 about 0.4 percentage point of the
3.2 percent growth rate for the private-business economy, more than 12
percent of the total, came from the shift. In 1947 over 19 percent of the
total hours of all persons in the private-business sector were in agriculture. By 1966 only 7 percent were in agriculture.

However, since 1966 the percentage has dropped only to 5 percent so that the shift effect accounted for only 0.1 percentage point of the productivity trend in the last decade. Thus, a significant part of the reduced rate of productivity growth since 1966 has resulted from the ending of this movement from the farms.

Because agriculture now represents a smaller and relatively stable proportion of the work force and because the productivity levels for the farm and nonfarm sectors are now much closer than they had been, it is doubtful that any discernable gains in overall productivity growth from this shift of resources will occur.

Within the nonfarm business sector, shifts among major sectors have had virtually no impact on productivity change. From 1947 to 1966 there was absolutely no overall effect on the productivity growth rate of any such shifts, and since 1966 the effect has been to reduce nonfarm business productivity growth by less than 0.1 percentage point.

Table 2. Effect of Shifts in Industry Composition (Average Annual Percent Change).*

Period	Total Productivity Change	Effect of Productivity Growth within Sectors	Effect of Shifts in Hours among Sectors
Private-Business Sector Farm-to-Nonfarm Shift Only			
1947–1977	2.81	2.47	0.34
1947–1966	3.36	2.91	0.45
1966–1977	1.86	1.74	0.12
Nonfarm Business Sector Shift to Services—Narrowly Defined†			
1947–1976	2.36	2.37	−0.01
1947–1966	2.80	2.80	0.00
1966–1976	1.52	1.54	−0.02
Shift to Services—Broadly Defined‡			
1947–1976	2.36	2.35	0.01
1947–1966	2.80	2.80	0.00
1966–1976	1.52	1.48	0.04

*Growth rates calculated on the basis of compound rates over terminal periods.

†Business and personal services only.

‡Broadly defined services include transportation, communications; public utilities; finance, insurance, and real estate; wholesale and retail trade; business and personal services; and government enterprises. Nonservices, then, consist of mining, construction, and manufacturing.

Source: Bureau of Labor Statistics, U.S. Department of Labor.

The shift of employment and hours to services as a whole has often been cited as a major source of the productivity slowdown, because services have been increasing in importance and are characterized by lower-than-average labor productivity. There are, however, various ways of defining the service sector—either very narrowly, to include only business and personal services, or very broadly, to include all noncommodity-producing sectors, such as trade, transportation, communications, utilities, finance, as well as business and personal services. In either case, the shift to services can be viewed only as a very minor source of the slowdown in the rate of productivity growth in the private sector. Table 2 shows the effects of these shifts on productivity growth for the private-business sector as a whole. As can be seen, under the narrow definition, the effect was very slightly negative, less than 0.1 percent for the three decades. Although there is substantial difference between the measured productivity levels of business and personal services and the other sectors, the relative importance of this sector is small, 6 percent of the private-business sector, and did not affect the total rate significantly.

Using the broad definition, to include the other sectors, the effect was also small, but it was positive—0.1 percent. In this case, although the importance of the service component was large (51 percent), the difference in the productivity level of the service versus the nonservice components was not as great.

Therefore, the impact of the shift to services has not been important as a determinant for the deceleration of the productivity growth rate in the private sector. Since much of the shift to services has been to state and local government employment, the effect on productivity growth for the total economy, that is, private plus public sectors, could be greater.[7]

As to the future, it would appear that additional movement of employees to the service type of industries will not have any appreciable effects on the growth of productivity. However, taken together, the effects of intersectoral shifts imply an expected productivity growth rate about 0.3 percentage point lower than the long-term growth rate has been, primarily because of the end of movement from the farm to the nonfarm sector.

Changes in the Capital—Labor Ratio

Historically, a major source of the growth in output per hour has been the increase in the capital stock that the labor force has had available to generate increased output. Over the last three decades real capital stock has grown at a rate of 3.0 percent per year in the private-business sector.[8]

Labor input, as measured by the number of persons employed, has risen only 1.0 percent per year, so that the stock of capital per worker over the entire period has been increasing at a rate of 2.0 percent per year. Because of the decline in annual hours per person, the capital–labor ratio in terms of aggregate hours shows a somewhat higher increase, 2.4 percent per year.

Within the period, however, the increase of total capital stock was greater in the last decade than in the preceding two. When total capital stock is disaggregated into its equipment and structure components, each of them shows accelerating growth rates in the latter decade.

Hours also grew at a higher rate in the decade 1966–1976 and for the private-business economy tended to match the acceleration in capital stock. The capital–labor ratio grew at almost the same rate from 1966 to 1976 as it did from 1947 to 1966 in the total private-business sector. However, in nonfarm business and manufacturing, because the increase in rate of growth of capital stock exceeded the increase in the rate of growth of hours, the capital–labor ratios actually accelerated in the latter decade. Thus, production in the private-business economy not only continued to increase in capital intensity during the period of the productivity downturn, it actually did so at a faster rate in the nonfarm business and manufacturing sectors.

Table 3 separates the change in labor productivity into the portion associated with changes in the capital–labor ratio and the portion associated with changes in output per unit of capital. As can be seen, whether on a gross or net basis, the change in labor productivity associated with the change in the capital–labor ratio was virtually the same in private business in the first two decades as it was the last. In nonfarm business and manufacturing, the growth in productivity associated with growth in the capital–labor ratio was actually higher. The decline in labor productivity growth reflects the reversal in capital productivity growth and the factors underlying that change.

The outlook for capital formation per hour in the next decade is uncertain because of difficulties in projecting investment. The expected growth in labor input alone, however, should lead to further acceleration of the capital intensity in industry. As mentioned earlier, the labor force is projected to grow at a substantially lower rate than it has over the last decade. Consequently, if the capital stock growth rate that prevailed over the entire three decades should continue, the ratio of capital to labor would accelerate, contributing positively to labor productivity growth.

Table 3.   Effect of Changes in the Capital-to-Labor Ratio on Output per Hour of All Persons in the Private-Business Sector.

Period	Productivity Change	Gross Capital Stock Attributed to:			Net Capital Stock Attributed to:		
		Capital–Labor Ratio	Output–Capital Ratio	Inter-action	Capital–Labor Ratio	Output–Capital Ratio	Inter-action
1947–1966	3.4	2.5	1.0	−0.1	3.0	0.5	−0.1
1966–1976	1.8	2.6	−0.8	−0.1	2.7	−0.8	−0.1

Source: Bureau of Labor Statistics, U.S. Department of Labor.

The amount of business fixed investment likely to be generated over the next decade under the existing structure of tax laws and economic incentives is difficult to predict. The projections of the Bureau of Labor Statistics on the percentage of GNP devoted to investment show it rising from 10.7 percent in 1973 to 11.3 percent in 1985.[9]

Kendrick, in an assessment of the outlook for tangible capital formation, concludes that the rate of increase in real stocks of capital after the 1973–1975 contraction should approximate past trends, if after-tax rates of return are restored to a normal range.[10] These projections support the expectation that the growth rate of the capital–labor ratio should continue to increase and have a positive effect on productivity growth.

The Council of Economic Advisors, in examining the question of capital adequacy, commissioned the Bureau of Economic Analysis to conduct a study of the capital that would be required to achieve a real output level consistent with full employment in 1980. The capital stock necessary was assumed to include facilities to meet present environmental and safety standards. The ratio of required investment to GNP from 1971 to 1980 was raised to 11.4 percent—higher than the 10.4 percent ratio that prevailed from 1971 to 1974. On the other hand, the general historical trend over much of the last three decades has been toward a gradually increasing share of GNP devoted to investment, and the projected proportion is in line with the growth in the ratio that has prevailed.

An increased proportion of GNP devoted to fixed investment would result in a reduction in the average age of the capital stock. The meeting of these needs would result in an additional contribution to productivity, since the greater proportion of newer capital would incorporate more recent technological changes.

At the same time, an increase in the amount of investment related to environmental antipollution standards, occupational safety and health standards, and energy conservation has taken place and will continue to occur for some time over the next decade. These investments would have a retarding effect on productivity growth since the outputs of these activities are not reflected in productivity. It could have accounted for some part of the deceleration in productivity growth in that, although the capital–labor ratio continued to grow, it was related in part to the use of the increased capital stock for activities that did not directly result in final output.

A rough assessment of the direct impact on industries having the largest air- and water-pollution problems was made recently in a Bureau of Labor Statistics study.[11] These industries were identified by the Environmental Protection Agency and accounted for 11 percent of total nonfarm employment. To establish some indication of the impact, an arbitrary assumption was made that the productivity growth rates in these industries had been cut in half. The resulting effect on the productivity growth for the nonfarm sector was to reduce it by only 0.12 percentage point.

However, in recent years, particularly since 1973, the impact on productivity growth has been much greater with regard to increased expenditures, including capital expenditures, on pollution control, occupational safety and health regulations, and crime control. Denison has estimated that from 1948 to 1969 the effect of these factors on productivity change was only 0.02 percentage point. From 1969 to 1975, however, the cost of the three determinants subtracted 0.26 percentage point from the growth rate in output per unit of input, and from 1973 to 1975 the cost of these factors subtracted 0.47 percentage point.[12] This measurement does not take into account the objectives of these expenditures, such as the improvement in the quality of life.

CONCLUSIONS

After examining the effect of the various factors contributing to the decline in productivity growth in the last decade, some general observations can be made concerning the direction and effect of these factors on future productivity growth. First, part of the slowdown was associated with cyclical factors, and some of the growth in productivity over the next few years should reflect continued recovery from the last recession.

Second, a significant part of the reduction in the productivity growth rate was attributable to the end of the farm–nonfarm shift—about 0.3

percentage point of the 1.6-percentage-point decline. Productivity growth in the future will not have the contribution that arose from this source. Other intersectoral shifts had a minor effect on productivity growth, and there is no reason to suspect this would change.

Third, little, if any, of the slowdown in productivity growth could be attributed to changes in the rate of capital formation and in the growth rate of the capital–labor ratio. In recent years, the capital formation devoted to pollution control, occupational safety and health regulation, and crime control has increased, and this has reduced the productivity growth that would have taken place. However, if expected reductions in the growth rate of the labor force materialize over the next decade and if capital formation continues at the relatively stable rate that it has for much of the last three decades, there should be a positive effect on productivity growth from this source.

Finally, the prospect for the effects of changing labor-force composition on productivity growth over the next decade is positive. The postwar baby-boom cohort will have been completely absorbed, and the greater predominance of the more experienced age groups should contribute to greater productivity growth. In addition, with increased participation rates, the movement of women into more productive occupations should also aid in this growth, in contrast to the effects of the employment of women over the last decade.

In summary, it would seem that productivity growth during the next decade, the late 1970s through the mid-1980s, will be stronger than it was during the past decade, reflecting some continuation of cyclical expansion and the mitigation of many of the factors depressing productivity growth after 1966. However, it is doubtful that it will return to the rate of the two decades prior to 1966. This observation rests in large part on the expectations relating to the factors associated with the downturn and on the continuation of the impact of changing technology on overall productivity growth.

These expectations could change and productivity growth could be increased if public and private policies having a positive effect on productivity growth were strengthened. Since productivity gains depend in large part on increased investment in the education and quality of the labor force, in the amount and quality of the capital stock, and in the application of new technology, policies stimulating these factors could be effective in enhancing productivity growth rates. For example, given the importance of capital formation on productivity growth, the adoption of tax programs and development of savings incentives to accelerate the growth in real capital stock could strengthen the growth of productivity.

Similarly, programs aimed at the development of new technology and its application could be effective. Although the linkage between research and development and applied technology is by no means clear, the establishment of incentives for further research (particularly applied research) could reverse the decline in the percentage of GNP devoted to research and development and, in turn, stimulate new technology.

Many programs for both the private and public sectors suggested by the National Commission and later the National Center for Productivity and Quality of Working Life could also alter these expectations. (The National Center for Productivity and Quality of Working Life was dissolved in September 1978 at the completion of the authorization period.) These programs not only encompass the development of human and capital resources and improvements in technology, but also the institutional arrangements under which production is generated. For example, in its statement on national policy, the center said that "greater cooperation between labor and management offers significant and largely untapped potential for increasing productivity in all sectors of the economy."[13] It also supported an "open exchange of ideas between labor and management occurring outside the formal collective bargaining process, and in a nonadversary environment."[14] The formation of labor–management committees, which attempt to solve such problems as how to improve performance; how to eliminate excessive waste of energy, materials, supplies, or equipment; how to avoid equipment breakdowns and improve product quality; and how to enhance worker satisfaction, is an example of this type of exchange.

Another area in which programs for improvement can be introduced involves government regulation. An examination of many government rules, standards, and requirements that currently may be impeding productivity growth could possibly lead to some improvements. The problems of assessing the trade-off between various social and economic goals, finding approaches to improving the efficiency of our regulatory processes, and finding ways to accommodate those who have legitimate vested interests in regulations that might otherwise be considered counterproductive are matters that require extensive and informed deliberations.

NOTES

1. The private-business sector excludes the activities of general government, private households, and nonprofit institutions.
2. In a recent econometric study of productivity change since 1973 Connor and Gough substantiate this observation by concluding that their tests show "no evidence to support arguments for a cyclically adjusted productivity slowdown within the last four years." James Connor and Robert Gough, "Another Productivity Slowdown?" *The Data Resources Review of the U.S. Economy* (November 1977): 115.
3. Edward F. Denison, *Accounting for United States Economic Growth, 1929–1969* (Washington, D.C.: The Brookings Institution, 1974), pp. 114, 118.
4. Edward F. Denison, "Some Factors Influencing Future Productivity Growth," in *The Future of Productivity* (Washington, D.C.: National Center for Productivity and Quality of Working Life, 1977.).
5. George Perry, "Labor Structure, Potential Output and Productivity," Brookings Papers on Economic Activity, 1971; and more recently, Frank M. Gollop and Dale W. Jorgenson, "Measuring Total Factor Inputs in U.S. Industry," Conference on Research in Income and Wealth, National Bureau of Economic Research, Williamsburg, Virginia, 1975.
6. Howard N. Fullerton, Jr., and Paul O. Flaim, "New Labor Force Projections to 1990," *Monthly Labor Review* (December 1976).
7. At the present time there are no official measures of productivity for the total economy—that is, including both the private and public sectors—because of the difficulties of measuring government output.
8. As measured by gross capital stock, net capital stock, which excludes depreciation, shows a 3.5 percent per year rate of gain.
9. Jerome A. Mark, Ronald E. Kutscher, and John R. Norsworthy, "Productivity Outlook to 1985: Summary of BLS Productivity Projections," in *The Future of Productivity* (Washington, D.C.: National Center for Productivity and Quality of Working Life, 1977).
10. John W. Kendrick, "Productivity Trends and Prospects," in *U.S. Economic Growth for 1976 to 1986: Prospects, Problems and Patterns,* Volume 1, Joint Economic Committee, Congress of the United States, October 1, 1966, p. 14.
11. Mark, Kutscher, and Norsworthy, *op. cit.*
12. Edward F. Denison, "Effects of Selected Changes in the Institutional and Human Environment Upon Output per Unit of Input," *Survey of Current Business* (January 1978).
13. *A National Policy for Productivity Improvement* (Washington, D.C.: National Commission on Productivity and Quality of Working Life, 1975), p. 14.
14. *Ibid.*
15. *Ibid.*, p. 32.

11.

The Impact of Changing Technology on the Working Environment

WICKHAM SKINNER

James E. Robison Professor of Business Administration
Graduate School of Business Administration
Harvard University

In the 1980s technological changes will undoubtedly affect working environments massively, powerfully, often unpredictably, often perniciously. In these ways, technology will run according to form. Nevertheless, some new forces may begin to alter the consistent historical pattern, a pattern in which technology has been an irresistible prime mover that inevitably defines working tasks and working environments.

Many companies have recently begun to try to manage this process instead of simply letting it happen. As they do, and as the purposes for which technology is developed expand, these companies are likely to have an increasing variety of technologies from which to choose. For example, the need for technologies that save materials and energy is rising relative to the traditional labor-saving motive. At the same time, management assumptions, values, and techniques may be shifting in the direction of no longer taking for granted that the quality of working life (QWL) must be subordinated to the choice of equipment and process.

These are interesting developments with potentially far-reaching consequences. But they are new, and their imminence and future impact are both uncertain, so that, as we look ahead, some important questions arise. Can industrial managers cushion or manage the impact of technological change for the benefit of working environments, and how? Are there inherently inevitable and difficult choices between equipment and process technologies (EPTs) that benefit the working environment, and EPTs that are more productive and economical? Finally, can technological de-

204

velopment be influenced or managed in order to produce EPTs which improve the working environment and QWL?*

In trying to look ahead a decade, we must form some judgment on these questions. But the subject described by the title is a complex one even before facing these challenging questions. Its complexity derives from the many interdependent issues that are involved. For example, what technological changes will take place? How will these changes bear on the working environment? What is the process by which technology affects the work environment? When these impacts take place, what will be the result? To begin to get at these issues, this chapter first focuses on the basic relationship between a firm's equipment and process technology and its working environment.

TECHNOLOGY AND THE WORKPLACE

A given EPT places demands on a company's operating policies and practices which are often rather difficult to overcome. For example, a plant using a basic oxygen steel process is apt to be a hot, noisy, and potentially dangerous place in which to work. In an oil refinery, where most work involves a team effort, an individualized incentive pay scheme would be hard to develop. And in a clothing factory, rich, broad jobs, such as making entire shirts, are hard to arrange. Jobs tend to become specialized because shirts have so many parts, making it difficult to keep them separated by size and fabric, and because the sewing operations are so varied. These kinds of constraints, by and large, have made the working environment dependent on technology throughout industrial history. But more is involved in the quality of working life.

A steel mill is a different place in which to work than an electronics plant, that is clear enough. But working in a computer factory for Honeywell might be perceived by some workers as quite different from working in a computer factory for Burroughs, because although the two companies (let us assume) may be using the same EPTs, a worker might feel

---

*Throughout this chapter, I use "working environment" and QWL (quality of working life) nearly interchangeably, but with the implicit intention that QWL is a value judgment (by workers or anyone else making the judgment) of the working environment. The term "working environment" represents all that a worker observes and feels at his/her workplace including the job tasks, physical conditions, the impact of the supervisor, unions, colleagues, pay schemes, pay rate, controls, work rules, pressures, and discretion, to name a few examples.

that one of these plants had "nicer people, a better pay system, kind and understanding supervisors, more chances to use one's judgment, or more interesting jobs."

So the QWL depends not only on the EPT, but on what I will call "operating policies and practices," that is, the web of procedures, such as work rules and pay systems, followed in the factory. A "good" EPT with "poor" operating policies and practices might not make a good working environment, and vice versa. The working environment, therefore, is a function of both the EPT and the resulting network of operating policies and procedures, which must be designed and managed so as to be internally consistent with and supportive of the EPT.

Because of the EPT's influence on operating policies and practices, as well as its impact on jobs and the workplace, the process of choosing an EPT can also change in the future. This choice is a management decision process depending on the premises, ideology, and strategy of the company on the one hand and the available technological alternatives (and management's awareness of these alternatives) on the other. Since the development of new technology depends partly on the needs and demands of business, informed managers, who are beginning to make the quality of working life a criterion in choosing EPTs, may influence the efforts and directions of scientists and engineers who design technology.

Any and all of these actors, factors, and processes will influence QWL during a decade of changing technology. And to add just one more variable, the quality of a work environment is a human perception dependent on each worker's personal sense of what makes a good working life. Exhibit 1 attempts a simple graphical picture of the dynamics of these elements in a changing work environment.

Our assignment is the decade ahead, but we must first see what we can learn from the past. The balance of this chapter discusses conventional and present practices first, then the future, and finally puts the two together for some conclusions.

HOW TECHNOLOGY AFFECTS THE WORKING ENVIRONMENT

Basic to the study of technology's impact on future working environments is an understanding of the mechanisms by which technology has affected jobs and work in the past.

Equipment and process technology has been the prime determinant of working environments for several fundamental reasons. The first is the pervasive effect of an EPT on the whole operating system. The second is

Exhibit 1.   Technological change and the working environment.

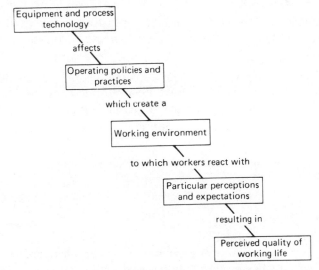

that the process of developing and selecting from the stock of existing technologies has generally left the working environment as a dependent variable. The third reason is that, until very recently, operating policies and practices have not been developed to cushion or modify the impact of an EPT.

Because a given equipment and process technology creates demands on and requirements for all other elements of an operating system, all parts of the system must be designed and managed to be congruent and compatible with the chosen EPT. The choice of EPT is, therefore, normally the primary determinant of every operating system, and its influence pervades the system.

Since most products can be manufactured in more than one way, choices generally exist in the selection of the equipment and the process. Once a new choice is made, however, virtually every element in the superseded production system is apt to change. At the center is the workplace, where the technological changes are physical and tangible. Changes then ripple out into the entire system, the institution, and sometimes an entire industry.

The pervasive impact of equipment and process technology is illustrated by the differences between plastics-molding technology and metalworking. Making flashlights of plastic instead of metal, for example, is entirely different for the worker, the supervisor, and all support groups.

The ordinary flashlight casing may be made in many ways. One would be by drawing metal out in a tubular shape on a press using a die, another by molding plastic resin by injection. Exhibit 2 suggests the different skills, the management systems, and the operating problems demanded by a metal-flashlight-casing operation compared to a plastic-based one. Two distinctions are particularly striking. The first is that the scheduling and inventory-control system is vastly more complex in the metalworking plant, where several operations must be performed on the same part. Paperwork is necessary to take care of parts moved from machine to machine, and capacity must be planned and scheduled. In plastics, with

Exhibit 2. Contrasting production systems for manufacturing a flashlight casing: metal versus plastic.

	Metal Drawing	Plastic Molding
Equipment	Punch press	Injection molding machine
Raw materials	Metal sheets	Plastic resin pellets
Tools	Die set—male or female	Split halves of a mold
Building	Heavy foundations to handle weight and impact	Ordinary floor
Manufacturing engineering	Mechanical, metal expertise	Plastics, hydraulics expertise
Maintenance	Mechanical, hydraulic	Mechanical, hydraulic
Operator	Heavier work, higher skill	Lighter work, lower skill
Supervisory skills	Managing male work force, scheduling	Mixed work force, machine troubleshooting, quality checking
Inventory	Sheet metal and work-in-process	Plastic powder and finished goods
Operations	May require several plus finishing	One
Scheduling	Potentially complex	Simple
Safety	Dangerous	Safer
Quality/ precision	Depends on die and machine setup	Depends on molds, timing set into machine
Costs	Depends especially on die conditions and setup	Depends especially on short cycle and changeovers
Flexibility-product change	Die change necessary	Mold change necessary
Volume change	Add dies, machines, shifts or move to higher speed equipment	Add dies, machines, shifts; cycle limited
Potential for automation	Combine operations with transfer dies, install part location sensors, etc.; can be largely automatic	Largely automatic

but one operation on one press, production scheduling is much simpler. The second difference is in the working environment: the job content, skills, training, and supervision. The lighter, cleaner, more automated work in the plastics plant would ordinarily be suitable for a less skilled, lower-paid employee, with key technical and personnel skills lodged in relatively higher paid employees.

Thus, each EPT brings with it its own demands and characteristics. A given EPT choice spreads its effects from the workplace to the entire operating system and, finally, to the ability of the system to perform in a competitive environment. This comes about because of the powerful economic advantages that occur when all parts of the system reinforce one another. An alert management recognizes the requirements the EPT places on the various management systems by its initial impact on the basic manufacturing process, and then develops an appropriate structure. The usual practice is to choose the EPT and then to design or adjust the system's operating policies and practices. The effects of an EPT, then, take place on three levels:

Primary.   Direct effects on the work, worker, working environment, product, costs, investment, and basic requirements.

Secondary.   Demands on the operating system infrastructure: wage and work force management, production planning, scheduling, and control, quality control, production organization.

Tertiary.   Effects on the performance ability of the operating system, that is, what the system can and cannot do well.

These three levels are illustrated in Exhibit 3.

The same ripple effect seen in one company from a change in technology usually spreads out over entire industries as each business firm gains cost, delivery, quality, or product advantages.

What have been the effects of technology's classic historical dominance of the workplace? Often the results are seen as harmful to QWL. Mass production, for example, usually means repetition and, therefore, potential boredom. Assembly lines, conveyors, and automation generally reduce skills and narrow job scopes. Because machinery does its work faster, humans are paced and pressured to keep it producing.

On the "good" side, however, most people would probably agree that life in both manufacturing and service/office industries is a great deal better in 1978 than in 1928. Industrial history is full of examples of technologies developed for such conventional objectives as improved profit potential and a better product, which have also resulted in better working environments and improved QWL. For example, most new

Exhibit 3.   The influence of an EPT on an operating system.

operating system elements INFLUENCES	COSTS	QUALITY	INVESTMENT	FLEXIBILITY product/volume change	CUSTOMER SERVICE	WORKING ENVIRONMENT
PRIMARY direct effects	operator skill level labor cost material energy requirement setup & change-over maintenance skills mgt. scheduling control	precision reliability appearance maintenance	capacity original cost economic life inventory utilities & buildings certainty-stability of technology	product range producible setup & change-over time lead times	cycle time total lead time	physical conditions job content skills & experiences needed safety industrial health pace required social elements of job
SECONDARY operating policies & practices	purchasing system burden rates cost control system work force mgt. mfg. eng. reqs. mfg. organization structure	maintenance system QC system supervision mfg. eng. reqs.	inventory control system capacity planning system capital budgeting system	production planning & scheduling system new product capacity & lead times	customer promise system organization for new product introduction into mfg.	wage system supervision labor contract personnel policies grievance procedures knowledge needed at workplace communications
TERTIARY performance ability	total costs cost flexibility with volume change, product change	quality performance reliability	return on investment	ability to be profitable with changes in volume and/or products	ability to compete by short lead times & reliability of delivery promises	productivity morale effort ingenuity creativity flexibility competitiveness responsibility assumed at working level

mechanization for the reduction of labor also reduces or eliminates repetitive human tasks or actual physical work. Offices and factories are cleaner, quieter, lighter, and more comfortable than they were fifty years ago.

This reduction of tedious, repetitious work has probably been the major fringe benefit of mechanization and automation. Numerically controlled machine tools, computers, word-processing systems, containerized shipping, automatic testing, wave soldering, and automatic component insertion (in electronics), mechanical fruit picking, the bulldozer, and direct telephone dialing are examples of technology which have reduced tedious and/or strenuous operations. Yet, none of these technological innovations, it seems safe to say, were developed primarily for the purpose of improving working environments.

Nevertheless, that turned out to be a major and primary effect of these new EPTs. Job contents were changed from specialized, narrow tasks, low in skill and sometimes physically demanding, to ones requiring more skill and experience. Low-level operating skills were replaced by setting up, maintenance, troubleshooting, and other high-skilled operations. True, a residue of very low-level repetitive jobs remains, such as loading and unloading automatic machines, but these jobs are substantially fewer.

The disappearance of messy carbon paper and blue reproduction fluid in office work came about largely as a side effect of the development of copy machines for cutting labor costs. Coal-mining equipment which mechanically claws out coal was developed because the high wages of unionized miners offered mining firms an incentive to find savings. The chief beneficiary, however, was the miner himself, whose physical work was much reduced.

Although the history of technology abounds with such examples of serendipity, the working environment has been determined by EPTs selected for reasons other than their influence on QWL.

Why is it that consideration of the working environment has come last in both the development and selection of EPTs? Some of the assumptions implicit in the corporation's traditional method of choosing an EPT are as follows:

- Someone will turn up able and willing to do nearly any job if the wage is right.
- People are adaptable to a wide variety of tasks and conditions.
- People match themselves with acceptable jobs.

- Problems with any negative job reactions can be handled with
  - careful selection
  - adequate training
  - wage adjustments/monetary incentives
  - proper supervision
  - good discipline
  - open communications
  - proper grievance procedures.

These assumptions boil down to one idea, namely, that an otherwise successful and profitable EPT may present personnel problems, but such problems can be overcome. These assumptions appear to have been valid much of the time and, indeed, have held factories together for many generations.

In the last decade, however, these premises have grown vulnerable. Workers' perceptions of what is acceptable are clearly changing, and their expectations of working life are more demanding. Today our society is generally suspicious of single, overriding motives such as "growth," "profits," "efficiency," and unmanaged technological innovation.

For these reasons, many managers are now asking some new questions about EPTs: Are a good working environment and highly competitive, profitable EPTs mutually exclusive? Granted that the corporation must profit and compete successfully to survive, cannot EPTs be designed, selected, and operating practices developed for the purpose of better work environments? These questions are now explored.

If good QWL and productive EPTs are mutually exclusive, then we must choose between them, and where poor working environments would result, cushion the impact with better operating practices, such as job restructuring, better tasks, pay systems, communications, and others. If they are not mutually exclusive, we can learn to develop EPTs that improve productivity and QWL and also develop better operating policies and practices for the workplace.

To explore these questions, we need to be more precise about the elements of a high-productivity EPT and its effect on the workplace. An attempt to describe the characteristics of a high-productivity EPT is shown in Exhibit 4. The left column lists twenty common descriptors of an equipment and process technology which, it is conventionally assumed, produces high productivity. Not all readers will agree with the author's assessment of the effects on productivity, nor with the effects of each quality on the working environment and QWL. Nevertheless, the two

Exhibit 4.   EPT descriptors related to productivity, working environment, and QWL.

EPT Descriptor	Conventionally Assumed Effect on Productivity	Conventionally Assumed Effect on W-E and QWL	Comment Re: Productivity	Comment Re: W-E and QWL
1. Large volume, scale	Good	Bad	Generally true	Not necessarily bad
2. Standardized product	Good	Bad	Generally true	Not necessarily bad
3. Highly mechanized, automated	Good	Bad	Depends on worker reaction	Can eliminate boring jobs
4. Highly fixtured, maximum use of figures and tools	Good	Bad	Depends on worker reaction	Can make jobs easier
5. Easy to maintain	Good	Bad	True	But if easy, operator can maintain
6. Dependable, predictable mature technology	Good	Bad	True	But if so, operator can take charge
7. Special purpose (vs. general purpose)	Good	Bad	Depends on product mix or cost of changeover	Can be more interesting
8. Easy to setup and change over	Good	Bad	Generally true	But if easy, operator can do it
9. Straight-line layout	Good	Bad	Easier to control but may cost more in space and inventory	Workers may like ease of control if given more latitude
10. One-level building	Good	Bad	Easier to control but no major advantage in materials handling	Depends on architecture, noise, social groupings
11. Requires little skill to operate	Good	Bad	Depends on worker reaction	O.K. if matches worker interest and skill to job
12. Continuous vs. batch	Good	Bad	Depends on product mix and technicians	Not necessarily less interesting
13. Automatic material handling load, unload	Good	Bad	Depends on its reliability and flexibility	Can make jobs easier
14. Paced operations	Good	Bad	Depends on consistency, balance	Depends on rate and pace
15. Specialized, narrow, job content	Good	Bad	Depends on worker reaction	Not bad for everyone
16. Little worker discretion	Good	Bad	Depends on worker reaction	Not bad for everyone
17. Low in-process inventories	Good	Bad	Depends on absence of problems and variations	Depends on pace, variations, and problems
18. Standard methods	Good	Bad	Depends on worker reaction	Not bad for everyone
19. Requires little knowledge of other operations	Good	Bad	Depends on steady flows	Not bad for everyone
20. Central scheduling	Good	Bad	Depends on what knowledge is needed for good scheduling	Not bad for everyone

right-hand columns with the author's comments point out the uncertainty of the effects.

Several conclusions can be drawn from this analysis:

- There are many myths about technologies and QWL which need more precise and contextual thinking. For example, assembly lines are not always necessarily highly productive. It depends on worker reactions, product mix, the physical elements of production, and 1,001 other factors. And assembly lines are not necessarily bad for QWL either, depending on job content, pace and rate of flow, particular workers, use of buffer inventory, and another 1,001 factors.
- Many of the assumed positive productivity effects of certain EPTs depend substantially on worker reaction to the EPT and, indeed, to the whole working environment. Hence, old "principles" of industrial engineering must now be seen as dependent on workers, management, and the situation. High productivity cannot be automatically achieved or guaranteed by any technology if worker cooperation and effort are negative.
- Similarly, many of the presumed negative effects of so-called high-productivity EPTs on working environments and QWL need not take place, depending on how EPTs are structured, managed, and accepted. For example, a mature, dependable, low-maintenance EPT can be boring if the operator only watches it, or interesting if the operator has complete charge of scheduling setup, changeover, and maintenance. The operator's expectations, interests, skills, and attitudes partly determine the impact of the EPT. Conversely, "job enrichment" policies, as demonstrated by many researchers, do not guarantee high QWL.

The answer to the basic question, therefore, is that there is no inherent conflict between high productivity and high QWL. Both working environment and productivity are dependent on the technical, human, and workplace infrastructure. The fact that conflicts have surfaced so often between the EPT and the working environment is due to the social and personal impacts of industrialization per se, the low priority given to the effects on the work environment in both EPT development and selection, and operating policies and practices.

To conclude, technology has been powerful in its effects on work environments in the past and, more often than not, has had a negative short-term impact.

However, poor work environments are not inevitable in the future, for any or all of the factors affecting work environments are susceptible to change. For example, the analysis so far suggests the following possible influences which can change the future impact of technology on the workplace:

- Scientific and engineering knowledge and skills leading to new technologies.
- Sociological/ideological forces inducing new technologies.
- Economic forces inducing new technologies.
- New objectives for management selection of EPTs.
- New criteria for management selection of EPTs.
- New weighting of criteria in management selection of EPTs.
- New operating policies and practices to cushion or improve the impact of existing EPTs.
- Legal and governmental influences on EPT choices and operating policies and practices.
- New perceptions of existing workers about what makes a good work environment.
- Perceptions of new workers about what makes a good work environment.
- New worker reactions to working environments they perceive as poor.

These factors and their interrelationships are pictured in simplified form in Exhibit 5. We turn now to the future.

NEW FORCES WHICH MAY ALTER THE FUTURE

Although our view of industrial history shows how the work environment has been the slave of technology and management operating policies and EPT selection decision processes, it also shows the way to future change. We saw three critical factors in the technology/work environment interface:

- How the impact of technology on work is managed.
- What motivates and influences the development of new EPTs.
- How EPTs are selected by management.

All three of these key factors now appear to be undergoing changes which are going to affect the future.

Exhibit 5.   Factors influencing future impact of technology on the workplace.

PRESENT		NEW		CHANGE
EPTs	+	"Mothers of invention"	=	NEW EPTs TO CHOOSE FROM →
MANAGEMENT DECISION PROCESS	+	Objectives, ideologies, premises, processes	=	DIFFERENT, MODIFIED EPTs SELECTED →
				These will produce NEW EPTS and with →
OPERATING POLICIES AND PRACTICES	+	Techniques, concepts, objectives, legal requirements	=	REVISED OPERATING POLICIES AND PRACTICES →
				NEW WORKING ENVIRONMENTS will result. These will combine with →
WORKER PERCEPTIONS, MOTIVES, AND REACTIONS	+	Changing values, expectations, and goals of workers	=	NEW WORKER ATTITUDES AND PERCEPTIONS OF QWL

216

Improved Techniques for Managing the Impacts of Technology
on the Working Environment

Although the future will be determined by new technologies influenced by
a variety of changed forces and revised managerial decision apparatus, let
us assume for now that the working environment continues to be the dependent variable of technology which it has been in the past. Also assumed for the moment is the classic premise of corporate managers and
scientists/engineers that whatever working environment may result can be
managed or contained.

Perhaps because new EPTs were designed and selected without regard
to the work environment in the past, a new body of knowledge and set of
techniques have emerged over the past ten years or so which are now assisting some managements first to cushion and then to improve working
environments.

Driving this new thrust for better management at the working level are
various engines of change, most of which are described elsewhere in this
book in detail. For example, corporate profits can become an incentive to
develop better ways to manage the impact of technology when a firm's
large investments in facilities are threatened by worker dissatisfaction and
unrest, for these conditions have a multiplier effect and can render such
investments disastrous. Changed social attitudes toward working
environments, widespread shortages of qualified workers, or militant
unionism will lead managers to develop new techniques for improving the
working environment. Federal and state laws, such as OSHA regulations,
as well as industrial problems, such as low productivity, inflation, and
foreign competition, are spurring the development of new techniques.

As a result of these forces which affect profits, industry is learning to
manage the working environment, and to manage it better. More management and staff attention is being placed on "people." Many companies have hired top-level corporate officers, called "managers of human
resources" or the equivalent. An increasing number of these officers are
listened to and exert power and influence as never before.

These forces are inducing the development of important new intellectual and analytical concepts that are providing useful frameworks for
management to develop tools and techniques for improving the working
environment. In particular, a rich literature has grown up describing how
work may be "restructured" within a given technology.

Work restructuring generally includes changing job tasks and content, compensation schemes, the scope of workers' responsibility, social structure, status hierarchy, and procedures for vertical and horizontal mobility. Knowledge is growing about indicators of and ingredients affecting QWL, and strategies are being devised for diffusing successful work restructuring into the organization. Professor Richard Walton has identified eight criteria for a high QWL, which can motivate such strategies:

- Adequate and fair compensation
- Safe and healthy working conditions
- Immediate opportunity to use and develop human capacities
- Future opportunity for continued growth and security
- Social integration in the work organization
- Constitutionalism in the work organization
- Work and the total life space
- The social relevance of working life[1]

The results of work restructuring experiments are receiving attention in the literature as a result of a large number of pilot programs that have taken place in the United States and in Western Europe. Experiments in work restructuring have been carried out in companies such as Corning Glass, General Foods, General Motors, General Electric, and Cummins Engine.

The experiments have involved nonsupervised work groups; new pay systems; increased participation in decisions affecting group teams; job enlargement; group-developed tools, systems, procedures, and work methods; and the provision of additional information for cost analysis and cost control. Although these experiments have generally been considered successful, their diffusion into broader usage has sometimes proved difficult.

All in all, it is growing clear that many managements are making modest but increasing progress in learning how to improve poor working environments created by technologies that were developed or chosen without regard to the working environment. It is now reasonable to assume that this promising work will continue, will be gradually diffused into new practice, and that the small nucleus of existing experiments and new work structures will grow at least modestly over the next decade. Progress will be gradual rather than revolutionary, it appears, because these experiments now cover only a tiny fraction of the work force and will take years to gather more momentum.

It is important to define what progress in work restructuring means. Although the goal of restructuring work is to improve work environments, the process is essentially one of adapting the tasks, rules, and practices affecting work to improve the status quo under existing technology. That is, the EPT is given, and the job of improving QWL is one of scrambling to adjust human work to the technology in the best way possible. But since, as we saw earlier, a given EPT determines to a great extent the entire operating system and sets up physical and technical constraints, the benefits of work restructuring are severely limited in many cases. When the EPT dictates a poor QWL, as in the case of the typical foundry of the 1950s, work restructuring is little more than a Band-Aid. At best, when the technology of the process is more neutral, as in electronic assembly work, work restructuring can result in substantial improvements.

These notions lead to the next question. Since a given EPT is typically so pervasive and, therefore, the benefits of better operating policies and practices such as work restructuring so limited, can we expect to come across or develop new technologies which themselves may be more conducive to better working environments?

Factors Influencing the Development of New Technologies

Increasing the Stock of Available Technologies. The flow of new technologies available for selection is stimulated and directed by a variety of forces (Exhibit 6). Some have effects which can turn out to be fortunate.

Exhibit 6.   Factors affecting innovation in equipment and process technology.

 1. Scientific knowledge
 2. Engineering skills
 3. Corporate investment
 4. Government investment
 5. Corporate objectives
 6. Productivity
 7. Economics/cost mix
 8. Resource availability
 9. Product changes
10. Product quality
11. Safety and health
12. Environment

One quickly developing technology appears to show promise for a favorable effect on QWL—that is, the explosion of computers, minicomputers, and communications. The effect is fortuitous, for the main purposes of such technology are improved production and inventory controls, cost and quality controls, and information systems. But side effects are already beginning to be seen at the workplace.

Until now, the machine operator has generally been servant to hard-and-fast orders, specifications, and decisions. He or she is given an order, material, and equipment typically set up and ready to go; inserts the material; runs the machine; stacks up the finished pieces; and gets another order. The parts produced will either pass inspection or be rejected, and if rejections are high or sales improve rapidly, another order may have to be produced right away. With the minicomputer, workers can be given the opportunity for intelligent participation; in effect, they can have an ongoing discussion with an advisor, the computer. They receive feedback from the computer about the quality of the work being produced, can make adjustments to improve quality, and can give the computer suggestions for improved operations.

In effect, workers can respond intelligently to information they need for doing their jobs better and more easily. Classical "supervision" is superseded by an information system that answers questions and gives rapid feedback for the workers' own improvements of performance. Currently, the best trained and most well-intentioned supervisor is forced by lack of time and the limited information one person can possess to issue definitive orders. The intelligent worker sees other alternatives and raises many questions to which the supervisor now must give a limited, narrow, and often hurried response.

The "system," then, seems arbitrary or downright stupid to the worker who sees firsthand, for example, that yesterday he or she was pressured all day for production and today has to stretch the work out to make it last. The use of minicomputers can change the supervisor's response to workers from a blunt "don't ask questions—do as you're told" to an accommodating, "here's what we need—please work it out your own way, use your ingenuity, and ask us any questions." The supervisor becomes a helper, colleague, teacher, or coach. His or her task of disciplining workers to follow orders can be reduced or eliminated.

So once again, some technologies which come along benefit the workplace. But another question now arises: Are there new or different forces at work which may develop substantially new equipment and process technologies from those currently available?

Changing Factors Motivating New EPT Development. There are many "mothers of invention" besides necessity, and it looks as though some new motivating forces, in fact, will result in a flow of EPTs to the workplace which may differ substantially from those of the past. At least seven changes are already working:

- Until recently it seems safe to say that saving labor has probably been the most common and powerful motive of technological development in equipment and processes. In many industries, however, materials are now the greatest expense, and, therefore, the new target for cutting costs. The United States has drifted toward becoming a material-short nation; we export fewer materials, import more, and move more materials longer distances. We are increasingly guarding our supplies of iron, cotton, copper, wood pulp, water, and petrochemical feedstocks. Costs of materials have outpaced and fueled inflation and, as a result, new technologies in metalworking, construction, chemicals, and cryogenics have developed, to mention but a few.

- A second major change in the economics of many industries has been the substantial increase in overhead costs relative to direct labor. As labor-saving technologies have been introduced and managements have invested more in overhead, the ratios of these costs to direct labor have gradually increased so that now overhead is a prime area for cost savings.

A growing portion of overhead costs is, of course, energy. Energy not only represents a rising cost, but, in fact, is becoming such a scarce resource that the present level of consumption could again result in the shutdown of entire factories and industries, as in the winter of 1976–1977. For this reason, many of the large and well-managed companies are going through their entire EPTs step by step and reprocessing with energy-saving technologies.

- A third new factor resulting in new technologies is the increased emphasis on asset management (in contrast to cost management). Increased costs of capital, combined with more opportunities for putting capital to work than can be financed, are resulting in a search by management for technologies that use assets more effectively. Increased capacity per dollar invested is one goal of asset management. Others are EPTs that are faster and thereby require less inventory, or those that offer improved flexibility for producing more product varieties with fewer pieces of equipment.

- Law and the courts are of growing importance in EPT design. The Environmental Protection Act and the Occupational Safety and Health

Act are typical. For example, companies mandated by law to cut pollution are developing new EPTs rather than pay fines and risk being shut down.

Enlarged protection for consumers by the courts has begun to have an effect on EPT development in many industries, as companies attempt to produce safer and more reliable products.

- "Mature" industries, such as steel, textiles, automobiles, and chemicals, are generally becoming less competitive in the United States, whereas industries characterized by a high rate of technological change and innovations, such as computers, industrial electronics, specialized plastics, cryogenics, and industrial and construction equipment, are holding unique competitive advantages. Assuming this trend will continue, we can foresee more emphasis on EPT development, characterized by higher skills, more information, more on-the-job problem solving, shorter runs and order quantities, greater product varieties, and hence a changed working environment which most analysts would predict to be an improvement.

- According to Abernathy[2] and Hayes and Wheelwright,[3] productive units in less mature industries tend to have small-scale capacity with a low level of backward integration, flexible but inefficient general-purpose equipment, skilled labor, and a loose and entrepreneurially based form of organization. Productive units in firms with low unit volumes or large numbers of multiple products tend to have disconnected or jumbled flows, as in a job shop, compared to the connected line flows of assembly lines. Therefore, technologies motivated for this kind of industrial product and process matching will tend to produce working environments that require less monitoring, more skill, and a higher judgment level.

- Supporting this conclusion, although arriving at it differently, some economists observe that U.S. capital spending over the past five years has tended to lag behind GNP growth, particularly in the construction of giant-scale plants needed to achieve competitive cost levels in bulk-process industries. High cost of capital, combined with the enormous capital investment and risks inherent in such ventures, has caused this slowdown relative to development and investment in EPTs in the non-commodity industries.

- A force gradually becoming more powerful in influencing technology development is society's beliefs and values. Our period of history is frequently called "postindustrial," with business no longer predominating over government or allowed to neglect human values, and with reduced confidence in science and technology to solve problems. We feel a new need for the development of human capital. The service-industry sector, which is more dependent on people than machines, has been growing faster than manufacturing. New ideologies are replacing individualism, property rights, competition to satisfy consumer desires, the limited state, and scientific specialization. One of these, communitarianism, which focuses on the rights and duties of membership in the community, community needs, the active planning state, holism, and interdependence, is already having an influence on workers and working environment.[4] Earlier chapters deal with these changes in values and the work ethic, and our task here is limited to noting that ideology, values, and societal objectives are bound to influence EPTs. This influence will be felt in many ways.

The Possibility of Developing and Selecting Technologies for Better Working Environment

There is no question that managers, engineers, and scientists can develop and select technologies which produce better working environments, for this is already being done in isolated instances today.

We are not talking about "work restructuring," which we noted earlier is adapted to a given equipment and process technology. But in situations in which the working environment is considered intolerable, as in paint spraying, coal mining, and nuclear power installations, EPTs have, in fact, been designed around the human operator. Not only was tooling, for example, usually "human-engineered," but the basic technology of the operation was developed from the start with the working environment in mind.

In these examples, work environments were so potentially harmful that improvements were essential. This illustrates that design objectives are critical and that if a satisfactory environment is given a high priority in the design and selection process, the EPT will meet these objectives. In the Volvo Kalmar plant, the EPT and engineering of the car itself were specifically designed in part for a team assembly process. The same thing occurred in the General Foods pet-food plant in Topeka, where the EPT design was influenced from the start by the prime objective of making the plant a good place to work.

To be successful, however, this process takes more than a new ideology, a firm policy, good intentions, new objective functions, and design criteria that are heavily weighted toward a good work environment. Also necessary are several other management skills that are still rare: an ability to anticipate the effect of a technology on the working environment and the skills to design EPTs which produce favorable working environments without sacrificing conventional objectives of cost, delivery, and quality. Our only knowledge base for these skills derives from experiments in restructuring work. There managers are learning which factors in an EPT cause problems in the working environment.

At Cummins Engine Corporation, managers, assisted by Professor Richard Walton, have set forth some principles for the design of EPTs which result in better work environments:

Some Work Restructuring Criteria in the Design of Machines and Plant Layouts[5]

1. Knowledge and skill will be required (not eliminated) by complexity and challenge in the task.
2. Variety will be allowed in operations performed, skills required, physical location, and working conditions.
3. Judgment and discretion will be permitted.
4. "Free space," that is, time, is created, for example, by buffer inventories between stations, permitting meetings, self-pacing, action independent of others, teaching–learning interchanges, and so on.
5. Operations will be grouped so as to allow team responsibility for an integrated task, incorporating support activity such as scheduling, maintenance, and inspection.
6. Jobs will be similar to avoid a hierarchy of jobs and to allow a pay scheme based on "what you know."
7. Interpersonal contact and communications will be facilitated by layout, noise level, and "free space."

So the necessary knowledge is developing although this is a new art. Certainly many years of experimentation and refinement will pass before EPT designers will be as capable of producing good working environments as they are at reducing direct labor and increasing volume and quality.

Several other impediments stand in the way of the development of better EPTs. One important and particularly sticky problem results from the disaggregation of many industries. For example, a small electrical equipment manufacturer must figure out how to get machine tools which have been designed, let us say, so that operators can do much of the maintenance, setup, and sharpening. In such a disaggregated industry, the EPTs are usually purchased from suppliers who are not easily influenced by a small fraction of their customers, so until enough manufacturers specify that they want equipment providing better work environments, it will be a slow process.

Further, the nearly universal practice in large divisionalized corporations of budgeting and controlling on a monthly basis, according to an annual plan, induces a cautious, low-risk, short-term approach on the part of division managers. This attitude is hardly conducive to experimental development of new technologies to improve working environments.

With regard to another obstacle, we may be more optimistic. Until the 1970s, conventional manufacturing decision making was done by factory specialists. Decision criteria were dominated by a strongly technical, "nuts and bolts" productivity point of view. This resulted in manufacturing policy decisions which were often in conflict or simply out of touch with corporate strategy and competitive marketing requirements. Dominated by cost and efficiency, manufacturing policies often resulted in plants which become corporate problems, limiting a firm's ability to compete flexibly as markets changed because bricks and mortar and the wrong expensive equipment in place had to be amortized over many years. Narrow thinking resulted from the isolation of manufacturing as a function, and from policy decisions made to optimize functional rather than corporate objectives.

In the 1970s, one new emphasis in corporate management is on a strategic, integrated approach to the management of all functions. There has been a steady trend to multiproduct, divisionalized, corporate organization and recently some firms have adopted a new approach to manufacturing that links it to the corporate strategy.[6] These factors may be leading manufacturing managers to new decision criteria and processes in forming manufacturing policy.

This new approach to manufacturing policy recognizes the inevitable trade-offs in designing and operating technology-based systems and requires that managements be more explicit in recognizing and choosing trade-off positions in the achievement of a "manufacturing task" that is derived from corporate strategy. A major contribution of this new approach toward the improvement of working environments is the promise it offers of movement away from the single dominating goal of cost or efficiency. The new approach is better able to handle, sort, weight, and balance a multidimensional set of criteria. As the old limited approach largely neglected the human factors (as well as many others) in choosing EPTs, the new approach can include consideration of the working environment, with appropriate weighting.

On balance, then, what is the likelihood of managers and engineers moving proactively to increase the stock and influence the choice of available EPTs that improve the working environments? On the positive side it is happening, albeit slowly and cautiously. The technology is developing as well, although it is still in its infancy. New forms of decision making in corporate manufacturing policy may provide a vehicle for the consideration of many objectives, while at the same time the trend toward decentralized corporate divisions has weakened the excessively function-oriented organizational structure of the past.

On the negative side, there are still barriers between suppliers and users of technology that make more difficult the task of managements in improving working environments. Further, the state of the art is that it *is* an art and not a science. We do not know how to do it: Managements and engineers are surprised by "good" designs that do not work and by side effects of ordinary EPTs that unexpectedly do work. It is still too mysterious and complex for most companies to risk more than experimentation.

It appears that public pressure and the new interest in QWL on the part of managements and employees are becoming a pivotal factor. For to improve QWL will take more firm involvement on the part of top management than the effort now receives. More labor crises, skill shortages, sick industries, and stalled productivity, on the one hand, and glowing examples of profit improvement from the intrepid, on the other, may also speed the process.

For these reasons, we judge that the proposed development of new EPTs conducive to better work environments is in an early experimental stage with no clear trend in view. At least five years of proven results, diffused widely across a substantial number of leading companies, will be necessary before industry reaches the takeoff stage where "everybody's doing it."

Changes in the Management Decision Process for Choosing Equipment and Process Technologies

Exhibit 7 lists factors involved in these management decision processes. As stated earlier, many of these factors are changing or are apt to change.

Exhibit 7.   Factors involved in the management decision: Choice of equipment and process.

1. Ideology—values
2. Objectives
3. Risks/uncertainty
4. Choice of criteria
5. Weightings of criteria
6. Judgment of anticipated results
7. Costs
8. Investment
9. Capacity policy
10. Resource reliability
11. Cycle—delivery

In particular, a powerful influence in management selection of EPTs favorable to QWL will be the expectation of profitable results. In other words, an efficient worker who gets more production out of a given investment in fixed assets is a profitable worker. The changing cost mix moving toward a lower percentage for labor and a higher percentage for overhead and materials will induce the same effect. The ancient clash over production and pay on the part of management and workers, respectively, will cool when there is a higher multiple of value added per employee, and when both parties are pushing for better utilization of material, overhead, and energy. Such considerations would indeed induce a manager to choose an EPT that provides a favorable working environment.

SUMMARY AND CONCLUSIONS

When changing technology moves across an industry, its effects on operating systems are usually pervasive and powerful. The choice of an EPT is the single most influential decision a management makes in determining QWL in a manufacturing or service-operations system. Once made, many other elements of the system are adapted to serve the EPT, or, if left unchanged, become incongruent and dysfunctional. The working environment is similarly affected by a change in EPT. All systems of work, including job content of individual jobs, pay schemes, the role of managers, and decision-making processes, are influenced and constrained by a choice of EPT. For these reasons EPT has been the major factor in determining QWL in a given work situation.

A second but always critical factor which acts as a modifier of the impact of EPT on the work environment is the set of operating policies and practices surrounding the workplace. A third and also critical factor is the decision processes by which managers choose an EPT. The fourth critical ingredient is that of worker perceptions, both individually and in groups. Exhibit 4 suggested the relationship of these four factors acting together.

The following paragraphs summarize the conclusions developed in this chapter:

For most of the industrial history, technology has dominated the working environment. The effects have been good and bad. Machines replacing labor do not, in themselves, produce poor working environments, for machines may remove drudgery and monotony as well as create them. Some technologies help and others hurt, and the working environment has been a haphazard result of the choice of EPTs from whatever stock of EPTs has been available.

An unusually rapid enlargement of EPT stock may now be forthcoming because of the changing mix of cost factors now taking place, emphasizing material, energy, and capital and deemphasizing labor costs. A possible, indeed probable, effect is a work environment in which the goals of labor and management may be less in opposition than they have been.

Some managements are developing skills and experience in adapting to EPTs, largely through restructuring the work content and infrastructure governing work and workers. Experiments have generally worked out well, but diffusing the innovation usually has proven difficult. Unions usually have been cautious and skeptical concerning these experiments.

A few managements are attempting to influence the stock of EPTs for the better by intentionally developing EPTs that may be conducive to better work environments. This takes new knowledge and judgment which are only beginning to be developed.

The management decision processes for selecting EPTs are being changed in some corporations by objective criteria that include anticipated effects on the work environments and the weighting of these criteria more heavily relative to traditional economic criteria. The new manufacturing policy/corporate strategy approach to EPT decisions facilitates the use of broader criteria related to longer term strategic considerations and may move traditional manufacturing management thinking away from a functional and toward a strategic corporate viewpoint.

Changes in ideology, worker insistence on participation, and management belief in the potential of better management of human resources will further the whole process, including better adaptation to existing technologies, affirmative development of new technologies, and more decisions influenced by QWL in choosing EPTs.

Disaggregation of industries and EPT suppliers, and inadequate knowledge of cause-and-effect relationships between the EPT working environment and the monthly divisional performance focus still cause substantial barriers to development of better EPTs.

Altogether, these conclusions add up to a scenario in which we can expect incremental change in the form of more new EPTs, more experimentation, more risk taking, and more management investment, concern, and involvement in EPTs and the work environment. Probably the greatest single factor that is beginning to change the process at many points (exhibit 7) is managers' premises and objectives—premises about people and their potential and objectives that include better development of human resources. The choice of technology is now beginning to be influenced by these considerations.

There are many signs that a growing number of U.S. managements are no longer going to let the working environment just happen. Some are going to try to manage that sector of their business just as they attempt to manage markets and finance, costs, and assets. The profit motive will be the driving force largely because of the multiplier effect that a turned-on, released, and cooperative work force can have on production.

What will be the effect of changing technology on working environment in the 1980s? Managements will slowly begin to react to existing technologies and to whatever technologies come along with better operating policies and practices; they will gradually produce better working environments. Many will not be content merely to react, however, and will instead begin to select and innovate new technologies that offer advantages for the working environment. They will be stimulated, partly by the ongoing change in factory costs, material, and energy, partly by changes in ideology and intention, and, finally, perhaps most of all by the recognition that achievement of profitable competitive productivity is steadily demanding a more competitive, dedicated, and committed work force, free of the resentments which fester and restrain in a poor working environment.

NOTES

1. Richard E. Walton, "Quality of Working Life: What Is It?" *Sloan Management Review* (Fall 1973): 11–21.
2. William J. Abernathy, *The Productivity Dilemma* (Baltimore: Johns Hopkins University Press, 1978).

3. Robert H. Hayes and Steven Wheelwright, "Matching Manufacturing Process Structure to the Product/Market Structure," working paper, Division of Research, Harvard Business School, Harvard University, 1977.

4. George C. Lodge, *The New American Ideology* (New York: Alfred A. Knopf, 1975).

5. Internal document of Cummins Engine Company. Also adapted in Richard E. Walton, "QWL Indicators—Prospects and Problems," *Studies in Personnel Psychology* (Spring 1974).

6. Wickham Skinner, *Manufacturing in the Corporate Strategy* (New York: Wiley, 1978).

12.
Emerging Trends in Collective Bargaining

IRVING BLUESTONE
Vice-President, International Union-UAW
Director, General Motors Department, UAW

Free collective bargaining is a powerful engine for progressive change—at the workplace and in society. In their richest sense, the goals of collective bargaining, if they are to be morally just and economically sound, should be consonant with the needs of society and their fulfillment. Human need and social change, therefore, constitute the major driving force in determining the direction of union–management relations. Intertwined with these forces is the changing nature of the worker and the workplace.

The past thirty years of collective bargaining have reflected this response to social need. Clearly recognizable during these three decades has been the emphasis on the development and refinement of income-security provisions, commonly given the misnomer of "fringe benefits." These have been designed largely to fill the vacuum created by the failure of society to meet national needs through adequate and universally applicable legislation. A few well-recognized examples will serve to establish the point:

- Every human being has a right to health-care protection. With the exception of the elderly and disabled, society has failed to provide this basic service. Through collective bargaining health-care programs have been negotiated to fill the void.
- No social legislation exists to assure income replacement for a worker who falls ill and is absent from work. Through collective bargaining weekly sick-and-accident benefits have been established to help sustain the family when there is no paycheck.
- Social legislation provides a woefully inadequate life insurance

231

benefit to the survivors of workers, barely covering funeral costs. Collective bargaining, once again, has been used successfully to obtain life insurance coverage to supplement meager federal benefits.

• Retiring workers cannot make ends meet with the low level of Social Security benefits provided by national legislation. Private pension plans, negotiated at the collective bargaining table, supplement the national benefit, not only for the retiree but for the surviving spouse as well.

• The plant or office closes down to celebrate a national holiday. Holiday pay is negotiated to assure a full paycheck.

• A worker is called to fulfill his or her civic responsibility as a juror. Through collective bargaining appropriate makeup pay has been provided to insure against loss of income.

The total list of benefits is long; many are ingenious. All are designed to meet a human need and, at the same time, a social need.

Collective bargaining must be given credit for bringing these fundamental financial bulwarks into the economic life of the nation. Moreover, as the minority of workers represented by unions have come to enjoy these socially desirable, family-sustaining benefits, employers have felt constrained to extend many of these benefits (if they were not already doing so) to nonunionized workers as well.

The process of fulfilling these human and economic needs is comparatively slow; the coverage is varied and by no means universally or equitably applied. But it is inexorable. Not too many decades ago these emoluments hardly existed. Some, such as health-care insurance, were not even available. All were resisted by employers. Yet today, workers—whether in production or skilled trades, in clerical or professional jobs, in supervision or management—with few exceptions, would not consider taking a job which did not provide a range of benefits, over and above the paycheck, designed to ameliorate their day-to-day concerns over security for themselves and their families. They seek the security that human beings demand to meet the measure of individual dignity and economic stability promised by a free and democratic society.

It is altogether fair to ask, Why is so huge a burden placed on the collective bargaining process in the United States? Is it not a moral and economic imperative that human beings and their families should enjoy certain basic benefits of life? Should not society provide both the agricultural worker and the president of a mammoth corporation the same health-care protection? Should not such a worker have the privilege of vacation with pay, or time off without loss of income when there is a death in the family, or assurance of continued full income while performing a citizen's duty as a juror? Some types of protection may vary in the amount of dollars and cents, but they should be universal in kind.

Other industrialized countries have long since legislated these kinds of income-security assurances and have made them universal. In the United States we still lack even the rudiments of a national health-security program which is comprehensive and universal in design. As long as our society fails to meet these human and special needs, collective bargaining will move in to try and fill the void.

As we look to the future, we must assess what social changes are impending, the more properly to predict what directions the union–management relationship will take. A few projections concerning American society are in order.

THE CHANGING WORK FORCE

Today nonwhite minorities make up 11 percent of the work force. It is estimated that by 1985, they will represent 14 percent. Today, about 41 percent of the work force is comprised of women. This proportion is growing, and if current trends continue, as they no doubt will, women will exercise a continually growing influence upon labor–management relations and on the political and legislative life of the nation. They will also doubtlessly play an increasingly significant role as union leaders. Unions that have not already done so would do well to heed the rising clamor for women to take positions of leadership, both appointed and elected.

Thus, in a few years white males will be a minority in the employed.

Moreover, the work force is, on average, becoming older. In 1968 workers 45 years of age or older comprised about 37 percent of the work force. Current projections are that in seven or eight years that percentage will rise to about 42 percent. This means a decline in the proportion of younger workers.

The worker entering the labor market today is estimated to have, on average, four years more of schooling than was the case a generation or two ago. In the decade ahead a worker entering the work force will have even more years of schooling. As older workers retire, their replacements will be younger and more educated. Since education tends to narrow the gap between minorities and the majority and trains people to be less accepting of outmoded ways of thinking, there will be qualitative as well as compositional changes in the work force.

THE ECONOMY

The failure of U.S. society to create a full employment–full production economy is probably the most persistent and most pervasive problem in its history. Despite the enormous economic expansion of our nation over the past forty years, largely stimulated by war—World War II, the Korean War, and the Vietnam War—we have never achieved a full employment economy in peacetime.

Even more troubling is the fact that since the end of World War II, the American people have suffered a series of six recessions. With each of these recessions the economic gap has grown wider between what our economy actually produces and what it is capable of producing. This loss of gross national product has reached staggering proportions. Leon Keyserling, chairman of the Council of Economic Advisers under President Truman, has calculated that "during 1953–1975 inclusive, by failing to maintain full employment and full production, we forfeited almost 3.355 trillion dollars of national production, measured in 1975 dollars, and relinquished also 61 million man-years of employment opportunity."[1]

The peak official (an underestimated) figure for unemployment during the Nixon–Ford recession years was 9.1 percent, seasonally adjusted in May 1975. Despite the resurgence of the economy since 1975, it is at a seasonally adjusted rate of 5.88 percent (January 1979). Six million (a conservative figure) without work in our affluent society is inexcusable. Even more startling is the fact that among our young people aged 16 to 19 unemployment officially stands at 17.1 percent, seasonally adjusted. Therein lie the seeds of future disaster. The economy must create at least 2½ million jobs per year just to keep abreast of the expansion of the work force, and another 2 to 3 million jobs per year to reduce unemployment sharply.

The uncertainties of an economy that has evidenced a fundamental inability to provide enough jobs at decent pay for people who are able and willing to work inevitably have an impact on the collective bargaining arena. For, once again, a societal failure to meet human need leaves a vacuum for collective bargaining to attempt to fill.

We must recognize, moreover, that continuing new developments in technology erode the number of jobs available. Discoveries of new products and new services must keep pace with these job losses and create new industries to replace them. The automobile made the horse and wagon obsolete but brought us into a new era. Perhaps solar energy will constitute the next major new job-creating development. Technological job erosion must be counterbalanced by new job-creating scientific and engineering advances.

Organization of the Workplace

For the individual worker, the workplace, even where a negotiated union contract prevails, is still dominated by authoritarianism. The methods, means, and processes of production or delivery of services remain essentially a management prerogative. The worker's role is to follow orders.

For decades the organization of the workplace has been predicated on the principles of so-called scientific management. This system is rooted in the drive for more output per work-hour by breaking down each job into its simplest, most repetitive, specialized tasks, with the shortest possible learning period, limited to the greatest efficiency in space and time. Such a system requires little more from the worker than to follow instructions to the letter and to perform precisely in a manner prescribed over and over again, so that each motion and each task are performed to mechanical perfection.

The aim of thus organizing the workplace "efficiently" has emphasized economic rather than humanistic criteria. The motivation has been "minimizing the unpredictable human element, to design systems that do not require a great deal of trust."[2] The fact is that management does not trust its workers and therefore places a variety of restraints on them. Its greater trust is in the machine.

Times and circumstances are changing, however, and some management executives are reevaluating these traditional concepts of work organization and efficiency. In part this may be due to the phenomenon described earlier, the worker's increasing challenge to the authoritarian climate of the workplace and its structure, and in part to a more valid definition of productivity, which measures it not only in terms of output per work-hour but in the humanistic concepts of social effectiveness, which honor the dignity of the human being and provide for the broader needs of society.

Three distinct yet overlapping directions in the collective bargaining process point to the nature and content of subjects that will concern unions and management in the days ahead.

First are the hard-line controversial issues. These include, of course, the traditional issues of wages and other economic benefits and certain conditions of employment. No doubt these will remain strictly adversarial in nature, much as they have been since the advent of collective bargaining as the vehicle for resolving disputes between management and labor. Then there are subjects that may be adversarial at the bargaining table but that, after agreement is reached, will lend themselves readily to joint, cooperative effort in their implementation. Third are the subjects that are of such mutual interest to the parties that they fall into a category of non-controversy and call for the joint, cooperative initiation of programs aimed at common goals for the ultimate benefit of the workers, the union, and the management. The latter two subject areas supplement the hard-line controversial issues—but all three are designed to improve the quality of working life. My purpose is not to cover extensively the issues that might fall within each of these categories, but rather to provide examples of what the future might hold for each.

HARD-LINE CONTROVERSIAL ISSUES

Creating Enough Jobs

The first concern of the worker, and it should be the first concern of society, is to earn a decent living and provide for his or her family. Food, clothing, housing, and health precede all other considerations. Workers want jobs at decent pay and job security. A healthy economy needs workers at work, earning and spending. Unemployment is the major scourge of any economic system, for to keep the unemployed supplied with the necessities of life is to pay people who are not producing.

Our economic system has never solved the problem of persistent unemployment. The spotlight is on this issue as never before; and the political battle lines are forming around the legislative struggle to assure a job at decent pay for anyone willing and able to work. The Humphrey–Hawkins Act (1978) addresses itself to this issue.

Full employment is a national issue of such dimensions that it requires a national solution. Collective bargaining alone cannot find a universal solution for it any more than it could achieve the equivalent of universal national health-care protection. However, here again, the societal failure to create enough jobs compels collective bargaining to attempt to fill the vacuum.

In the next few years, even if full-employment legislation is passed, the demand for finding ways to create more job opportunities will dominate much of the labor contract negotiating process. The labor movement's approach is to reduce work time, for to produce the same amount of goods and services in less time requires more workers, or at least saves workers from becoming superfluous by reason of technological labor-saving advances. The reduction in work-time formulation has been in process for many years.

It manifests itself in various ways: by the hour, by the day, by the week, by the year, or over the span of working life. Relief time on the job, paid holidays, annual paid vacations, even jury duty, bereavement, and military reserve duty pay are formulations to reduce work time. Retirement programs, especially those designed to stimulate voluntary early retirement, are also means of reducing work time.

The initial moves have already been made to permit retirement at an early age with decent income, with special supplements related to years of service. This provides a triple advantage: It meets the demand for leisure time, creates promotional opportunities for younger workers, and simultaneously either opens up job opportunities for the unemployed or saves the jobs for workers who might otherwise be unneeded.

Currently the major thrust lies in the attack upon the forty-hour workweek. Continuing progress will be sought to reduce work time and thereby create more job opportunities by improving upon already well-established time-off-with-pay provisions, including voluntary early retirement. Still, the demand to alter the traditional forty-hour week will probably take priority. It is already in effect in some industries, and is gathering strength as the realization grows that the economic system, despite all its successes, will not solve the problem of unemployment without dramatic change in its direction and motivation.

Any consideration of reducing the workweek should bear in mind two essential ingredients. The first, of course, is that the individual worker should not lose income by reason of the reduction in time worked. The other is that the firm should be able to continue to utilize its capital equipment for the full normal forty hours of the week. At first glance, these two ingredients would appear to be contradictory. In fact, however, they are not. Management's resistance to reducing the workweek emanates not only from the cost factor involved but from the denial of full utilization of capital investment. Management wants to be able to use its equipment fully, and this means, under normal circumstances, forty hours a week.

In the 1976 contract negotiations between the UAW and the automobile industry, a strong beginning was made toward the achievement of a four-day week for the individual worker, while maintaining a forty-hour week for production purposes. This was done by designating days off for each individual during the period of the contract year as paid personal holidays. Workers absent from work while on paid personal holidays are replaced by additions to the work force. Moreover, each worker rotates his or her paid personal holidays in such a way that all workers enjoy the same number of long weekends and midweek days that they have off. Through these devices, management continues the full utilization of its equipment. The workers enjoy days off which over the years the union will insist be increased in number to effect eventually a four-day work-week; the result of this reduced work time will be to create job opportunities in order to help alleviate the serious problem of unemployment.

It remains to be seen whether this device for reducing work time, increasing employment, and maintaining full production hours will be adopted in other industries. However, whether or not this approach is utilized, it is evident that in the years ahead collective bargaining pressures will be brought increasingly to bear upon the demand for reducing work time in order to increase job opportunities for the unemployed.

Plant Shutdowns and Plant Movement

Management controls the decision to shut down a plant or move all or part of it to another location, often hundreds of miles away or overseas. The union bargains for severance pay, early retirement, the right of the worker to transfer with the job and to receive a moving allowance, and so on. But the workers, often with long years of service, are the victims of management's decision. They are permanently thrown out of work, or, if given the right to transfer with the job, must pull up stakes, cut their roots in the community, leave family and friends, and begin a new life in a strange place, with no assurance of permanence. Management wields the decision-making authority; the workers (and the community) dangle at the end of that decision. The community in which the workers live suffers from economic dislocation.

In some other industrialized nations movement of plants or parts of plants is regulated to some extent by law. In the United States, no legal restrictions exist on management's right of decision in this regard. Workers, therefore, demand protection for themselves and their communities through the collective bargaining process. We can anticipate that this issue will continue to fester, particularly in light of the failure of the nation to produce a full-employment economy and the search by management to reduce labor cost, transfer to new market locations, move to more readily available sources of energy, and so on.

Subcontracting

As a rule, management controls the final decision to subcontract work out (often motivated by the enticement of lower costs at home or abroad) or to move work about among its many facilities in a multiplant corporation. It is the worker who faces the ultimate insecurity.

Increasingly, contract negotiations are taking account of the insecurities that workers feel as a result of management's unfettered right to subcontract out work that can be performed by the workers. This is a highly controversial subject for collective bargaining and will continue to be so.

New Technology

The never-ending yet necessary introduction of technological innovation and the concomitant alteration of jobs, cutbacks in the work force, and effect on skill requirements are a constant source of new problems, emphasizing the concern workers naturally have for their job security.

Most unions have long since recognized that resisting the introduction of new technology is a futile and regressive exercise and that, instead, ways must be found to create enough jobs to replace those jobs eroded by scientific and engineering discoveries. The protection of the job security of the workers against the encroachment of the machine gives rise to incessant friction within the collective bargaining scene.

Production Scheduling

Production scheduling can be a serious source of friction, especially in moving-line operations. In an auto assembly plant, for instance, changes in line speed to meet changes in production schedules, or changes in model mix, require the rebalancing of jobs and operations. This in turn gives rise to disputes over production standards and the work force. Frequent changes in line speed or model mix disturb agreed-upon production standard settlements and work force agreements, often resulting in crisis bargaining and, on occasion, strike action.

The cyclical nature of the economy of certain industries makes this a most difficult problem to resolve. Yet, at the collective bargaining table the parties must think through possible ways and means of leveling out production schedules to provide continuity in operations and to avoid the intermittent confrontations over work force requirements that arise from unilateral changes in production schedules.

Day-Care Centers

With the continuing strong influx of women into the workplace, new issues for collective bargaining are gaining force. Capturing increased attention is the need for management to develop day-care centers to provide care for children while their mothers are at work. Progress in Europe and Japan on this issue has moved far faster than in the United States. As union women mobilize their power both within the labor movement and their communities, the demand for day-care centers, established through labor negotiations or by legislative action, will become more prominent.

Prepaid Legal Services

In the past several decades, unions have devoted close attention to negotiating benefit programs to protect the health of the worker and the worker's family; to provide income replacement in case of illness, death, or layoff; and to care for the worker in retirement. As these programs mature, unions will turn to other areas of worker concern to be covered by union contract provisions. Auto insurance coverage is one such area of interest. Another is prepaid legal services. A handful of such programs now exist, the most recent one negotiated between the UAW and Chrysler Corporation. We can anticipate that these will be areas for serious negotiations in the years ahead, adding coverage for these personal services provided by professionals to those already provided by doctors, hospitals, dentists, optometrists, psychiatrists, and psychologists.

Challenging the "Double Standard"

The double standard that exists between managers and workers is being seriously questioned. Symbols of elitism, traditionally taken for granted in an industrial society, are being challenged: salary payment and its normally recognized advantages, rather than hourly payment and time

clocks; paneled dining rooms, rather than plain Spartan types of caf-
eterias; privileged parking facilities close to the plant entrances; and so
on.

Similarly, the issue of organizing work schedules to enable workers to
manage their personal chores will be raised. Visiting the dentist or doctor,
getting the car repaired, discussing the children's problems with the
teacher, keeping appointments with repairmen, arranging to buy a home,
and other problems could be met through flexible working hours, a concept widely used in West Germany and beginning to find some measure of
acceptance in the United States.

Business executives, as we know, hold zealously to their so-called
management prerogatives. Each provision written into the collective bargaining agreement represents in one way or another an assault upon these
prerogatives; and, to be sure, there is really no end to the ingenuity of
workers in making demands upon the employer. The examples just described by no means exhaust the list of hard-line bargaining issues, nor do
they necessarily take priority over other subjects which might well have
been noted.

The point is that the adversarial issues for collective bargaining are almost endless in number and kind and will continue to play the key role in
relationships between management and labor.

ISSUES FOR JOINT COOPERATIVE PROGRAMS
TO IMPROVE THE QUALITY OF WORKING LIFE

Despite the intensity of the bargaining process in attempting to resolve
issues of a harsh adversarial nature, there are many subjects of mutual
concern and interest that simultaneously call for joint, cooperative effort.
Some must first be pounded out in principle in traditional bargaining
forays, such as the establishment of joint committees on health and safety;
others are not at all conducive to solution in the heat of a collective bargaining crisis, but in the inception call for reasonable parties to work together to achieve a commonly desired end. In the latter category we find
the recent joint efforts to promote work reorganization and the meaningful
involvement of workers in the decision-making process.

We may fittingly describe these as issues for joint, cooperative programs to improve the quality of working life. Many examples already
exist involving joint programs undertaken by the union and management.
To cite some of these is to explore the vast possibilities that exist for
cooperative union–management effort.

Alcoholism Rehabilitation

Alcoholism, long a festering problem, was traditionally handled by management as a matter for progressive discipline. Yet discipline could not and did not change the alcoholic. Succeedingly severe disciplinary measures simply aggravated the illness until discharge resulted. Thus, management lost the employee's training and skills; the employee lost his paycheck—and often his family as well. Society lost the benefit of a productive citizen. Joint alcoholism rehabilitation programs have been established which now recognize that alcoholism is an illness like other illnesses. Management and union representatives with training and expertise work together to assist the alcoholic who seeks or is induced to seek help. Thousands of ill workers thus have been restored to health, to their jobs, and to their families. They are once again contributing to the welfare of society.

A similar activity is developing with regard to the illness of drug addiction. True, the cures are still uncertain. Nevertheless, workers who seek help are being provided a measure of assistance through cooperative union–management programs.

This idea of cooperative effort to assist troubled employees is now expanding to cover family problems, emotional problems, and others as well. Essentially this approach represents an endeavor to meet human problems through humane methods, jointly undertaken.

New Employee Orientation Programs

Joint programs to help orient new employees in their jobs are another cooperative undertaking. In such programs knowledgeable management and union representatives jointly meet with newly hired workers and provide them with pertinent information concerning their job, the union, and so on. Thus, they enter upon a new and often strange world armed with comforting knowledge concerning the workplace and its surroundings and the people with whom they will be thrown into contact.

Preretirement Informational Programs

Joint preretirement programs have been initiated involving not only the prospective retiree but the spouse as well. Here again instruction and pertinent information are provided jointly by management and union representatives in meetings in which the agenda is carefully designed to assist workers contemplating retirement.

The Sensible Handling of Discipline

Experiments in which union and management think through together how best to handle problems of discipline regarding individual workers are also finding their place in the labor–management scene. How successful they will be remains to be evaluated, but the fact that in some instances management is willing to seek the assistance of the union in correcting the behavior of straying workers before any discipline is invoked is an interesting development and a recognition that humane understanding of a worker's personal problems and a willingness to assist him or her in resolving them can be a more effective deterrent to aberrant behavior than the mailed fist of the discharge threat. How often have foremen come to the realization that the habitual absentee prefers disciplinary time off as the penalty because it provides more time away from the job, in this instance "sanctioned" by management!

Apprenticeship Training

Joint apprentice training programs are of long standing, with the union and management making certain that apprentices are properly selected and that their training is appropriate to their trade.

Administration of Benefit Plans

Joint administration of worker benefit plans, such as pensions and health care, is also not new to the union–management relationship.

Together the parties determine the facts in each disputed situation, apply the provisions of the program, and correct errors in the administration of payment or coverage. In some UAW contracts there has developed an independent medical arbitration procedure to resolve disputes between doctors over eligibility for sickness-and-accident weekly benefits or total and permanent disability. The procedure of determining the eligibility of workers for retirement benefits, calculating the amount of the benefits, and then providing prospective retirees with information on their rights and other matters lends itself well to the joint union–management approach.

Health and Safety

Perhaps the most significant development in cooperative effort of the union and the management is the establishment of joint health and safety committees. The worker, after all, is the first-line victim of inadequate health-and-safety conditions at the workplace. With the proliferation of joint committees, health and safety programs have been elevated in importance and urgency. Literally thousands of corrective actions are being taken each year as a result of the joint efforts of union–management health and safety teams.

The establishment of joint programs on health and safety normally arises out of the heat of tough collective bargaining, but once the provisions are written as part of the labor contract, their implementation becomes a matter of mutual concern and cooperative effort in the workplace. Admittedly, this does not mean that all controversy over health and safety matters disappears—not at all. But it does direct the parties to a more wholesome appreciation of the need to work together to remove or ameliorate hazards to life and limb and create a safe and healthful workplace. Health and safety matters represent a unique mixture of cooperative effort on the one hand and tough controversy on the other.

WORKER PARTICIPATION IN DECISION MAKING

The joint and cooperative programs described in the preceding section represent sound progress in developing areas of mutual effort between union representatives and management representatives. They are healthy developments designed to be advantageous to the worker, the management, and the union. They have inestimable value, therefore, in enhancing labor–management relations. However, they do not involve the worker directly in the decision-making process, which is the essential next step toward improving the quality of working life and expanding at the workplace the fundamental concept of our democratic way of life.

Changing Views in Management

Time and circumstances are beginning to change the old authoritarian habits of management, due in part to the fact that workers' attitudes toward the meaning of work are changing and in part to the fact that society as a whole is paying closer attention to the totality of its environment and the quality of life.

In the days of the elder Henry Ford the worker lived, inside and outside the factory, under the autocratic rule of the owner of the enterprise. Mr. Ford's employment practices were strict and stifling inside the plant, and no less so outside the plant. No women were permitted to work in his factories; they belonged at home in the kitchen and with the children. Men who failed to support their dependents would find no work at Ford. Similarly, divorced men or others who were "living unworthily"—that is, those who smoked or drank hard liquor—were not welcome.

Once hired, the workers were subjected to a spy system. "Social workers" on the Ford payroll would enter the workers' homes and report on living habits: whether the worker raised his own garden as instructed; whether his family housed male boarders, a practice that was taboo; whether the worker complained to his family about his job and factory conditions; and so on.

Contrast Henry Ford's stifling authoritarianism with the promise expressed in 1972 in the words of Mr. Richard Gerstenberg, chairman of the Board of Directors of General Motors Corporation:

> Productivity is not a matter of making employees work longer or harder. . . . We must improve working conditions and take out the boredom from routine jobs. . . . We must increase an employee's satisfaction with his job, heighten pride of workmanship and—as far as is feasible—involve the employee personally in decisions that relate directly to his job. (April 26, 1972)

Management has historically paid lip service to the slogan that it is the people performing the work who are the most important in the productive process. In fact, however, the treatment given workers belies the rhetoric. As often as not, management places little trust in the worker to do the "right thing" in the performance of his job. It surrounds the worker with rules and regulations, instructions and orders, precise requirements for performing in a prescribed manner—all in the authoritarian atmosphere of the workplace. Typically, supervisors are taught to give "direct orders" and to discipline or discharge for "failure or refusal" to obey them. So little is the worker trusted to produce a quality product that management devises innumerable complicated quality-control systems to oversee the job—the more complex the system, the greater the pride on management's part over its ingenuity in monitoring the worker and the product. Let us face it, management places more trust in the machine than in the worker, and therein lies one reason that over the years the worker has become more an adjunct of the tool than its master.

At the same time that management thus demeans workers and their capabilities, it traditionally exhorts them to cooperate in increasing productivity and improving the quality of the product. Actually, the other face of the coin is more appropriate, namely, that management should cooperate with workers to find ways to enhance the human dignity of labor and to tap the creative resources of each human being in developing a more satisfying working life. Rather than excluding workers from making decisions, management should give them every opportunity to participate meaningfully in the decision-making process.

The concept of participation in the decision-making process is fundamental to the democratic way of life, which is the lifeblood of our society. In a democratic society workers as citizens enjoy broad rights of decision making that are denied to those living in autocratic societies. They have the right, through their vote, to determine who their leaders will be. With their vote they can also turn those same leaders out of office. As family members and residents of their community they participate in a myriad of decisions affecting their lives and the well-being of their loved ones, their neighbors, and their fellow citizens. Within the rational restrictions of living within a society of people, they are decision makers every day of their lives. In the workplace, however, they are the obeyers of orders. Suffice it to say, it is time that a social order anchored in democratic principles ensured to each individual at the workplace a significant measure of the dignity, self-respect, and freedom enjoyed as a citizen. The citizen as worker should be afforded similar opportunity for self-expression and participation in the decisions that shape the quality of working life.

In recent years, an increasing number of management executives have been pondering this problem, perhaps not in philosophic terms related to democratic values, but in the light of the harsh reality of a new work force, which increasingly resists the authoritarianism of the workplace. Regardless of the motivation—increased absenteeism, high labor turnover, declining product quality, a better educated work force—some managements are coming to the realization that life at work must change, that perhaps the traditional adherence to "scientific management" is obsolete. This has led to a wave of experimentation to improve the quality of working life. Some projects are unilaterally undertaken by management; some are joint efforts by union and management. Some are cynically designed to thwart successful union organization in nonunion facilities; others are genuine attempts by union and management to create a new, deeper sense of worker dignity and satisfaction at the workplace.

The Union View

Union attitudes toward these developments are mixed. Unions in the United States traditionally have moved in the direction of improving wages, benefits, and working conditions. As a general rule, they have left "managing the enterprise" to management, reacting to managerial decisions objectionable to the workers. They have not embraced a political philosophy to motivate their overall policies and programs. This is not to say that unions in the United States hold no socio-politico-economic concepts. Quite the contrary. But they are not married to an "ism" or a dogma governing and directing their behavior.

Unions in the United States move to meet practical problems with practical solutions. It would be highly improbable that they would approach the problem of worker participation in decision making by way of a fierce ideological struggle founded in socioeconomic theory. They are not prone to beat their wings in ideological frustration.

When workers feel victimized, they combine their forces to correct the situation, case by case, problem by problem. Gradual, persistent change, not revolutionary upheaval, has marked the progress of the American worker. When explosions do occur, as they did in the 1930s, they are responses to specific problems in the search for specific solutions. They are not revolutionary reactions founded in ideological concepts of the class struggle.

We can anticipate, therefore, that worker participation in the development of programs to improve the quality of working life will manifest itself as a step-by-step effort to enhance the welfare of workers and to uplift their human dignity.

Unions will make a grave mistake if they stand aloof from these developments and fail to participate in experiments and demonstration projects to increase the role of workers in decision making, for these new directions will have significant impact on life at the workplace. Unions, therefore, should welcome the introduction of such programs and insist that they be jointly developed and implemented, with the union an equal partner in the process, providing direction and leadership as to the nature and substance of the total program.

Decisions regarding purchasing, advertising, selling, financing, and so on, are more remote from the immediate problems facing workers than are decisions concerning their jobs. In the vast range of managerial decisions that must be made, the immediacy of impact on workers varies enormously. Thus, the average worker in a gigantic enterprise usually displays less interest in the selection of the chairman of the board of directors than in the worker's own right of transfer and promotion. If workers should come to recognize these and other "managerial functions" as imminently important to their welfare, they will then move to participate in them also.

For the present and foreseeable future, however, worker participation in decision making will more readily spring up with regard to the more immediate and noticeable aspects of working life. "Managing the job" is more immediate and urgent. Worker concern for "managing the enterprise" is more variable and is best measured by the immediacy of impact on the worker's own welfare.

Human Development and the Humanistic Concept of Productivity

Experiments are underway in both Europe and the United States that are designed to alleviate the deadening routine of the work process. Some appear more successful than others; some are utter failures. Important, however, is the fact that these experiments exhibit a desire to stress the fulfillment of human development as much as and sometimes even more than the achievement of productive efficiency.

Concomitant with this "new mood" in structuring work is an equally significant challenge to the views held regarding the definition of productivity. It is not enough to define productivity simply in terms of units of production per work-hour. Dr. Michael Maccoby, for instance, suggests a broad, humanistic concept of productivity, in terms of overall social effectiveness and creativity, which to my mind is far more attuned to twentieth-century society.

As we couple the idea of human development at the workplace with a humanistic definition of productivity, we must arrive at a different, if not altogether new, view of the relationship between management and labor.

As management executives either reach a similar conclusion or at least become willing to engage in demonstration projects that recognize the worker as a decision maker, the opportunities become brighter for the development of a new look in the labor–management relationship, one in which workers are treated not as substitutes for machines to perform the bidding of the foreman without question, but rather as "co-partners" in the decision-making process.

It must be clear from the beginning, however, that any projects or programs designed to enhance worker involvement in decision making must not become simply another gimmick designed essentially to fool the worker and having as their primary goal an increase in worker productivity. Manipulation of the worker will be recognized for what it is, another form of exploitation. It will breed suspicion and distrust and it will fail. The essential purpose of any program should not be tied to increasing productivity. Rather, it should be geared to creating human satisfaction at the workplace. And if the result is reduction in absenteeism, reduction in labor turnover, reduction in the use of disciplinary action, and improvement in the quality of the product, these will be fallout advantages to which there can hardly be any objection.

Worker participation in decision making should result in a departure from the miniaturization and simplification of the job to a system which embraces broader distribution of authority; it should increase rather than diminish responsibility and accountability, and also engineer more interesting jobs, with the opportunity to exercise a meaningful measure of autonomy and to utilize more varied skills. It requires that management permit workers every opportunity to exercise their creative and innovative ingenuity to the maximum extent of their capabilities.

Worker Participation in Decision Making

Some experiments in worker decision making have been widely publicized, such as the UAW-Harman International Industries project at Bolivar, Tennessee; General Foods in Topeka, Kansas; Rushton Mines Osceola Mills, Pennsylvania; and others. Less publicized, but making steady progress, are the demonstration projects being undertaken jointly by the UAW and General Motors Corporation in several of its plants.

Usually the introduction of a program requires a two-step procedure. First, there must be built up a relationship of trust between the union and management in the day-to-day handling of their collective bargaining disputes. This requires not a "cozy" relationship, but rather an understanding of each other's problems and a willingness to try to work them out at the level of the workplace itself. With such a relationship developed (and it does not come easily), the way is cleared to introduce programs involving workers directly in "managing the job."

The joint union–management programs that are in existence have not yet proven themselves in any permanent sense. They must be subject constantly to review and change as management, the union, and the workers learn by doing. Although it is not possible to set forth a precise blueprint to ensure the successful participation of workers in the decision-making process, experience already indicates certain criteria that are basic:

- The programs should be voluntary. Workers must have the free opportunity to decide whether or not to participate in the program. To order compulsion is to invite resistance and failure.
- Workers should be assured that their participation in decision making will not erode their job security or that of their fellow workers, that they will not be subject to "speed up" by reason of it, and that the program will not violate their rights under the collective bargaining agreement.
- Workers should genuinely experience that they are not simply adjuncts to the tool, but that their bent toward being creative, innovative, and inventive plays a significant role in the production (or service) process.
- Job functions should be engineered to fit the worker; the current system is designed to make the worker fit the job on the theory that this is a more efficient production system and that, in any event, economic gain is the worker's only reason for working. This theory is wrong on both counts.
- The worker should be assured the widest possible latitude of self-management, responsibility, and opportunity for use of "brainpower." Gimmickry and manipulation of the worker must not be employed.
- The changes in job content and the added responsibility and involvement in decision making should be accompanied by an effective reward system.
- Workers should be able to foresee opportunities for growth in their work, and for promotion.
- The role of workers in the business should enable them to relate to the products being produced or the services being rendered, and to their meaning in society; in a broader sense, it should also enable them to relate constructively to their role in society.

In the ensuing years, while hard-line collective bargaining continues on its traditional course, the scope of union–management relations will be enlarged and will simultaneously embrace those aspects of working life that advance the concept of human development of the individual and target in on enhancing the dignity, self-worth, and job satisfaction of the worker. Such endeavors will be to the advantage of the workers, the management, and the union. In the final analysis, all of society will stand to gain.

The Assault on the Labor Movement

The changes that are taking place in society, the economy, and the work force obviously affect considerations which the labor movement must give to its future directions.

Unions must face up to the fact that the public image of the labor movement is, according to various reputable polls, far from satisfactory. Although studies indicate that a majority of the people agree that unions are necessary to advance and defend the rights of workers, at the same time the once high regard in which the public held the labor movement as a positive force for constructive change in society has been waning. The question is not whether in fact this image is deserved; the fact that large sectors of the public are turned off suffices to make this a problem not to be ignored.

The antilabor forces in the country have mounted a multifaceted attack upon the labor movement. Not since the thirties have they been so blatant in their assault, utilizing not only the various propaganda and legal devices available to resist organizing drives and the harassing tactics of legislative action (so-called right-to-work laws) but even firms with well-established relations with unions are vigorously fighting efforts to unionize their newly established operations.

The challenge is evident. The labor movement has an urgent twofold task: to refurbish its tarnished image as a socially constructive force, overcoming community resistance to unionism, especially in the Sun Belt, and to mount vigorous organizing efforts to bring the unorganized into the fold. The Industrial Union Department of the AFL–CIO and the UAW have embarked on such a program in certain areas that have thus far proven almost impervious to union organization. The program shows initial progress; but the total task will still prove slow and painstaking and will require dogged persistence, applying new organizing techniques both among the workers to be organized and the communities in which they live.

The purpose behind labor's thrust to organize workers is rooted in the need to improve the quality of life for workers and their families and to bring a larger measure of democracy into the workplace. Increased membership adds strength to the achievement of these goals. There is more to it, however.

Historically, a free labor movement is in the vanguard of the struggle for democratic freedom and the rights of the individual. It is the sworn enemy of dictatorial oppression. In every country in which a dictatorship has been established, among the first victims are the leaders of free labor unions. This was true in Hitler's Germany, in Franco's Spain. In the Soviet Union free and independent labor unions are not permitted. (Recently, a small, lonely group of workers has declared the establishment of an independent union; their future remains obscure.) In China labor unions, independent or captive, do not exist at all. Where there is dictatorship, there are no free unions.

The American people must understand that the most vocal antilabor forces in the country are intent upon weakening or destroying unionism. Should they succeed, they will clear the path for unfettered authoritarianism at the workplace; they will have weakened the sensitive fiber of our democratic heritage. Simply put, we need free, independent, strong unions to maintain a strong democracy.

NOTES

1. Leon Keyserling, *Toward Full Employment within Three Years* (Washington, D.C.: Conference on Economic Progress, 1976), p. 10.
2. Michael Maccoby, "The Bolivar Project: Productivity and Human Development," a report from the Harvard Program on Technology, Policy, and Human Development, 1977.

13.
Public Policy and the Quality of Working Life

A. H. RASKIN
Associate Director, National News Council
Former Labor Columnist, The New York Times

In this post-Watergate era of apologetic government, Uncle Sam is trying to keep a low profile in the workplace. Democratic leaseholders in the White House and in the governor's mansions of most states and city halls across the country vie with Republicans in proclaiming that government meddles too much in people's personal and business affairs and that most of what it does it does badly. As part of the retreat from the imperial presidency, an attempt is being made to translate the doctrine of "small is beautiful" into "less is better" in the top-level approach to the whole regulatory field.

All such efforts to bring back Adam Smith's "invisible hand" as the principal arbiter of industrial conduct are, however, doomed to failure, for the worldwide persistence of high levels of inflation and unemployment and the proliferation of problems growing out of dislocations caused by trade and technology point toward much more, not less, public involvement in determining the conditions and quality of working life in the United States. Far from easing government out the door of factory and office, Americans will have to accommodate to what seems likely to be a future of increased governmental involvement in everything from the creation of jobs to their character.

The great question is whether that thrust toward a more assertive federal presence takes its direction from the kind of tripartite cooperation reflected in the activities of such groups as the Work in America Institute, where labor, management, and government attempt to fuse their best thoughts on how to tackle novel challenges, or whether it will be imposed

253

externally under conflict circumstances ill adapted to the successful emergence of new patterns of industrial democracy in an environment of freedom.

HOW DID IT ALL START?

A useful starting point for exploration of this pivotal question is a recognition of the formidable dimensions of the current governmental presence in the workplace. Franklin D. Roosevelt's New Deal unleashed a tide that slackened a bit in the three decades after World War II but not enough to invite any serious attempt, even under the most enterprise-minded of Republican administrations, to chop away the underpinnings of a new structure of shared authority.

The main building blocks of that structure were trundled out even before FDR got to 1600 Pennsylvania Avenue. In December 1932, he called New York's industrial commissioner, Frances Perkins, to his New York City townhouse and urged her to accompany him to Washington as secretary of labor. The idea did not intrigue her. She pointed out that the American Federation of Labor was insisting that the new head of the Department of Labor come from labor's own ranks, a requisite she did not fulfill. Moreover, the federation had a very specific idea of who the new secretary ought to be. Its nominee was Dan Tobin, president of the International Brotherhood of Teamsters, who ranked alongside "Big Bill" Hutcheson of the Carpenters as the principal mover and shaker inside the AFL executive council.

When Roosevelt brushed aside this line of argument, Miss Perkins turned to another that she felt would certainly chill the president-elect's enthusiasm for appointing her. She proceeded to tick off a legislative agenda that included a federal program of aid to the states for direct unemployment relief, a statutory floor under wages, a ceiling on working hours, public works, unemployment insurance, old-age security, abolition of child labor, and creation of a federal employment service. To Miss Perkins' considerable astonishment, Roosevelt, whom she knew as a pragmatist, raised no question about the practicality of instituting so many ambitious reforms in a period of depression and mass joblessness. On the contrary, he gave the whole list his hearty endorsement and said he wanted to carry it out.

That decision, converted into law within a half decade, represented a fundamental turning point in American industrial relations, one that put the federal government irrevocably into an activist role as definer and enforcer of employee rights, guarantor of basic levels of economic decency in the workplace, stimulator and stabilizer of the economy. It was not a revolutionary turn; just the reverse, its frank purpose was to defuse the forces of despair that were pushing many Americans toward the revolutionary nostrums of political extremists—the Communists, the Townsendites, the Coughlinites, and the disciples of Huey Long, with his siren song of "every man a king."

For all his denunciation of "economic royalists" and his admonitions to drive the money changers from the temple, Roosevelt had no wish to junk capitalism. He was an experimentalist, distrustful of rigid intellectual theories, and opportunism bulked large in his arsenal of tactics. But none of that stripped him of a sense of social direction. Impatient as he was with moralistic cant, the reforms with which he was identified were predicated on concern for promoting and safeguarding human values in an industrial structure built on the pursuit of profit. The integrating premise of the New Deal was a concept of governmental intervention to keep the economy healthy, to protect the poor, and to curb abuses by private power blocs.

Collective Bargaining

Out of that came sponsorship by FDR and enactment by Congress of every one of the initiatives put forward by Miss Perkins three months before inauguration day, plus another that had perhaps the most far-reaching impact of all in altering the quality of working life. This was the passage in 1935 of the Wagner Labor Relations Act, aimed at assuring workers the right to organize in unions of their own choosing and to bargain collectively with their employers.

It is easy more than forty years later to forget how dramatic a turnaround all of this was in traditional notions of the proper boundaries of governmental responsibility. As late as 1930 William Green, president of the AFL, was testifying before congressional committees against unemployment insurance. A year after the stock-market crash, with unemployment on the rise everywhere, the head of the labor movement still felt justified in telling the legislators on Capitol Hill that job insurance was paternalistic, a form of dole that stultified individual initiative and murdered hope. "The real cure is employment," was his pious dismissal of the whole idea that governmental cushions might come in handy as the idleness total climbed toward 13 million, a quarter of the work force.

Social Security Act

Even the most popular feature of the original Social Security Act, its provision for bailing out state and local old-age relief programs, most of which were inoperative or verging on bankruptcy, had some rough going initially. Southern Democrats, in key committee posts, held the entire bill hostage until they exacted a commitment to delete a proposed requirement that federal funds for the needy aged go only to states that met federal minimum standards for "health and decency." The Southerners viewed any such mandate as an insupportable invasion of state's rights. Not until 1974 would Congress move enough on this issue to permit nationwide establishment of a uniform minimum allowance for aid to the elderly, disabled, and blind under the Federal Supplemental Security Income plan. For mothers with dependent children and others on the general relief rolls, thoroughgoing welfare reform will have to emerge from the never-never land of White House and congressional delay before any comparable bedrock can be put under their living standards.

Wage–Hour Legislation

Inside the workplace the first upward thrust of the minimum wage and the first federal lid on basic working hours came at the very dawn of the New Deal as part of the codes of fair competition adopted by many industries under the National Industrial Recovery Act. But the Blue Eagle of the NRA was shot down by the Supreme Court in the Schechter "sick chicken" case.

The Court's invalidation of the recovery act stalled any major presidential push on the wage–hour front until 1937. In that year a switch by Justice Owen J. Roberts, a pillar of the conservative majority, on the constitutionality of a state job-insurance law provided the swing vote needed to turn the Court from a chronic five-to-four margin against such legislation as an infringement of "freedom of contract" under the Fourteenth Amendment to a five-to-four margin in favor. Up to then the Court's invariable position had been that the moral right of workers to a living wage could not take precedence in law over an employer's right to pay whatever he deemed a "just wage."

Even after the Court flashed its green light on wage–hour legislation, Southern Democrats and their Republican allies in Congress remained unconvinced that the federal government should interfere with the market system by attempting to set a living wage for the working poor. They warned then, as their lineal descendants do today, that the cost in higher prices and job extinction would make all such efforts counterproductive. The New Dealers won after much tactical maneuvering on Capitol Hill, but the first minimum wage was set at only twenty-five cents an hour, effective October 24, 1938. It took five years to boost it to forty cents on an across-the-board basis.

Congress was bolder when it came to a ceiling on hours. In the hope that a shorter workweek would effectively spread opportunities for employment, it fixed an initial minimum of forty-four hours before premium pay became mandatory at overtime rates of time and a half or better. The timetable called for reducing the maximum to forty-two hours after one year and, a year after that, to the forty-hour standard that remains the cutoff point today. By contrast, the statutory minimum wage has increased more than tenfold since 1938. The current minimum wage is $2.90 an hour, and it is scheduled to step up to $3.35 on January 1, 1981.

Labor–Management Relations

By the yardstick of democratic practice to effect changes in the work environment, no element of the New Deal compares in significance with the legislation it fostered to put a firm legal foundation under unionization and collective bargaining. For the first time the workers, through their unions, were guaranteed a voice in determining their conditions of labor if they chose to exercise it. The mass-production industries, which had maintained private armies of goons and labor spies to frustrate that elementary right of industrial self-expression, reluctantly bowed to the law. So did many of the smallest of small businesses, along with thousands at every level of size and power in between. The face of American industry was fundamentally changed in the process.

The principle of federal responsibility in policing labor–management relations had established a limited toehold through the Railway Labor Act of 1926 and the Norris–LaGuardia Anti-Injunction Act of 1932, but the "great divide" came with congressional passage of the Wagner Act in 1935 and the upholding of its constitutionality by the Supreme Court two years later. Pending that judicial seal of approval, many employers had withheld compliance out of expectation that the labor law would prove as short-lived as had the National Industrial Recovery Act. That judicially aborted law had included union guarantees akin to those in the Wagner

Act as a counterbalance to its provisions exempting businesses enrolled under the NRA codes of fair competition from antitrust prosecution.

The Wagner Act itself ran into trouble in the period immediately after World War II, when the termination of labor's wartime no-strike pledge and the collapse of wage-and-price controls brought a rash of strikes in most basic industries and an inflationary settlement pattern engineered in large measure by the White House. The congressional response was passage, over President Truman's veto, of the Taft–Hartley Act of 1947. It kept in place the essential provisions of the Wagner Act, but added many new features aimed at checking union excesses. Revelations of underworld penetration and undemocratic practices in some unions brought additional amendments to the basic law in the Landrum–Griffin Labor Reform Act of 1959. In 1977 and 1978 organized labor clashed bitterly with a united front of business over yet another revision. This one, endorsed by President Carter, was directed at reinforcing the original guarantees of freedom to organize and bargain collectively, a full turn of the circle back to the precepts of four decades ago. The House of Representatives approved the measure, but an industry-fostered filibuster killed it in the Senate.

The battle left a residue of acute ill feeling in the upper echelons of unionism, but the bill's demise will not erase the impact on the workplace of two generations of federal support for collective bargaining. Unions have steadily extended the boundaries of bargaining in ways that curtail the authority of management to make unilateral decisions on the conditionsand quality of work. A thousand items, from job transfers to coffee breaks and toilet time, are in the bargaining orbit, and each contract round sees the list made more inclusive.

It is improbable that anyone ever will succeed in building a fence around the bargaining table. As long ago as 1945, when Truman called a summit conference of labor and management in an attempt to work out a formula for industrial peace and stability, the union chiefs balked at employer proposals that a line be drawn beyond which labor would not go in seeking to share prerogatives traditionally reserved to management. The unionists disavowed a desire to socialize business under any scheme of outright worker control but added: "The experience of many years shows that with the growth of mutual understanding the responsibilities of one of the parties today may very well become the joint responsibility of both parties tomorrow."

The same statement is applicable to the extensions of governmental involvement in the workplace. Areas once regarded as subject to control only by industry and workers, with any essential monitorial role confined to the states or localities, keep moving under federal surveillance, even though the rate of movement has been measurably less brisk than it was in the breathtaking early years of the New Deal. The importance of the new fields over which regulatory authority has been established underscores the potentialities for even more arresting extensions of federal supervision, if the formulators of public policy decide that activist solutions are necessary to meet the problems of the 1980s.

Equal-Employment Opportunities

Unquestionably, the most mine-strewn area of federal monitorship of the workplace has been in the field of equal-employment opportunity. Employers and unions alike have repeatedly found themselves in bitter conflict with blacks, Hispanics, and women who are demanding compliance with the nondiscrimination requirements of Title VII of the Civil Rights Act of 1964. Yet the statutory insistence on equal treatment in hiring and promotions never would have been in the law at all had George Meany not put all the lobbying strength of the AFL–CIO behind a demand for its inclusion. President John F. Kennedy and Attorney General Robert F. Kennedy were convinced that it would be difficult enough to get an omnibus civil rights bill through Congress without unleashing the intense emotions stirred by a ban on job discrimination. The correctness of that view was demonstrated by the fact that the law did not pick up momentum until the shock of the president's assassination made rejection unthinkable.

Occupational Safety and Health

Almost as much controversy has been stirred by the enforcement of the Occupational Safety and Health Act of 1970—and by its nonenforcement. The multiplicity of chemicals used in industry has vastly added to the death-dealing hazards attendant on earning a living in many fields. Certainly, nothing bears more intimately on the quality of working life (or, in the baldest terms, its continuance) than the reduction of all such hazards. By the same token, no assessment of the cost-effectiveness of remedies is more troublesome, necessitating, as it often does, an impossible balance between the value to be put on the survival of jobs and on the risk to human health.

WHERE ARE WE GOING?

It is the necessity for just such choices in a fast-broadening spectrum of activities that makes probable a steady expansion of governmental influence in the workplace in the next decade. That probability is increased by the prospect that a combination of internal and external constraints, ranging from concern for the environment to the intensified competitiveness of world trade, will oblige the American economy to adjust to an indefinite future in which overall living standards will, at best, stand still.

Such a freeze in standards will not set the United States apart from the rest of the industrialized countries, but none of the others worships so totally at the shrine of "more and better." Looking down rather than up in real purchasing power is a shock for which most Americans remain poorly prepared. The average worker is worse off today than he was five years ago in terms of how much his paycheck will buy, but two cuts in federal income taxes have kept the squeeze from becoming too painful. Now another tax cut is in prospect, partly to pep up the economy and partly to neutralize the dent put into workers' budgets by the bite of higher Soecial Security taxes. But worries over inflation have taken first place in popular concern and give every indication of remaining paramount in public policy determination in the years immediately ahead.

Inroads of Foreign Trade

Many of those who up to now have been "winners" in the inflationary sweepstakes because they had leverage sufficient to push wages up faster than the consumer price index are being thrust into the ranks of "losers" by the inroads of imports. Workers in steel and electrical manufacturing, once in the vanguard of a blue-collar elite, are joining apparel and textile workers on the shutout list.

The government, riding to the rescue in response to anguished appeals from union and industry leaders, is faced with problems that could involve it deeply in the determination of new patterns of industrial organization. These will have a profound bearing on such issues as the degree of worker participation in every aspect of management decision making, including investment policy and products to be made or services supplied.

The likelihood of government involvement arises out of the acknowledged inadequacy of traditional methods of adjustment assistance to plants that are being forced out of business by the foreign takeover of their markets. In order to save these businesses and the jobs they sustain, new solutions are needed. The crucible for a new adjustment pattern may be provided by the shutdown of the Campbell Works of Youngstown Steel, which resulted in the layoff of 5,000 members of the United Steelworkers of America. Under pressure from the community, the federal government is exploring the practicality of reviving the Ohio mill under some form of cooperative ownership.

The cost in plant redesign and modernized equipment is bound to prove high, but investments of great size may prove inescapable if the United States is to evolve a supportable policy of fairer, freer trade—one that does not throw a crushing burden of sacrifice on particular sectors of the economy in the process of advancing the total national interest. Indeed, the government's task may extend to underwriting the development of entire new industries, such as solar energy, especially if trade policy in this interdependent world requires that certain industries be phased out in return for guarantees of secure markets for others in which the United States can compete more effectively. Undertakings of that dimension would parallel the space program at peak priority.

Full Employment

The quest for full employment, whether through the Carter-backed Humphrey–Hawkins Act or some alternative approach, will represent another insistent prod toward governmental involvement in the workplace. In and of itself, this belated effort to make real the commitment so artfully fudged in the Employment Act of 1946 deals with the foundation stone of any concern for the quality of working life, the right to a job for everyone willing and able to work. It may be disingenuous to believe that any democracy can enter into a compact with its citizens to hold unemployment inside a 4 percent ceiling, but no administration dedicated to human rights can shrink from the duty of mapping programs calculated to test the feasibility of such a goal.

Reduced Workweek

One question that will require an answer as part of such planning is whether it is not time to lower the forty-hour ceiling on the workweek that Congress decreed fully forty years ago. If the country could go from a six-day basic workweek to five days in the depths of the Great Depression, why is it preposterous to believe that a gradual stepdown toward a universal four-day week would not necessarily prove a calamity today? As the first reporter hired at *The New York Times* when the NRA code for the newspaper industry ushered in a five-day schedule in 1934, I can offer firsthand testimony that a government-induced cut in working hours is capable of spreading employment without undermining the viability of an enterprise.

The United Auto Workers is already well launched in pursuit of a four-day workweek in the automobile industry. Its contracts with the Big Three companies now provide forty days of paid leisure time each year, just twelve days short of the desired total if they were spread out on a day-a-week basis. But what may be practical for Detroit may be ruinous as a pattern for less prosperous industries. That is why governmental delay in studying the problem could be dangerous.

When the economy is already tipped in a seventy-to-thirty ratio toward the predominance of service industries and when billions of dollars in productive capacity go unused year after year, there is ample warrant for a tripartite inquiry under presidential auspices into the feasibility of inflation-free approaches to work sharing through reduced basic work schedules. The much-battered work ethic might be the principal beneficiary if heightened job satisfaction results from enlarged opportunity for the enjoyment of leisure within a framework of employment.

A prompt step in that direction is particularly desirable because the presence of 40 million women in the job market, with the number still soaring, has already brought a sharp rise in people wanting to work part time or demanding flexible schedules to accommodate family needs or personal preferences. Younger workers of both sexes, rich in creativity, tend to be obstructive when the rigidities of factory or office routine provide no outlet for deviation from the norm. The conditions of near anarchy within the United Mine Workers, once the most autocratic of unions, indicate that even the highest of pay scales coupled with secure employment in a booming industry do not still the restlessness of a youthful work force steeped in free-swinging life-styles and impatient of authority.

A host of additional forces are pulling government deeper into the work arena. One is the impossibility of mounting a systematic drive toward full employment and toward more substantial indemnity against the casualties of foreign trade, without an incomes policy to guard against a drastic worsening of inflation. Another is the need for public intervention to salvage such distressed industries as the railroads, first through the already completed consolidation into the Conrail system of the Penn Central and other bankrupt carriers in the Northeast and Midwest, and now through the projected fusion of other troubled roads elsewhere in the country.

Technological Change

The dislocations caused by technological change, the shift of job opportunities into the Sun Belt states, and the need for environmental protection all produce a clamor for increased federal intercession. The staggering cost of retirement benefits will force attention to the need for integrating private pension programs with Social Security in much the manner already done to save the railroad retirement system from insolvency. Similarly, the advent of some form of national health insurance will involve dovetailing the new governmental program with those already in place under employee welfare funds. The mounting pressure for better bridges between the worlds of education and work emphasizes the need for more embracing links between government and the workplace.

Occupational Safety and Health

The most dislocative thrust in its impact on existing production practices, costs, and jobs is likely to be the one an industrial society committed to the improvement of human values has too long neglected, the definition of enforceable limits of tolerance for carcinogens and other menaces to occupational health and safety. Secretary of Labor Ray Marshall and Director of Occupational Safety and Health Administration Eula Bingham have left no room for doubt that their thinning out of regulatory underbrush at the beginning of 1978 was not intended as a backward step but rather as a clearing of the decks for more rigorous action to eliminate the major causes of death, sickness, and physical impairment due to the work environment. The elaborate scope of the programs currently in force in Sweden and Norway, to protect the mental and psychic as well as the physical well-being of workers, provides an indication of the unchartability of future federal involvement in health and safety in a world of changing technology and changing human expectations.

The assertiveness of the public role in controlling private work practices in the United States could be expanded tremendously without approaching the encyclopedic range of laws now common in the Scandinavian countries and the European Economic Community, which prescribe posts for employees as corporate directors or as joint architects of production policy, job design, and wage systems at the shop level.

The ways in which Uncle Sam gets into the act will continue to grow as the problems facing both industry and labor increase in importance and in intractability. The futility of seeking constructive solutions to all of them through private means alone brings to center stage the query raised at the outset of this chapter: Will the search for more secure and satisfying jobs be conducted under conditions of labor–management cooperation with government, or will it degenerate into conflict and confrontation, with tests of political and economic muscle substituted for rationality?

Labor–Management Relationships

At the moment the answer is not totally reassuring. Top-level relationships between industry and unions, after several years of steady movement toward a cordiality founded on mutual respect, have been sliding downhill under the bruising impact of repeated clashes in the very area that is under question, the appropriate extent of government involvement in the workplace and the overall economy.

The battle has been joined principally on the legislative front, where every major initiative for governmental job creation or alteration of the status quo in the workplace has found management and labor on opposite sides of the ideological barricades. The disappointing fruit of forty years of learning to live together in increasing harmony has been to leave management and labor incapable of reaching any measure of consensus even on the proposed revision of the basic law governing labor–management relations.

The polarization that developed on that issue from the moment the labor law reform bill was sent to Capitol Hill with President Carter's blessing has left lasting scars. George Meany, whose support for capitalist institutions is as firm as that of the most rock-ribbed free enterpriser, was so irked by the united front of big and small business against the bill that he began to compare American industrialists to the German and Italian tycoons who helped bring Hitler and Mussolini to power before World War II.

Uncharacteristically lurid as the Meany language may have been, labor's disappointment at the near universality of industry opposition was understandable in the light of the goodwill that had supposedly been established in three years of close contact between the heads of the largest of U.S. multinational corporations and the presidents of the country's strongest unions. With John T. Dunlop of Harvard, secretary of labor in the Ford Administration, as coordinator and catalyst, the two groups had first come together as a top-level advisory committee to President Ford. They stayed together even after Professor Dunlop resigned as secretary of labor in protest against Ford's about-face veto of a 1975 bill to extend picketing rights at construction sites. Operating without any kind of formal ties to government, the industry and union chiefs found their periodic discussions beneficial not only in promoting mutual regard but also in enabling them to achieve common positions on such controversial issues as nuclear energy and methods of controlling the skyrocketing cost of hospital care.

The recent reversal in this cooperative trend has also been reflected in a harsher management stance at the bargaining table and a chillier climate in general relationships. One signpost of such a change for the worse came in 1977 in steel, an industry that won richly deserved acclaim during the last decade for its substitution of reason for force in the negotiation of wages and other contract terms. Its long-term peace treaty, the seven-year-old Experimental Negotiating Agreement, barely survived a 1977 strike of iron ore miners that dragged on even longer than the 116-day industry-wide strike of 1959, a tie-up both sides regarded as the strike to end all strikes in their beleaguered industry. In the dismayingly long coal strike of 1978, representatives of the steel industry were the hardest of the hard-liners on the industry side.

Increased combativeness has similarly been manifest in aerospace, meat packing, and big-city newspapers, where employers have demonstrated that they will no longer accept a union strike call as inescapable notice that they must shut up shop. They actively encourage employees to come through the picket lines and maintain operations. In a similar vein, management consultants are finding a brisk market all over the country for seminars that provide sophisticated instruction to employers in such topics as "How to Maintain Non-Union Status" and "Making Unions Unnecessary." The National Association of Manufacturers has itself joined this phalanx of adult educators by setting up a Council of Union-Free Environment. Perhaps the most interesting aspect of this development is that it represents the first major initiative of the NAM's new president, Heath Larry, who as vice-chairman of United States Steel was co-parent of the Experimental Negotiating Agreement with I. W. Abel of the United Steelworkers.

It is possible, however, to read too much into these signs of reversion to conflict. The pulls in the opposite direction remain compelling, and nowhere more so than in the necessity for joint industry–union action to keep the United States strong in world trade competition. Building that strength will require all the ingenuity and creative energy of both sides, not an intensification of ritualistic calls on government to establish import quotas or other expensive forms of protection for domestic producers and unions unwilling to make any independent contribution to their own survival.

For all the reasons previously noted and for others of irresistible urgency, such as the insistence of the Third World on a less lopsided distribution of the world's wealth, public policy will play an ever more important role in marshaling the country's resources and fixing its priorities. One part of that redefinition of national purpose and practice almost certainly will be aimed at a fuller tapping of the reservoirs of creativity located in the minds and muscles of the nation's workers, much of it stifled by the present paramilitary lines of industrial command.

The success of any endeavor to infuse the workplace with more democracy will, in the final analysis, depend on how convinced rank-and-file employees are that their employers and unions are genuinely interested in getting their ideas and putting them to constructive use in modifying the work environment. And that conviction, in turn, will depend on how ready management and labor are to shed atavistic fears of lost prerogatives in favor of collaboration with legislators and administrators on programs that will encourage experimentation, while keeping intact the essential freedoms of both sides. Laws of the kind now general in Western Europe, which require worker representation on boards of directors, do not seem probable in this country, but that leaves open a wide area for government-fostered exploration of new areas of shared authority at the shop level.

Unfortunately, the lines of administrative direction within government for activity in this field are now atrociously scrambled. The short-lived National Center for Productivity and Quality of Working Life represented an ideal instrument for ironing out this tangle, but it died on September 30, 1978—victim of precisely the kind of bureaucratic infighting between the Labor and Commerce departments and the lack of sustained commitment by either the White House or Congress that had kept the center from ever attaining full usefulness.

If the needed commitment to forward movement finally does emerge, the Federal Mediation and Conciliation Service could serve as the coordinating agency that the National Center was originally intended to be.

The instrumentality is less important, however, than the openness of horizons and the sincerity of dedication at the topmost levels of organized labor and industry to the desirability of making those at the bottom full partners in the problem solving and decision making that directly affect their jobs.

14.

Conflict and Compression: The Labor-Market Environment in the 1980s

ARNOLD WEBER

*Professor of Economics and Public Policy
and Provost, Carnegie-Mellon University*

Labor-market institutions and practices are seldom the product of perfect foresight and rational design. Rather, they reflect a series of imperfect adjustments to changes in ideology, interest, and the environment. Moreover, the labor market rarely offers a *tabula rasa* on which new institutional arrangements may be directly inscribed. More likely, changes in the environment create tensions that alter existing institutions in some unpredictable manner. Plotting these shifts and the process of adjustment is the metier of labor-market analysts. In the next decade we will enter a period of far-reaching change in the labor-market environment that will strain our capacities for both forecasting and institutional adjustment.

The dominant aspect of the labor market during the 1970s was the flood of new job seekers. This condition reflected the confluence of two streams: young people, who comprised the baby boom of the late 1940s and 1950s; and women, responding to both economic necessity and the exhortations of Gloria Steinem. From 1969 to 1976 new entrants moved into the labor force at an average annual rate of 2.3 percent, nearly double the rate that prevailed in the early 1960s. This rapid expansion of the labor force, combined with the failure to achieve sustained economic growth, engendered the persistent, high levels of unemployment in the 1970s.

During the decade of the eighties, the contours of the labor force will be altered in a dramatic and diverse manner. First, there will be a sharp drop in the growth of the labor force, from the current 2.3 percent rate to

1.1 percent over the ten-year period. This precipitate decline, of course, mirrors the reduced birthrates of the 1960s and the early 1970s. The Bureau of Labor Statistics estimates that by 1990 the number of people in the labor force aged 16 to 24 will have diminished by about 16 percent and the fraction of the total labor force comprised by this group will have fallen from 23.9 percent to 18.4 percent.[1]

Second, the legions of young people who earlier trooped into the labor market will now move into the 25–44 age bracket, creating a bulge of unprecedented proportions. The number of jobholders and job seekers in this cohort will jump by one third from 1980 (by 50 percent from 1975) so that by 1990 they will constitute about 53 percent of the total work force.

Third, the number of people aged 55 and over will continue to rise from 40.8 million in 1975, to 44.1 million in 1980, and to 47.7 million by 1990. During the same period, the participation rate of this group is expected to fall so that it constitutes a smaller proportion of the labor force. The decline is largely attributable to the continued fall in the labor-market activity of males aged 55 to 64, which is projected to ebb from 74.3 percent in 1980 to 69.9 percent in 1990.

In contrast to most economic projections, these will have a high degree of reliability. The young people who will come into the labor market in the 1980s have already been born, and those who will impact the 25–44 age category have moved off the assembly line and onto the street. The most tenuous estimates are those involving the continued rise in the participation rates of women and the decline for men 45 and older.[2] Any deviations from the projections, however, are unlikely to be of sufficient magnitude to alter the basic trends.

By now, these prospects are well known to demographers, labor-force analysts, and casual readers of *The Wall Street Journal*. But we have not yet begun to consider seriously the probable impact of these changes on prevailing practices and policies. Indeed, our track record in recognizing and reacting to obvious labor-force trends has been inauspicious. The recent influx of young people into the labor market was perfectly predictable but, with the exception of a few observers such as James Conant who warned of the "social dynamite" of youth unemployment, our policymakers were generally caught with their options down when the anticipated events took place. To some extent, our attention was diverted by what now seems like interminable discussions of automation. But simple myopia also helped to create the policy gaps in dealing with the problem of youth unemployment.

In addition, both the labor-force trends and the policy issues they pose will be far more complex in the 1980s than they have been during the 1970s. As we look ahead from the vantage point of the late 1970s, a critical question relates to the likely effects of short-run efforts to deal with the current labor surplus on our ability to adjust to the sharp decline in labor-force growth and the prospect of labor shortages in the 1980s. Similarly, what are the implications of labor shortages at the entry levels, a superabundance in the 25–44 category, and the decline of full-time labor-force participation by older workers? Labor-market institutions in the 1980s will have to navigate powerful crosscurrents generated by the impact of short-term policies on long-term trends and the differential position of various age groups in the labor force.

This chapter explores the probable implications of the new labor-market environment. The lines of analysis are clearly speculative—futurism legitimizes conjecture—but the inferences are related to expected institutional needs and behavior. In any case, the precise nature of the adjustments is not as important as an appreciation of their magnitude and probable direction.

THE COMING LABOR SHORTAGE

Assuming a reasonable performance by the economy, labor-force trends will afford a fair chance of reaching nominal full employment during the eighties. To apply past relationships, a moderate growth rate in real GNP of 3½ percent per year should be sufficient to absorb the new entrants arising from demographic factors and changes in participation rates. Although recent experience does not support a high degree of confidence in our capacity to manage the economy successfully, this goal is not unreasonable. During the period 1980–1985, for example, an annual increase in employment of 1.3 million should keep the unemployment rate in the 5 percent range.[3] By contrast, total employment increased by approximately 2 million per year in the period 1970–1977, despite the setbacks associated with the 1974–1975 recession. Hence, for the economy as a whole, full employment appears within reach. Parenthetically, it should be noted that the changing balance of labor supply and demand cannot be expected to ameliorate completely the problem of black unemployment. Many of the black teenagers unemployed in the 1970s will have lost any constructive linkage with the labor market, and remedial programs will still be necessary.

The pressures of labor supply will be intensified by the practices put in place during the seventies, when chronic unemployment prevailed. In this period, workers, individually and through their unions, have sought economic cover both within and outside of the labor market. Unions have pressed for the expansion of what the Bureau of Labor Statistics antiseptically calls "pay for time not worked"—holidays, extended vacations, and personal leave—to reduce the absolute share of employment opportunities claimed by any individual worker. During the 1970s, the cost of this component of compensation has been growing half again as fast as the basic wage rate. The most dramatic gain in this area was the exaction of twelve days of additional personal leave by the United Automobile Workers in its 1976 contract with the Big Three auto makers. Similarly, six weeks' vacation for long-service employees is no longer the sign of employee indolence or employer generosity. Recent studies reveal that during the post-World War II period there has been little disposition to reduce weekly work schedules to less than forty hours.[4] But many workers have approached an effective four-day week within an *annual* framework through the elaboration of various elements of pay for time not worked.

Unions also have led the way in winning early retirement plans to induce attrition from the labor force. In 1977 the Steelworkers negotiated a plan whereby workers who are age 45 or more and have twenty years' seniority can receive a special pension in the event of plant or departmental shutdowns. This comes on top of a regular pension plan that permits retirement after thirty years of service, without age restrictions. Some variant of the "thirty-and-out" approach to retirement has become increasingly widespread. And once the unions have attained this right, it is frequently extended to nonunion, white-collar workers. In General Motors, the average retirement age for both production and office workes is 56 years.

Government programs have provided other avenues out of the labor force. Between 1972 and 1977 the number of individuals receiving disability benefits under Social Security jumped by 45 percent, from 1.8 million to 2.8 million. The reasons for this increase are not clear, but many workers with minor incapacities probably have sought disability benefits rather than pursuing dim prospects for employment. In addition, 1.8 million workers between 62 and 64 are utilizing the early-retirement option under Social Security.

The various income-maintenance programs that have been built up during the period of high employment will also affect the availability of labor. Other things being equal, the greater the availability of income-maintenance programs, the less likely that an unemployed worker will actively seek other employment opportunities at a given wage. For example, a displaced aluminum worker who can draw 102 weeks of Supplemental Unemployment Benefits payments probably will be more deliberate in pursuing new job opportunities than in the absence of such benefits. This weakening of work incentives is a consequence of government programs as well as those negotiated through collective bargaining.

All of this is not to pass judgment on the social and economic desirability of such measures. Both unions and individual workers have been doing what comes naturally in the face of the perceived scarcity of employment opportunities. Nonetheless, the effect of these measures on the availability of labor supply seems inescapable and undoubtedly has contributed to the decline of participation rates of men over 45 years of age. In this manner, we will have put in place various programs that constrain the effective supply of labor as the demographic trends that underlie labor-force growth nose down.

In this context, employers will be forced to search for new sources of labor supply (in addition to more aggressively pressing the substitution of capital for labor). From the employers' vantage point, the labor market has had an indulgent quality during the 1970s. The persistence of high levels of unemployment and the ready availability of new entrants created personnel practices based on the assumption of labor abundance, a condition that is unlikely to continue in the eighties.

Employees who have nominally retired or otherwise withdrawn from the labor force will be a prime source of supplementary labor supply. This potential supply will be enlarged by the growing gap between retirement standards and retirement practices. As noted previously, there has been a widespread tendency toward the lowering of the actual retirement age through the extension of early retirement programs. At the same time, the mandatory retirement age has been raised by statute from 65 to 70, reflecting pressures from "senior citizens" organizations, if not from the older workers themselves. Thus, extended employment becomes a legal possibility for the older worker and a feasible source of labor supply for the employer. Recent changes in the so-called retirement test under Social Security further enhance this possibility. Individuals receiving old-age benefits can earn more wages than in the past without being subjected to a 50 percent benefit offset on these earnings. The BLS estimates that the participation rate for people 55 years or more will fall from 34.7 percent in 1975 to 30 percent in 1990. If this *rate of decline* is reduced by half, about 1 million additional workers would be available. Similarly, the maintenance of the participation rate that prevailed for males 45–54 in 1970 through the 1980s would add another half million workers to the labor force in 1990.

Under these circumstances, there will be greater discretion on both sides of the labor market to utilize more intensively the older components of the labor force. Moreover, the prospect of higher wages induced by the changing supply–demand relationships will make this alternative more appealing to those who otherwise would find it in their interest to remain out of the labor market.

Two adjustments will have to be made, however, before the way is clear to turn to this age group as an important source of labor supply. First, workers in this group are unlikely to want to work on a full-time, year-round basis. Thus, there will have to be innovations in work scheduling that go beyond the conventional notions of "part-time" work. Work arrangements may be developed that provide for the sharing of an individual job by two or more persons, or the intermittent distribution of work time over an annual period. For example, a "part-time" employee may now work full time six months of the year and spend another six months pursuing the pleasures of the golden years.

Second, consideration also will have to be given to the amendment of the Employee Retirement Income Security Act (ERISA). Under existing regulations, an employee who works 1000 hours a year generally must be covered by any private pension plan in effect in the employing unit. Moreover, vesting must be provided for covered employees within the ten- or fifteen-year schedule provided by law. Because the older workers involved are already likely to be drawing pensions from private sources and may further be enjoying Social Security benefits, the economic need is not as compelling. Although unions are likely to flinch at waiving pension coverage, pressures in this direction will be exerted to pave the way for wider utilization of such "recycled" workers and to prevent the excessive pyramiding of pension benefits. It is significant to note that, under the provisions of the law raising the mandatory retirement age to 70, employers apparently do not have to make pension contributions for workers who continue on the job beyond age 65.

The constraints on labor supply in the 1980s will also induce a close review of immigration laws. Again, short-run problems will collide with long-term needs. Currently, there are strong political pressures to curtail the flood of so-called undocumented, or illegal, aliens, many of whom have swept across the border from Mexico. At a time of high unemployment, these aliens are viewed as "taking American jobs" and threatening wage standards. In the eighties, immigration is likely to be perceived as an important element of supply, especially for the unskilled, low-wage positions that will become increasingly less attractive to indigenous workers with more appealing alternatives.

A case in point is the food-service industry. In 1977, there were almost 4 million people employed in food service. Traditionally, the industry has drawn upon young people and women as the primary sources of labor supply. Although it is not quite correct to say that one worker has been employed for each hamburger produced, these industries have adopted a low wage/high turnover personnel strategy based on the presumption of an abundant labor supply. During the 1980s, teenagers will find a wider array of opportunities open to them, and women will increasingly eschew low-level, dead-end positions. Thus, immigration will constitute an important element of potential labor supply. The same situation is applicable to other service industries at the low end of the wage structure, such as hospitals and retail trade. In order to provide workers for these low-level jobs, U.S. immigration laws, which have moved from xenophobia to an emphasis on skill qualifications, will have to become more permissive in the future. This policy shift took place in several Western European countries in the post-World War II period.

PRESSURES IN THE BULGE

If younger workers will be able to contemplate greener pastures in the 1980s, the outlook will be less comforting to those in the 25–44 age bracket, the critical state of career development for most individuals. As noted previously, they will have to jostle and elbow to find room in an increasingly dense labor-market environment. In most organizations, career progression takes place within pyramidic hierarchies. Thus, only a limited proportion of workers at a given occupational level will be able to progress to the next level. Because the number of workers in the 25–44 age bracket will increase by one third, competition will be intense and disappointment more widespread. This disappointment will be deepened by the fact that, on average, these workers will be better educated than many of their superiors. Competition to move up the organizational ladder will be sharpened further by the secondary effects of the antidiscrimination laws, which have brought women and minorities into the privileged corners of the occupational structure from which they were excluded in the past. Whereas in 1975 there may have been ten workers competing for a middle-management position, there will now be thirteen—and to this total you can probably add three women and three members of minority groups.

Some augury of economic life in the "bulge" can be inferred from the experience of the 1960s and the early 1970s when the baby boom hit the labor market. From 1967 to 1977, the index of median, real weekly earnings of wage and salary workers 25 years and over rose by approximately 15 percent. For men 16–24 years, this index fell by 5 percent. A similar experience was recorded for women.[6] The influx of young workers without commensurate increases in demand had the effect of diminishing the rate of gain for this growth. The rate of increase in real wages for most segments of the labor force was unimpressive in the face of inflation, but young workers clearly fared worse. This experience is likely to be replicated for sizable elements of the 25–44 group as they move into the 1980s. At the same time, the younger workers probably will enjoy the economic benefits of their more sparse cohort, compressing wage differentials.

The enormous size of the bulge—50 percent of the labor force—will make it impossible to ignore the plight of this group. In the first instance, there probably will be an increasingly strident backlash against programs for affirmative action. It is no accident that legal resistance to affirmative action has intensified as the implications of these programs have been felt at higher levels of the occupational structure. The defense of seniority systems for promotion, the complaints filed by indignant white male professors who believe that scarce academic positions have been given to less qualified women or minorities, and the *Bakke* case all serve notice that exhortations for social justice will have less appeal where there is sharp competition for limited positions in the upper reaches of the occupational structure. Expanded economic growth might temper the problem, but its statistical magnitude is such that economic growth alone is unlikely to be a sufficient antidote.

Second, this mass of midcareer workers will exert great pressure to expand their horizons by accelerating the withdrawal from the firm of the older workers who block their way. These pressures will become particularly acute with each rotation of the business cycle and induce the further extension of early retirement programs. The problem will not be employment opportunities per se, but the opportunity for progression. In one way or another, efforts will be made to entice or push from the labor force those workers who have had time in middle- and top-rung positions. Since the mandatory retirement age has been raised, the obvious avenue is to increase the inducement.

The cost of these expanded early retirement programs will be politically palatable as long as they are borne by the employer. There will be an obverse reaction, however, to public retirement programs, that is, Social Security. As Social Security has matured, the ratio of people working to those drawing benefits has declined precipitously. This decline will continue through the eighties and into the nineties as the rate of increase in the labor force diminishes. We already have seen the fiscal consequences of this trend in the form of sharply rising Social Security taxes. The negative political vibrations caused by the tax increases will be magnified when these increased taxes fall on a group with reduced economic prospects. This helps to explain why Social Security, which has long been viewed as a model of public virtue and intelligence, is now a topic of sharp controversy. The controversy initially has focused on the source of funding for Social Security, that is, a dedicated tax or general revenues, but another alternative has been raised by suggesting that the age be lifted at which retirement benefits would become payable. Significantly, this possibility was first floated by a cabinet official of a Democratic administration which has a deep commitment to the Social Security system.

The proposal was immediately assailed and withdrawn, but the issue is now out of the actuarial closet and will receive serious attention as the financial burden of Social Security increases. Moreover, the raising of the mandatory retirement age to 70 has diluted the historical legitimacy of age 65 as the chronological threshold for retirement. The fact that an increased number of workers will receive pensions at considerably earlier ages will further obscure the validity of retirement at age 65. No one quite expects firemen or members of the armed services retiring at age 45 to spend thirty years playing golf and watching television. At the same time, the increased availability of employment opportunities for older workers, on a part-time basis or otherwise, to deal with the shortfall in labor supply will diminish the economic pressures for Social Security to carry the full burden at age 65. For these reasons, it would not be surprising if the eighties saw definite action taken to raise the retirement age under Social Security by discrete increments sometime in the future.

In this tortuous way, the disparate pressures generated by labor-force trends are likely to transform the concept of retirement and, indeed, the entire work–leisure cycle in later years. Thus, some "retirement" will be provided at a time when there would otherwise be a normal expectation of work, while some work will be afforded at an age when we have anticipated permanent withdrawal from the labor force. The "linear" pattern whereby an individual goes to school, enters the labor market for an extended period of time (45 years), and then withdraws permanently to savor the ease of retirement is likely to be changed in unpredictable ways.[7] A worker may "retire" at a relatively early age and then return to the labor force in a new capacity and in other than on a full-time basis. In the 1980s new work–leisure patterns are likely to emerge that will change our standards and expectations.

OPPORTUNITIES FOR UNION ORGANIZATION

The consequences of the changing labor-market environment in the 1980s will present unions with an unparalleled opportunity to register major gains among the white-collar workers. This group generally has been resistant to union organization in the past. The group with the highest potential for unionization will be those who are compressed in the labor-force bulge. Their aspirations eroded by the extreme competition, their opportunities crimped by what they judge to be unfair advantages given to some groups at the expense of others, their economic gains dampened by their great availability, and their feelings of injustice heightened by the need to contribute to programs of income maintenance for others, these individuals are likely to view collective action as necessary to stake their claim in the labor market.

The climate for the unionization of white-collar workers will be enhanced by two unrelated developments. On the one hand, much of the class stigma associated with unionization has been removed by the widespread organization of public employees and other professionals. Two of the five largest unions in the labor movement today are the National Education Association and the American Federation of State, County, and Municipal Employees. Both unions contain a substantial number of professional, semiprofessional, and other white-collar workers. The traditional view of the union member as a blue-collar militant has been blurred by the increased visibility of teachers, nurses, social workers, and even doctors using collective action to advance their interests in the name of professionalism.

Second, the high proportion of women among the ranks of white-collar workers has been viewed in the past as an impediment to organization because women have not had a commitment to full-time, permanent employment. The explosion of female participation in the labor force clearly has altered that condition. Indeed, much of the increased participation of women in the labor force can be explained by the extended duration of their labor-market activity as contrasted to an increase in the number of new entrants to the labor force. Experience with organization in education and health services has demonstrated that this strengthened commitment can be reflected in a greater propensity for unionization.

Whether or not this improved climate for the unionization of white-collar workers will be translated into actual gains is uncertain. In a large measure, the success of unions in penetrating these areas will depend on their capacity to develop appeals and programs that are attractive to these constituencies. In addition, the unions must make the jurisdictional adjustments necessary to build structures congenial to these workers' interests. In view of the trade union movement's past lethargy regarding such matters, there can be no assurance that the necessary changes in tactics and structure will take place.

The appeal of unions to this group also will be conditioned by management's willingness to recognize their special problems and to fashion policies that will reduce the attractiveness of collective action. But to the extent that the problems besetting those in the bulge reflect broad demographic factors rather than the heavy hand of individual employers, the capacity of any individual management to provide amelioration will be limited.

PERSPECTIVE ON THE 1980s

It is an occupational attribute of futurists that they offer their prognostications with the same confidence, and probably accuracy, as TV weather forecasters. Obviously, this exercise may turn out to be fanciful, but in looking ahead, the general cast of the labor market in the eighties can be described with a somewhat greater degree of confidence.

The next decade will be a time of increased tension and potential conflict among the various groups in the labor force. During the seventies, the deficiencies in the performance of the labor market were manifested in the large-scale unemployment of young people. Because these young people did not have firm links to a job, the resultant tensions were expressed in the streets, the schools, and other forums for social protest.

In the 1980s, the primary arena for the resolution of intergroup conflict will be the labor market and the workplace, where young job seekers, those in midcareer, and older workers will have radically different perspectives on the world. These tensions will have to be accommodated as much in the minutiae of personnel administration and union contracts as in the halls of Congress. In fact, unions have had to deal with such problems as a matter of course; a more difficult adjustment will be necessary by managers, who are less skilled in, and less willing to play, the role of conciliator.

At the same time, the eighties probably will be a period of widespread experimentation with alternate "work-styles" (if that ungainly phrase can be used to distinguish the concept from life-style). Changing patterns of labor-market participation will blur the traditional discontinuities associated with a "linear" lifetime work pattern. New patterns will take shape, as employers scramble for labor supply and older workers exercise the discretion afforded by the availability of "retirement" income to alter the time distribution of their work. This changing environment also will stimulate a sweeping review of established public policies, including immigration laws, Social Security, ERISA, and Fair Labor Standards. And for the unions, the eighties will present an opportunity to break out of a shrinking blue-collar perimeter and gain the membership of large numbers of white-collar workers.

After the turmoil of the 1960s and 1970s, it was hoped that society would enjoy a respite during which it could refurbish its institutions. Within the labor market, at least, such a pause is unlikely to occur. Instead, labor-force developments will call into question existing practices and will require more ingenious ways to satisfy personal and social needs.

NOTES

1. This and the other labor-force projections are taken from *New Labor Force Projections to 1990*, Bureau of Labor Statistics, U.S. Department of Labor, Special Labor Force Report 197 (Washington, D.C.: U.S. Government Printing Office, 1977). For a more detailed discussion of labor-force trends, see Richard B. Freeman, "The Work Force of the Future: An Overview," Chapter 4, this volume.
2. See Michael L. Wachter, "Intermediate Swings in Labor Force Participation," *Brookings Papers on Economic Activity* (1977): No. 2; also pp. 9–10.
3. For a discussion of the relationship between labor-force trends and unemployment in the 1980s, see Leonard Lecht, "The Labor Force Bulge Is Temporary," *Across the Board (The Conference Board)* (December 1977): 15–22.
4. Albert Rees, *The Economics of Work and Pay* (New York: Harper & Row, 1973), p. 27 ff.

5. *Social Security Bulletin,* March 1978, Social Security Administration, U.S. Department of Health, Education, and Welfare, Tables M-3, M-14.
6. U.S. Department of Labor, "Trends in Weekly and Hourly Earnings for Major Labor Force Groups," New Release 77-955, November 2, 1977.
7. This line of thought is further discussed in Fred Best and Barry Stern, "Education, Work and Leisure: Must They Come in That Order?" *Monthly Labor Review* 100 (July 1977): 3–10.

INDEX

Abernathy, William J., 222

Abused spouse: incidence of, as related to unemployment, 144–145

Affirmative action: impact of on working women, 121

Affirmative action programs: backlash against, 275; *Bakke* decision, 275; in response to changing work attitudes, 56

Age: effect of, on job satisfaction, 43, on work values, 40; of workers, projected increase in, 50

Akabas, Dr. Sheila, 175

Alcoholism: in industry, 174; rehabilitation for, as issue for cooperative union-management effort, 242

Alternative society: effect of on orientation to work, 30–32; options in development of, 32–33

Alternative work schedules: as an aid to women employees, *xix–xx*; as an encouragement to older workers, 273; as a factor affecting quality of work life, 168–173; objections to, 169; predictions regarding, 172–173; types of, 169–172. *See also* flexible work schedules

Alternative work styles: projections regarding, 279

Annual salary plans: as a replacement for wage-and-hour pay systems, 160

Asset management: influence of on development of new equipment and process technologies, 221

Avocational counseling and education: use of in response to changing work attitudes, 55

"Bad" jobs, *ix*, *xvii*, *xx–xxi*

Behavioral analysis: as a technique to improve production, 184

Benefits. *See* employee benefit plans

Bernstein, Harry, 40

Bienstock, Penney, 184

Bingham, Eula, 263

Black youth: labor-market position of, 94–95; unemployment among, projections regarding, 75

Blacks: changing work attitudes of, 47; college graduates, compensation among, 109; employment levels of, projections regarding, 107–108; employment possibilities for, *xx*; growth of white-collar workers among, 62; income status of, 92, in the South, 98, relative to whites, 96, 98; labor force participation of, 50, ratio of male to female, 94; need for manpower policies for, 85; occupational trends for, 96; unemployment among, 3, 92, 95, 270

Blue-collar jobs: shift away from, 62

Brenner, Harvey, 145

Cain, G., 70

Campbell Works of Youngstown Steel: shutdown at, 261

Capital-labor ratio: changes in, as affecting productivity, 197–200

Capitalism: effect of on alternative society, 31–32

Carter, Jimmy, 258, 264

Cartter, Allan, 66, 75

Child abuse: relation of to employment status of parent, 144–145

Child care: effect of parental unemployment on, 141–145; need for, as a component of a family policy for working women, 130–132, 135; quality of, as affecting parental job satisfaction, 152

Child development: effect on, of working father, 146–148, of working mother, 145–146

Children's allowance program: as a component of a family policy for working women, 129–130

Collective bargaining: as a means of serving society's needs, 231–233; hard-line controversial issues in, 236–241; issues for joint cooperation in, 241–244

College enrollment: reduced rate of, 62; patterns of, relation of to wages and profits, 72

College graduates: black, job competition among, 109; job projections for, 121–123

College students: attitude of toward work, x–xii

Colletta, N., 145

Communitarianism: influence of on development of new equipment and process technologies, 223

Compensation: as a technique to improve productivity, 185. *See also* pay

Comprehensive Employment and Training Act (CETA): funding of, 83–84; goals and objectives of, 82–84

Conant, James, 269

Control Data Corporation: use of part-time employees at, 170

Corning Glass: work restructuring at, 218

Cultural trends: effect of on work attitudes, 47–49

Cummins Engine Corporation: design of equipment and process technologies at, 224; work restructuring at, 218

Day care: centers, as a collective bargaining issue, 240; effect of on child development, 145–146; governmental participation in the development of, 135; need for, 130–132; potential for innovative approaches regarding, 152

Decision-making: employee participation in, 176–180, 244–251, criteria for developing, 250, experiments with, 249–251

Democracy in the workplace: as a factor affecting the quality of work life, 180–182; employee attitudes on, 180, expectations of, 180–181; projections for, 181–182

Denison, Edward F., 193

Disadvantaged: black youths in the labor market, 95–96; manpower policy for, 91. *See also* black youths; blacks; hard-to-employ

Disaggregation of industries: effects of on equipment and process technologies, 224–225, 229

Discipline problems: in the workplace, as an issue for cooperative union-management effort, 243

Discrimination: changing concept regarding, effect of on employment systems, 101

DuBois, W. E. B., 92

Dunlop, John T., 66, 264

Early retirement: effect of on projected labor supply, 271; programs for, 276

Earnings: for women, relation of to educational level, 126; sex differentials in, 123–126

Economic conditions: effect of, on employment, 234, on labor-market prospects for minorities, 99, 102, on quality of work life decisions, 182

Economic participation: on the part of workers, as a factor affecting quality of work life, 159

Educational attainment: among blacks, quality of, 100, trend in, 100

Educational level: effect of, on job satisfaction, 43, on work values, 39–40; increase in as reflected in the labor force, 50, 61–62; of women, relation of to earnings, 126, relation of to labor force paticipation, 112; of the work force, effect of on productivity growth, 193–194; projected decline in rate of increase of, 75–76

Employee benefits plans: administration of, as an issue for cooperative union-management effort, 243; as a factor affecting the quality of work life, 161–165; difficulties of some employers in providing, 161; potential for innovative approaches regarding, 150–151; relation between employer and federal social programs, 162–165

Employee participation: as a factor affecting quality of work life, 176–180; in Western Europe, 176–177; obstacles to application of, 177–178; projections for, 178–179

Employee Retirement Income Security Act (ERISA): amendments to, as an encouragement to older workers, 273

Employer: potential for, as family strengthener, 148–153

Employment growth: influence on of energy policies, 104–108; varying patterns of for different occupational groups, 106–108

Employment levels: of blacks, projections regarding, 107–108

Employment opportunities: for women, 112

Employment policies: for minorities, new discrimination laws on, 101–102

Employment system: effect of New Breed values on, 16–20

Energy policy: as a factor affecting labor-market prospects for minorities, 104–108

Energy scarcity: influence of on the development of new equipment and process

Energy scarcity (cont.)
technologies, 221, 228
"Enriched" jobs: effect of on job satisfaction, 43
Entitlement: as a work attitude, 11, 12, 20, 29–30, 41, 47, 48, 180; psychology of, 54
Equal employment opportunities: effect of on labor-market status of minorities, 100–102; governmental participation in fostering, 259
Equal pay: placement of women in lower ranking jobs, 125. See also sex differentials
Equal Rights Amendment: importance of for working women, 133–134
Equipment and process technology (EPT): development and selection of for better working environment, 223–226; effect of, emerging concern over, 212; example of high productivity and, 212–214; future impact of on workplace, influences affecting, 215; impact of on working environment, 205–206, 214, 217–219, 227–228; impediments to development of better, 224–225
Erosion of modernity: as an alternate societal development, 32
Europe: governmental control of private work practices in, 263–264
Experimental Negotiating Agreement, 265
Extrinsic factors: diminishing importance of in job satisfaction, 45

Faerstein, Paul, 184
Family life: effect of parental stress on, 147–148
Family policy for working wives, 129–130
Federal-state employment service: manpower expenditures on, 81
Females. See women
Flexible work schedules: as a collective bargaining issue, 241; increased use of, 55, 132–133, 134. See also alternative work schedules
Flexitime: as a form of alternative work scheduling, 169–170; benefits of, 169; predictions for, 172–173; problems with, 169; supervisors' concerns regarding, 170; union experiennce with, 170. See also alternative work schedules; flexible work schedules
Ford, Gerald, 265
Ford, Henry, 244
Foreign competition: governmental involvement in coping with, 260–261

Forty-hour workweek: trend toward altering, 237–238
Four-day week: operation of, 238. See also reduced workweek; work time
Friedman, Milton, 19
Full employment: governmental participation in helping to secure, 261; in the 1980s, focus of collective bargaining on, 236–237, projections regarding, 270. See also unemployment

GNP: relation of to productivity, 199
Gallup, George, Jr., 44
Galston, R., 144
Gelles, R., 144
General Electric: work restructuring at, 218
General Foods: Topeka pet-food plant, 223; work restructuring at, 218; worker participation in decision-making at, 249
General Motors: work restructuring at, 218
Gerstenberg, Richard, 245
Gill, D., 144
Ginzberg, Eli, 16
Goal setting: as a technique to improve production, 184
Governmental regulations: effect of, on production, 200, 202, on quality of work life decisions, 182–183; in the workplace, 254–260, projected expansion of, 260–267; influence of on development of new equipment and process technologies, 221–222
Green, William, 255
Guaranteed jobs: in the 1980's, 17–18

Hard-to-employ: importance of manpower policy for, 86; manpower expenditures on, 81; supported work for, 86. See also blacks; minorities
Hard-line bargaining issues, 236–241
Harris, Seymour, 66
Hayes, Robert H., 222
Health and safety committees: as an issue for cooperative union-management effort, 243–244
Health care: cost control, projections regarding, 164–165; increase in in-house services, projections regarding, 165
Hoffman, L., 145
Horner, Matina, 135
Hours of work: potential for innovative approaches regarding, 150–151

Human resource planning: use of to avoid lay-offs, 167
Humphrey-Hawkins Act, 84, 236, 261

Illegal aliens: increased percentage of in labor force, 64; influencing labor-market prospects for minorities, 103–104. *See also* immigration laws
Immigration laws: review of, in response to projected labor shortage, 273–274
Incentive systems: boring jobs, effect of on, 3–4; devaluation of traditional economic incentives in, 22–23; faults of, 21–24; in relation to quality of work life, 23–24; New Breed values, effect of on, 20–24
Incentives: "executive type," 160
Income level: of blacks, 92
Income levels: three-tiered grouping for, *xvii*
Income-maintenance programs: effect of on projected labor supply, 271–272
Income status: of blacks, 96, 98
Income taxes: effect of on the incentive value of a pay raise, 159
Individual differences: effect of on job satisfaction, 53–54
Individual Retirement Accounts (IRA), 163
Individualism: need for, in the incentive system, 21–22. *See also* New Breed
Individuality: as a value, to New Breed, 14–15; depersonalizing aspect of old work-value system, 15; emphasis on, as affecting managerial efficiency, 15
Individualization of the work environment, 54. *See also* entitlement
Industrial composition: shifts in, as affecting productivity, 195–197
Inflation: effect of on the incentive value system of pay raise, 159
Innovative work practices: variables to consider in developing, 150–153
Intergroup conflict: projections regarding, 279
Intrinsic factors: growing importance of, in job satisfaction, 45, in formulation of work values, 42
Involvement in work: projected increase in employees', 52

Japan: lifetime security system in, 166
Job characteristics: effect of on job satisfaction, 42
Job content: sharing control for developing, 185
"Job control," *xviii*
Job-creation: incentives needed to encourage, 149–150. *See also* manpower policy
Job involvement: effect on, of work situation, 37, of worker's personal characteristics, 37–38
Job opportunities: creation of by reduction in work time, 237–238
Job performance: as related to job satisfaction, 43–44
Job redesign: as a means of improving productivity, 184; in response to changing work attitudes, 55
Job rotation: use of, in response to changing work attitudes, 55
Job satisfaction: age and, 43; facets of, 42; factors associated with higher levels of, 43; individual differences and, 53–54; job characteristics and, 42; off-the-job factors and, 43; projections for, by segments of the population, 44–54; relation of to job performance, 43–44; similarities in, by sex, 43; workers' values and, 42
Job security: as a factor affecting quality of work life, 165–168; early full-pension vesting to increase, 168; enhancing productivity and, 168; human resource planning to increase, 167; importance of to employees, 165, 168; in Japan, 166; incorporating labor force changes into plans for, 168; integration of private plans with government systems, 168; issues for employers, 167–168; layoffs, removals and recall under, 167; past service and performance as factors in, 167; pension portability to increase, 168; tenured employment patterns, 165–166; through worker reassignment, 168
Job sharing: increased use of, in response to changing work attitudes, 55
Jobs: demand for by New Breed, 3; desire for "good," *ix, xvii, xx–xxi*; projections regarding increased competition for, 76
Juvenile delinquency: relation of to quality of at-home supervision, 132

Kaemmerev, Christel, 132
Kahn, Herman, 32, 41
Katzell, Raymond, 184

Kendrick, John W., 199
Keyserling, Leon, 234
Keyserling, Mary, 130

Labor bulge: projections regarding, 274–277
Labor force: age structure of, *xvi*, 61, projected, 269; characteristics of employment, 62–64; current composition of, 58 64; changes in, economic explanation for, 69–74; decline of private-sector unionism in, 63; educational attainment level of, 61–62; ethnic composition of, 64; geographic distribution of employment, shift in, 62–63; governmental share of, 62; historical changes in composition and character of, *vii–viii*, *xii–xvii*, 60; illegal aliens in, 64; inadequacy of predictions regarding changes in, 64–67; mobility and flexibility of, 63; older workers in, 269; participation in, for blacks, 94, for women, 112–116; projections regarding, 74–77, 268–279; proportional increase in size of, *xvi*, 60; public-sector unionism in, 63; trends in, effects of, 277–278; women in, age of, 60–61. *See also* work force
Labor-management relations: governmental involvement with, 257–258, 264–267; improvement of, by joint effort, 266–267; increased combativeness in, 264–266
Labor market: in the 1970s, 268; projections regarding, effect of on minorities, 94–103
Labor movement: negative public image of, union efforts to combat, 251
Labor supply: determinants of, 67–74; new sources of, 272–274
Landrum-Griffin Labor Reform Act, 258
Larry, Heath, 265
Leisure: importance of to New Breed, 13
Lindblom, Charles, 66
Lippman, Walter, 32
Long, Huey, 255

Maccoby, Dr. Michael, 248
Machine design: criteria for development of vis-a-vis work environment, 224
Males. *See* men
Management: decision-making by, factors involved in, 223–227, 228; functions of, integrated approach to, 225; women employees in, factors influencing, 121

Manpower policy: Carter administration commitments to developing, 84–87; criteria for assessing, 80–82; displaced workers and, 85; effect of economy on, 88; goals of, 82–84; hard-to-employ and, 86; standards for evaluating, 81–82; trends in, 90
Manpower Training and Development Act, 87
Manufacturing: as related to corporate strategy, 225–226
Market wage: 67–68
Marshall, Ray, 263
Materialism: the work ethic and, 30–31
Materials shortage: influence of on development of new equipment and process technologies, 221–228
Maternity benefits: as part of a family policy for working women, 129–130
"Mature" industries: influence of on development of new equipment and process technologies, 222
Mayo, Elton, *xxii*
McLean, Dr. Alan, 173
McMurry, Robert, 40
Meany, George, 264
Men: older, decline in labor force participation of, 71
Mental health care: at the workplace, 173–174; model for company program providing, 175; obstacles to providing, 175; projections for, 175–176
"Meritocracy," 165–166
Midcareer workers: oversupply of, predicted, 75, 274–277
Mincer, J., 69
Minorities: employment status of, factors affecting, 93–94, effect of energy policies on, 104–108; equal employment opportunities for, public support of, 104; factors affecting labor-market prospects of, 94–98, 102, 103; self-help activities of, 94. *See also* blacks
Moynihan, Daniel P., 134
Myrdal, Alva, 129

National Industrial Recovery Act, 256
Neighborhood youth corps, 81
New Breed: concept of success of, 12; congruence of work values and social values of, 41–42; effect of values, on employment system, 16–20, on inncentive system, 20–24; importance of leisure for, 13; older symbols

New Breed (cont.)
    of success and, 10–11; work values of,
    12–15, 41
New careers: creation of, in response to
    changing work attitudes, 56
New employee orientation programs: as an is-
    sue for cooperative union-management ef-
    fort, 242
New technology: introduction of, as a collective
    bargaining issue, 239; job erosion caused by,
    235
Nonwhites. *See* minorities
Norris-LaGuardia Anti-Injunction Act, 257
Nye, F., 145

O'Brien, J., 144
Occupational level: effect of on job satisfaction,
    143
Occupational safety and health: governmental
    participation in, 259, 263–264
Occupational Safety and Health Act, 259
Occupational Safety and Health Administration
    (OSHA), 174
Occupational stress: as a factor affecting quality
    of work life, 173–176; consequences of
    ignoring, 174
Occupations: blacks and, projections regarding,
    107–108; nonwhite women and, 123; pro-
    jected trends, 104–108; working women and
    changes in, 116–123
Older people: labor force participation of, pro-
    jected increase in, 76
Older workers: as a source of labor, issues to
    consider, 273; employment opportunities for,
    xx
Operating policies: influence of equipment and
    process technology on, 209–210
"Operation Mainstream," 86
Organizational structure: redefinition of, in re-
    sponse to changing work attitudes, 56
Overhead costs: influence of on development
    of new equipment and process technologies,
    221, 228

Part-time employment: advantages of,
    170–171; as a form of alternative work
    scheduling, 170–171; attempts to organize
    employees in, 171; benefits under, 171; inci-
    dence of, 170; predictions regarding, 172;
    women and, 170; youth and, 170

Participative management: increased use of, in
    response to changing work attitudes, 55, 56
Pay: as a factor affecting quality of work life,
    158–161; effect of on job satisfaction, 43;
    policies on, predictions regarding, 160–161;
    raises, factors weakening the incentive value
    of, 159
Pension plans: private, as affected by revised
    social security regulations, 163–164
Perkins, Frances, 254
Phillips, Kevin P., 32
Plant shutdown and movement: as a collective
    bargaining issue, 238–239
Political rights: in the workplace, *ix*
Poverty: effect of on child care, 142–145
Prepaid legal services: as a collective bar-
    gaining issue, 240
Preretirement informational programs: as an is-
    sue for cooperative union-management ef-
    fort, 242
Production scheduling: as a collective
    bargaining issue, 239–240
Productivity: growth in, 192; projections re-
    garding, *xxii*, 201–202; reduction in, 192;
    humanistic concept of, 248–249; increase in,
    programs directed to, 184–185, 202; tech-
    niques to improve, 184–185; trends, conclu-
    sions regarding, 189; historical movements
    in, 190–192; projections for, 189
Property tax: as a factor affecting the incentive
    value of a pay raise, 159
Public service employment: as part of man-
    power policy effort, 81, 88; problems with,
    88–89

Quality of life: as an alternate societal develop-
    ment, 31, 33; as part of an incentive system,
    23–24
Quality of work life: criteria for effective, 218;
    noncontroversial issue for collective bar-
    gaining, 241–244; obstacles to changes in,
    182–184; projections for, 186–187

Railway Labor Act, 257
Reduced workweek: as a form of alternative
    work scheduling, 171–173; benefits of, 171;
    doubts about, 172; effect of on labor supply,
    271; governmental involvement in
    promoting, 261–263; predictions regarding,
    173; societal effects of, 172

Rehabilitation Act: affirmative action programs under, 174
Restoration: as an alternate societal development, 32
Retirement counseling: increased use of, in response to changing work attitudes, 55. *See also* preretirement informational programs
Retirement plans: increased flexibility of, in response to changing work attitudes, 55
Ricciuti, H., 145
Riesman, David, 30
Roberts, Owen, J., 256
Rockefeller, Nelson, 33
Roosevelt, Franklin D., 254
Rushton Mines Osceola Mills: worker participation in decision-making at, 249

Sales tax: as a factor affecting the incentive value of a pay raise, 159
Scandinavia: government control of private work practices in, 263
Second careers: projections for, 52
Self-development: for New Breed, importance of, 12
Self-fulfillment: as distinguished from success, 10; as a goal in the 1970s, 11–12; in the job, *ix, xii*; leisure as a factor in, 13; paid job as a factor in, 13–14; vis-a-vis the work role, 14–15
Service industries: economy's shift to, effect of on productivity, 197
Sex differentials: in earnings, 123–126; in work values, 40
Shadow wage: 67–68
Sheehy, Gail, 11
Single-parent worker: motivation of, 140
Social interaction: effect of on job satisfaction, 43
Social security laws: effect of, on employment patterns, 71; on labor supply, 276; implications of revised tax schedule, 162–164; Social Security Act, 256
Social security tax: as a factor affecting the incentive value of a pay raise, 159
Social service jobs: for blacks, 96
Society: failure of to meet national needs, 231–232
Soule, George, 36
Staggered hours: as a form of alternative work scheduling, 170; experience with, 170; predictions regarding, 172

Stress: on working parent, effect of on family life, 147–148
Structural unemployment: in the 1980s, 16–19
Subcontracting: as a collective bargaining issue, 239
Success: changing concept of, 10
Supervision: effect of on job satisfaction, 43
Supervisory personnel: attitude of toward flexitime, 170
"Supported work," 86
Survey of Working Conditions, 1969–1970, 39
Sweden: importance of leisure concept in, 13; rural unemployment in, efforts to combat, 16–17

Taft-Hartley Act, 258
Technological change: governmental involvement with, 263
Thrift and savings plans, 160–161
Tobin, Dan, 254
Trade Expansion Act: training and mobility provisions of, 85
Trade-induced unemployment: as a factor affecting minority employment, 103; manpower policy regarding, 85
Training: as a form of manpower policy, 87–89; eligibility for, 88; improving productivity through, 184
Transfer policies, 150–151
Transportation: potential for new approaches to, 152–153
Troubled employees: union-management efforts to assist, 242
Two-wage families, 140–141

UAW: pursuit of four-day workweek by, 262
UAW-General Motors Corporation: worker participation in decision-making at, 249
UAW-Harmon International Industries: worker participation in decision-making at, 249
Underutilized employees: changing work attitudes of, 47
Unemployment: among blacks, 92, 95; among women, 126–128; as a function of the economy, 234; current focus on, 236–238; cyclical differences in, for men and women, 127–128; of parent, impact on child, 142–145, relation to intrafamily violence, 144–145
Unionism: private-sector decline in, 63: public-sector growth in, 63

United States Joint Economic Committee: 1977 Report of, 102
University of Michigan Survey of Working Conditions, 1969–70, 39

Value systems: effect of on work, in the 1950s and 1960s, 6–9, in the 1970s, 9–24
Veblen, Thorstein, 4–5
Violence: intrafamily, relation of to employment status, 144–145
Volvo: Kalmar production plant, 223

Wage-hour legislation: governmental participation in fostering, 256–257; history of, 256–257
Wagner Act, 255, 257–258
Walker, Charls E., 80
Walton, Richard, 218, 224
Weber, Max, 30
Welfare reform: importance of, 134–135
Wheelwright, Steven, 222
White-collar jobs: for blacks, 62; shift to from blue-collar, 62
White-collar workers: unionization of, 277–278
Whitsett, David, 41
Williams, Harold, 183
Women: as white-collar employees, projected unionization of, 277–278; changing work attitudes of, 47; greater availability of jobs for, 112; in the labor force, age of, 60–61, 116, as part-time workers, 60, effect of productivity trends on, 194, married, 60, participation in, xvi, 50, 60, 76, 112–116, 262, relationship between and husband's earnings, 112–114, social changes resulting from, 60; nonwhite, occupational status among, 123; paid job for, symbolic significance of, 13–14. See also working women
Work attitudes: changes in, xvii–xviii, xix, 29–30, 55–57; cultural factors affecting, 47–49; dynamic nature of, 47–48; influence of personal experiences on, 47–48; major classes of, 36–46; patterns of, 132–133; projections regarding, 54
Work force: age of, 233; age-sex compositional ratio of, changes in, 194–195; altered nature of vis-a-vis quality of work life issues, 183; changing composition of, 193–195, 233–234, as a reflection of worker attitudes, 50–52; educational level of, 233–234; presence of minorities in, 233

Work restructuring: criteria for in plant and machine design, 224; experiments with, 218; within specific technology, 217–218
Work role: refusal of New Breed to subordinate to, 14–15
Work satisfaction: trend in, xvii. See also self-fulfillment
Work time: reduction in, as a means of creating jobs, 237–238
Work values: as affected by, age, 40, educational level, 39–40, labor-force composition, 52–53, sex difference, 40; improved leisure and, 41; interesting work and, 39; University of Michigan Survey of Working Conditions, 1969–1970, 39
Work-group size: effect of on job satisfaction, 43
Worker participation: effect of on job satisfaction, 43; in decision-making, changing management attitudes regarding, 244–246, union view of, 247–248
Worker values: effect of on job satisfaction, 42
Working environment: definition of, 205. See also quality of work life
Working father: conditions of work of, effect on child development, 146–148
Working mother: and child development, effect of employment on, 145–146. See also child care; family policy for working wives; juvenile delinquency; women
Working women: family policy for, 129–130; in the labor force, occupational changes among, 116–123; occupational placement of, 125, occupational segregation among, 116–123; marital status of, 128–129; sex differentials in earnings of, 123–126; unemployment among, 126–128
Workplace: impact of child rearing on, 147–148, 153; organization of, 235; subjects for collective bargaining regarding, 236–251
Workweek. See work time.

Yankelovich, Daniel, 48
Young people: as unmarried, jobless parents, 143–144; in the labor force, effect of on productivity trends, 194–195; jobs for, xx
Young workers: projected shortage of, 74–75
Youth Employment and Demonstration Projects Act (YEDPA), 84
Youth unemployment, xx, 85, 95–96, 143–144, 234, 269